Religion at Ground Zer

Also available from Continuum:

From Political Theory to Political Theology, edited by Aakash Singh
    and Péter Losonczi
A Grammar of the Common Good, Patrick Riordan
The New Visibility of Religion, edited by Graham Ward and
    Michael Hoelzl
Politics of Fear, Practices of Hope, Stefan Skrimshire
The Politics to Come, edited by Arthur Bradley and Paul Fletcher
Religious Cohesion in Times of Conflict, Andrew Holden

Religion at Ground Zero

Theological Responses to Times of Crisis

Christopher Craig Brittain

continuum

Continuum International Publishing Group
The Tower Building   80 Maiden Lane
11 York Road   Suite 704
London SE1 7NX   New York NY 10038

www.continuumbooks.com

British Library Cataloguing-in-Publication Data
A catalogue record for this book is available from the British Library.

ISBN: HB: 978-1-4411-0677-3
      PB: 978-1-4411-3239-0

Library of Congress Cataloging-in-Publication Data
Brittain, Christopher Craig.
  Religion at ground zero : theological responses to times of crisis / Christopher Craig
Brittain.
    p. cm.
Includes bibliographical references.
ISBN-13: 978-1-4411-3239-0
ISBN-13: 978-1-4411-0677-3 (pb)
ISBN-10: 1-4411-3239-2 (pb)
1. Religion and international relations. I. Title.

BL65.I55B75 2011
201'.727—dc22
              2011008209

Typeset by Newgen Imaging Systems Pvt Ltd, Chennai, India
Printed and bound in Great Britain

*This book is dedicated to **Anna Clausen**
and to all who raise children through times of terror.*
Your witness honours us all.

In times of terror, when everyone is something of a conspirator, everybody will be in a situation where he has to play detective.
    −Walter Benjamin

To live, to love, is to be failed, to forgive, to have failed, to be forgiven, forever and ever. Keep your mind in hell, and despair not.
    −Gillian Rose

Contents

Acknowledgements   ix

Introduction   1

Chapter 1: In the Wake of Lisbon, Katrina and Haiti:
           On the Limits of Theodicy   13

Chapter 2: The 'War to End All Wars':
           Religion in the Trenches of the Great War   39

Chapter 3: Jewish Theological Responses to the Shoah   62

Chapter 4: September 11, 2001: Religion
           Reviled and Revived   85

Chapter 5: Belief and the Trauma of
           Catastrophic 'Events'   112

Chapter 6: Religion as Ground Zero?   149

Chapter 7: Speaking of God in a Time of Terror   177

Afterword   208

Bibliography   210

Index   221

Acknowledgements

The issues explored in this book have been the subject of a University course I have taught over the past seven years. I am thus indebted to colleagues and students at the University of Aberdeen in Scotland, and Atlantic School of Theology and Saint Mary's University in Halifax, Nova Scotia, who have done much to contribute to my thinking during class discussions. Some students whose impact has been particularly significant should be mentioned here: Neale, Aaron, 'Karma boy', Elspeth, Kate, Robert, Colin, Sarah, Gareth, Andreas, Oliver and the 'Leipzig two'.

Numerous colleagues and friends have generously served as discussion partners as I have developed this material: Jody Clarke, Mark Davidson, Alyda Faber, Andrew McKinnon, Andy Odle and John Ramirez. Donald Wood and Philip Ziegler have tried (in vain?) to help me understand Karl Barth. Ken MacKendrick introduced me to Zizek's work, as well as that of Bruce Lincoln, and has long been a valuable conversation partner. I continue to be influenced by the time I spent in Marsha Hewitt's classroom, and now benefit from her ongoing research. Likewise does my research continue on a path initiated by Gilbert Allardyce during my undergraduate work on the Holocaust, and by earlier teahers like Richard and Sandi Thorne. I am grateful to David Alexander for the time he spent with me to discuss his work on post-disaster trauma. Brian Brock and Katja Stößel suffered moments of poor judgement when they agreed to read early drafts of these chapters, but the text is clearer than it would have been without their generous suggestions.

Research into issues and themes of the sort confronted in this book is only possible due to the support of family and friends who remind me that much of life can be celebrated. My parents Pat and Bob, and my grandmother Ruth have done much to shape the habits and instincts that guide my academic work. My brother Jonathan has tirelessly laboured to improve my sense of humour, as well as my writing. The Stößel family's wonderful support is most clearly demonstrated by their patient endurance of my spoken German. Clan Ziegler (Phil, Helena, Karl, Daniel and Thomas) do much to enrich my work and wide life, as does friendship with Andrew MacKinnon and Martina Klubal. Finally, in order to keep the peace, and out of deference to paternal authority, I am compelled to apologize to the Toronto Maple Leafs ice hockey team for remarks made of it in Chapter Five.

It is more than likely that this book would not yet be written without the determined support of my wife, Katja. For her understanding, love and courage I am immensely grateful.

Introduction

Still in the Aftermath

Following the fifth anniversary of 7/7, the British government organized a public inquest into the response of London's emergency services to the terrorist attacks that erupted in the public transportation network on 7 July 2005. Most of the survivors who were interviewed by the court, as well as by the sea of eager journalists, were hesitant to offer many details about their experiences: 'I looked and then I looked away, because I didn't like what I saw', is about as much as a dancer who was riding the 'Tube' that morning would say. Another man, from the third train that was attacked, told the coroner, 'I don't want to go into too much detail what I saw . . . it's a very difficult image to hold.' When a survivor – about whose injuries initially made rescue teams assume that he must be dead – finally did tell his own story in some detail, one of the sitting judges could only reply, 'you've reduced us all to silence.'[1]

Five weeks prior to these hearings, on September 11, 2010, a librarian from Fayetteville, Arkansas, stood at the former site of the World Trade Center in New York City, to commemorate the ninth anniversary of the al-Qaeda attacks on that city. She held a sign that read: 'Today is ONLY about my sister and the other innocents killed nine years ago.' When a journalist approached her to ask what the sign meant, she began to cry and spoke of the 'impossibility of closure'. After she regained her composure, she explained the motivations behind the message on her sign: 'I'm tired of talking about everything else, tired of the politics . . . Today is only about loss.' Just a short distance away, a medical analyst was heatedly protesting against the proposed construction of an Islamic cultural centre near the former footprint of the

Twin Towers; 'They've got no business being down there. It's wrong to put the mosque down there. This is a sacred place!' Further down the street, but still within sight of the ruins, a Morroccan head waiter and his friends chanted the *salat al-Ghaib*, the Muslim funeral prayer for the dead when there is no intact corpse.[2]

Just two weeks prior to this confrontation, the fifth anniversary of a very different catastrophe was observed in New Orleans. A former first lady appeared on the television programme 'Good Morning America' in order to defend her husband's record during the aftermath of Hurricane Katrina. When an eager reporter tracked down a young boy who had become a national celebrity after surviving the disaster on his own, the now fourteen-year-old adolescent did not provide a cheerful performance: 'New Orleans is not back to normal. A lot of people may think that it is, but it's not.'[3]

These stories from recent commemorations of devastating incidents of the last decade illustrate that the impact they had on individuals who were touched by them lingers for many years after the immediate drama has passed. They also demonstrate that however much the victims of such tragedies might wish to the contrary, the legacy of such events continue to be controversial and politically charged. Different groups tell the story of these disasters in differing ways. Not all agree on what lessons are to be learned from the incidents, nor on what meaning, if any, can be derived from them.

'Religion' at Ground Zero?

In their analysis of official public responses to mass atrocities in the modern age, Thomas Brudholm and Thomas Cushman suggest that 'religious discourse and practices have seeped into broader, public, and secular discourse and contexts.' Official commemorations of contemporary disasters encourage politicians to 'act like clerics'.[4] By this, Brudholm and Cushman refer to the fact that political leaders are increasingly expected to respond to a wide variety of disasters and upheavals, in ways which offer reassurance and future vision, and these messages frequently imply specific systems of value or meaning. Brudholm and Cushman suggest that in such a situation, the use of religious discourse following a disaster is ambiguous. It emerges as a result of being placed in a 'double bind': for a disaster demands a response from individuals and authorities, but this necessity emerges in the face of a situation in which it is virtually impossible to respond in a complete or adequate way. A catastrophe does not contain within it, nor does it permit, clear meaning or resolution. But the pain and disruption it leaves in its wake raises the demand for exactly such things as curative solutions or meaningful explanations. It is for this reason that Brudholm and Cushman argue that responses to atrocities frequently include a 'religious' dimension, which they define as the following: 'religion as a means for understanding what appears to be beyond the reach of our understanding'. They suggest that when faced with events that exceed a society's expectations and customary routines, people generally grasp for cultural 'reservoirs of meaning', which are often located in traditional religious beliefs and practices. Robert Wuthnow observes similar patterns of social behaviour, and suggests that when disasters confront human beings with an unprecedented awareness of the fragility of human life 'it is almost inconceivable that we are unaffected by this knowledge.'[5] Wuthnow observes how this results in a varied range of responses, including anxiety, denial and intense activity. Like Brudholm and Cushman, he refers to some of this activity as 'religious', due to the fact that 'Sense making in times of crisis also involves coming to terms with transcendence.'[6]

An old cliché that is often simplistically employed to describe this phenomenon is that 'there are no atheists in foxholes'. In times of fear and crisis, many turn to sources of consolation and hope, to some desired promise that the world – or at least the 'next' world – can be better than the present situation. Marx's description of religion as an 'opiate' contains an element of this perspective, as does Freud's concept of 'wish-fulfilment' and rational choice theory's understanding of religion as a system of 'compensators'. Theological traditions, by contrast, generally struggle to explain the existence of suffering in relation to the existence of a divine being by developing a 'theodicy'. That many find such accounts unconvincing or inadequate to the ongoing reality of historical disasters, as this volume will demonstrate, has done little to diminish the presence of theodicies, even in secular forms.

This book explores the troubled state of religion in the face of a variety of modern disasters and crises. It analyses moments in history when many people have lamented that, after what they have experienced, 'The world will never be the same!' The discussion examines how such emotive reactions impact on the way religion is understood and theorized. Since the terrorist attacks of September 11, 2001 (in the United States) and July 7, 2005 (in the United Kingdom), political and academic discussions of the place of 'religion' in the contemporary world have taken on an increasingly urgent and intense tone. Such events spurred a new interest in religion among secular philosophers like Jürgen Habermas, Jacques Derrida, Peter Sloterdijk and Slavoj Žižek.[7] The attacks have also provided the impetus for an energetic movement commonly known as the 'New Atheism', which has renewed a description of modernity as being inherently opposed to the 'violent' and 'intolerant' nature of religion.[8] Religion has thus received an enhanced level of attention in social and political discourse since the events of 9/11 and 7/7. Some leaders of religious communities have hoped that this will lead to a renewal within their traditions. Critics of religion, however, have at the same time become more determined to restrict the presence of religious practice in the public sphere.

One needs only to recall another recent tragedy to understand the anger behind such criticism. Following an earthquake in 2003 that killed 31,000 people in Bam, Iran, a prominent cleric named Hojatoleslam Kazem Sedighi declared that 'A divine authority told me to tell the people to make a general repentance. Why? Because calamities threaten us.' He recalled this event as presidential elections approached in April 2010, after President Mahmoud Ahmadinejad warned that Iranians had better vote for him or face the threat of a massive earthquake in Tehran. The conservative cleric explained his president's remarks by suggesting that women who dress immodestly risk causing earthquakes by invoking the wrath of God. 'What can we do to avoid being buried under the rubble?' Sedighi asked during a prayer sermon, 'There is no other solution but to take refuge in religion and to adapt our lives to Islam's moral codes.'[9]

Such a clear link between a theologically instrumental theodicy and a specific political agenda presents the basic problem confronted by this book: the way in which religion can and is used in situations of crisis and disaster to forward ideological agendas by those who speak of God. Following a catastrophe, religious adherents and critics of religion alike frequently use the fear and emotional disruption caused by a tragedy as rhetorical leverage for their theoretical or political positions. The outcome of such a dynamic is neither a deeper understanding of the tragic event, nor of the object of religious faith, but rather serves as only another venue for the ideological battles that emerge in the wake of a disaster.

The problem of speaking of God in face of a catastrophe is clear in the case of the Iranian cleric Sedighi, but the problem confronting religious adherents is deeper and more subtle than this illustration suggests. Lawrence Langer warns that common forms of reactive grasping of cultural 'surfeits of piety' following a catastrophe are frequently problematic.[10] He argues that the use of traditional religious language can often become a barrier to a direct and open encounter with atrocities. Religious discourse, in other words, can be reduced to a sentimental and reassuring cliché, which individuals use to maintain their existing understanding of the world in the face of confusion and disruption. When this is the function of speaking and acting religiously, Langer suggests that, in the face of a disaster, religion inhibits the development of deeper understanding and of change.

Background to This Book

The reflections that make up this volume began after I encountered quite directly the problems inherent to speaking theologically in times of crisis. Although I learned of the attacks on the United States on September 11, 2001 from the safety of distant Toronto, immediately following the crisis, I was, like most people, shocked and deeply disturbed. I left a university meeting after I first heard the news from New York to search for some place with a public television, in order to discover more about what was going on. On the way, I encountered a fellow theology student on the side-walk – a kind and gentle man who was training to be a Christian minister, and who always presented himself as composed, mature and wise in years. The man I encountered that day, however, had been completely transformed. He was pulsing with anger. 'Roger' had heard the news from New York and he was furious. He said to me,

> For too many years we have been naïve, and our bleeding hearts have let people take advantage of us. We have tried to be liberal and tolerant, but now we've had to learn the hard way. Maybe now we won't be afraid to punish terrorism and Iraq. It's time that we finished the job that the Americans were afraid to finish in the Gulf War. Maybe now we can finally bomb those bastards back into the dark ages!

I was shocked to hear this man – who up to then I had found to be a thoughtful and deeply compassionate Christian – present such an angry and hateful position. To me, his views were simplistic and based on fear and emotion, rather than informed reasoning. Trying to put his words into the context of the terrible events of the day, I attempted to calm him down:

> I understand your anger, but my worry about your suggestion that we use military force and bombing against entire countries is that, rather than punishing the people actually responsible for today's attacks, we will instead kill innocent people – women and children. . . .

Roger interrupted me impatiently,

> I don't care! Let's bomb them all! I don't care how many we need to kill! I'm tired of all this wishy-washy open-mindedness. The Muslims don't like us and never will! It's time that we faced reality.

Roger then angrily stormed off down the street. I found a cafe with a television at the front, and I stood with a crowd of about fifty people, watching the horrifying images on CNN. I was standing there watching when the first tower suddenly collapsed.

The basic questions that guide this book began to emerge for me on that day. The most immediate concern I had was: how can a Christian like Roger be so quickly and completely transformed into a ball of rage, demanding violent vengeance? I could understand his anger and his desire for the guilty to be punished, but I was shocked by the hatred I saw when I looked into his burning eyes. How do events like those on September 11, 2001 cause people to be cosumed by a hateful desire for violent revenge? More specifically, how does religion contribute to this reflex action? Is religious faith able to help people resist responding to tragedies and shock with violence and rage, or is it itself an inherent part of the problem of violence, as the 'New Atheists' suggest? If one argues the former position, however, then how does one avoid the danger that Langer warns of, or that the Muslim cleric Sedighi illustrates? How does one speak of God in times of terror, without having one's speech simply be shaped and dictated by the fears and anger one experiences during such moments?

The Structure of the Book

To explore such questions, this volume analyses theological responses to human tragedy and cultural shock by focusing on popular reactions to the terrorist attacks on the United States in 2001 and on the United Kingdom in 2005. It also examines the events surrounding the Lisbon Earthquake of 1755, the First World War, the Holocaust, the Tsunami in South-East Asia, Hurricane Katrina and the 2010 Earthquake in Haiti. Attention is given to themes such as the theodicy question, the function of religious discourse in the face of tragedy and the relationship between religion and politics. The book is particularly concerned to explore the tension that exists between religion's capacity to both cause and enhance the suffering and destruction surrounding historical tragedies, but also religion's potential to serve as a powerful resource for responding to such disasters.

Before proceeding further, it may be helpful to clarify what this book does *not* intend to do. It should be stated clearly that the volume does not develop an explanation of the motivations which drive terrorists, nor does it offer a precise theory of the relationship between religion and terrorism. For such a discussion, there are other useful studies available.[11] Similarly, this volume does not focus on therapeutic or 'pastoral' responses to disasters with a view to providing methodologies and practices that offer relief to victims.[12] The scope of this book does not include a broad survey of how all the major religions of the world respond to terror and tragedy. The primary religious tradition under examination is Christianity. Chapter Three focuses on Judaism, and there are some brief discussions of Islam at various points of the book, but there is no attempt to offer a thorough treatment of these latter two traditions, nor of any additional religious communities.

Within the academic study of religion, an intense debate rages over whether it is possible to define what is distinctly 'religious' about certain forms of subjective human experience, structures of discourse or communal practices.[13] The discussion here will not attempt to offer a thorough or systematic theory of religion, although Chapter Four does discuss issues relevant to such a question. I am aware of the contentious debate over the status of 'religion' as a concept and do not intend to treat it as either a universal or an autonomous category in the discussions in this volume. Rather than suggesting a specific theoretical definition of religion, references to 'religion' or 'religious practices' simply refer to the institutional existence of Christian, Jewish and Muslim communities, or to the experiences and activities of individuals who are practising members of those communities. References to 'theology' refer to the conceptual and theoretical elements of a religious tradition, through which adherents of those traditions attempt to articulate the object of their beliefs and practices.

Rather than developing a theory of the relationship between religion and violence, or a pastoral methodology for the treatment of victims of trauma, the central concern of this book is to explore how theological discourse is intertwined with political and ideological agendas, which is particularly in evidence during times of crisis. The discussion demonstrates that one of the primary ways that theology generally deals with human suffering – by constructing a theodicy – often reveals more about the person articulating the explanation for suffering than it does about either the world or a divine reality. A second agenda of the volume is thus to present a critique of theodicy. The third contribution of the book is to offer a sustained reflection on how one might contemplate speaking of the divine at all, given the dangers inherent in the use of theological discourse in times of crisis. This section of the book is primarily developed by engaging with the Christian tradition. The position defended is that the demand that theology speak 'positively' in times of disaster and catastrophe is itself ideological, so that it is both reasonable and faithful to proceed in a more negative mode of engagement with the theological traditions of Christianity.

The book is divided into two sections. The first four chapters focus on analysing different historical examples of modern catastrophes.[14] The purpose of these discussions is to illustrate different ways that theology and religion have become entangled with politics and trauma in the wake of a terrible tragedy. There is no attempt to compare or contrast these differing events, or to establish any hierarchy of significance between them. Rather, each event is presented in the order of its historical occurrence, with the intention of highlighting different ways that theology is confronted by the problem of suffering during times of crisis.

References in this book to 'Ground Zero' clearly brings to mind the term commonly used to refer to the footprint of the now-destroyed World Trade Center in New York City, but the volume also intends a more general and metaphorical meaning. The term 'ground zero' entered into common vocabulary after the end of the Second World War. It is derived from the term 'point zero', which was coined at the Trinity test site in New Mexico, where the first nuclear bomb was tested by the United States on 16 July 1945. 'Point zero' was the tower that housed the test bomb, and so the term 'ground zero' has come to refer to the precise point at which an explosion has occurred. One of the significant aspects of indentifying 'point zero' is to make it possible to measure the shock waves which emanate outwards from the primary explosion, but which cause considerable destruction in their own right. The former site of the World Trade Center is clearly a site of both a major disaster, as well as a point from which shock waves emerged and left a major impact on many people at some distance from lower Manhattan. Beyond the event of September 11, 2001, this book is concerned with many other locations and situations where a major catastrophe has emanated shock waves that have interrupted and scarred entire communities and cultures far beyond the site of the immediate impact. Speaking metaphorically, the 'Ground Zeros' of human history are locations where tragedies occurred whose destruction and capacity to inflict trauma and suffering far surpassed the immediate physical damage they caused, so that they shocked and wounded entire societies and cultures. The primary concern of the first section of this volume is to explore how such 'shock waves' have impacted on theological reflection and how religious adherents employ their traditions in reaction to an historical disaster.

The second half of the book is more theoretical in nature. Rather than focusing on historical disasters directly, the final three chapters examine concepts and problems that have emerged in the previous section: the nature of ideology, the impact of trauma on theology, the relation between witnessing and empathy, the limits of remembrance, and the demand to offer 'positive' hope and consolation in the face of a crisis.

The opening chapter offers a critique of traditional articulations of theodicy and an introduction of the idea that religion and politics are intertwined. This is developed via an analysis of an exchange between the philosophers Voltaire and Rousseau following the Lisbon Earthquake in 1755. The second task of the chapter involves revisiting those same issues by exploring popular responses to the disasters of the Asian Tsunami of 2004, Hurricane Katrina in the United States and the Haitian Earthquake of 2010. This discussion illustrates how many articulations of theodicy in these contexts are shaped by political agendas and concerns.

In Chapter Two, the concerns of the previous chapter are explored in more particular detail through an analysis of the reactions of Christian army chaplains to the horrors of trench warfare in the First World War. Particular attention is given to the writings of the British chaplain Geoffrey Studdert Kennedy and the German Paul Tillich. What emerges in particular in the recollection of the experiences of these two men is their emphasis on the idea of divine suffering and the concept of religion as ideology.

The Christocentric approach to suffering and theodicy developed by Kennedy and Tillich in the second chapter is challenged and problematized in the third chapter by exploring Jewish reactions to the

National Socialist 'Final Solution' during the Second World War. The debate over what to name this event ('Holocaust'/'Shoah') illustrates the contentious nature of commemorating such a devastating event, and particular attention is given to the writing of Elie Wiesel and to the philosophy of Emil Fackenheim.

Chapter Four explores reactions to the terrorist attacks in the United States in 2001. The focus here is particularly on how the attacks have enhanced criticisms of religion as aggressive and dangerous (Bruce Lincoln, Mark Juergensmeyer, Richard Dawkins) as well as efforts to encourage a greater appreciation for religion. The primary issue highlighted in the analysis in this chapter is how the use of religious rhetoric in the wake of the 9/11 attacks has often served to construct a dualistic distinction between 'Us' and 'Them' which served to portray the present global situation as a clash between two irreconcilable groups.

Following the opening four chapters focusing on specific historical disasters, Chapter Five analyses the concepts of 'ideology' and 'belief' as developed by the philosopher Slavoj Žižek. This discussion deepens understanding of numerous issues raised in the previous four chapters and assists with a description of the impact of the terrorist attacks as a 'cultural shock'. Žižek's work suggests an approach to 'belief' that regards it as both ideological and in need of critique, but also as essential for progressive politics. After highlighting the usefulness of his basic position, however, an analysis of Žižek's secular attempt to harness religion's capacity to motivate human action demonstrates that his position risks being reduced to the same 'religious' zeal that he generally criticizes.

The primarily philosophical discussion of Chapter Five is brought into dialogue with the Christian theological tradition in Chapter Six through a discussion of Barth's criticism of religion in *The Epistle to the Romans*. At this point, the discussion moves from a secular to a theological critique of religion. But while Barth's cautionary approach to the dangers of religion are instructive, his slogan that the theologian ought to carry on doing theology 'as if nothing has happened' is shown to be inadequate in the wake of a contemporary catastrophe. This point is developed conjuction with theologians who have brought theology into dialogue with trauma theory, as well as with the political theology of Johann Baptist Metz.

The volume concludes by highlighting the difficulties of speaking of God in a time of terror. The discussion develops around an examination of Rowan Williams's response to both 9/11 and also the bombings in London on July 7, 2005. The theology of Metz and the critical theory of Theodor W. Adorno are drawn upon to complement the examination of the challenge confronting theological discourse during such times of crisis, in order to challenge the demand that theology must speak 'positively' in the face of a disaster. By describing theology as an act of 'planned frustration' or 'hoping against hope', its task is conceived in a limited and negative mode. Thus, the book argues that not as much can be said about a situation as one would want to be able to say, nor will it be as positive a contribution as many will want it to be, or indeed, as many understandably will demand it to be. The discussion demonstrates, however, that this is the only adequate approach to speaking of God at ground zero in a way that one can realistically hope does not contribute further to the suffering of the world and which just might serve to illuminate, if only momentarily, a sense that the current catastrophe is not all that there is.

Notes

1   Esther Addley, '7/7 inquests: We know who did it and why. But this is more than just catharsis', *The Guardian* 27 October 2010.
2   Andy Newman, 'At a Memorial Ceremony, Loss and Tension', *New York Times* 11 September 2010.
3   Alessandra Stanley, '5 Years On, Katrina Dampens Coverage', *New York Times* 28 August 2010.
4   Thomas Brudholm and Thomas Cushman (eds), *Religious Responses to Mass Attrocity: Interdisciplinary Perspectives* (Cambridge: Cambridge University Press, 2009), 2–3.
5   Robert Wuthnow, *Be Very Afraid: The Cultural Response to Terror, Pandemics, Environmental Devastation, Nuclear Annihilation, and Other Threats* (Oxford: Oxford University Press, 2010), 8.
6   Ibid., 14.
7   Giovanna Borradori, *Philosophy in a Time of Terror: Dialogues with Jürgen Habermas and Jacques Derrida* (Chicago: University of Chicago Press, 2003); Peter Sloterdik, *God's Zeal: The Battle of the Three Monotheisms*, trans. Wieland Hoban (Cambridge: Polity Press, 2009); Slavoj Žižek, *On Belief* (London and New York: Routledge, 2001).
8   See, for example, Richard Dawkins, *The God Delusion* (New York: First Mariner Books, 2008); Christopher Hitchens, *God is not Great: How Religion Poisons Everything* (New York: Twelve Books, 2007). See also Amarnath Amarasingam (ed.), *Religion and the New Atheism* (Leiden: Brill, 2010).
9   Scheherazade Faramarzi, 'Iranian Cleric: Promiscuous Women Cause Quakes', *Washington Post* 20 April 2010.
10 Quoted in Brudholm and Cushman, 9.
11 For psychological explanations and analyses of terrorism, see Jessica Stern, *Terrorism in the Name of God: Why Religious Militants Kill* (New York: HarperCollins, 2003).

[12] For so me such discussion, see David A. Alexander, 'Psychological Intervention for Victims and Helpers after Disasters', *British Journal of General Practice*, 40 (1990), 345–8; Patric R. Spence, Kenneth A. Lachlan and Jennifer M. Burke 'Adjusting to Uncertainty: Coping Strategies among the Displaced after Hurricane Katrina', *Sociological Spectrum*, 27.6 (2005), 653–78; the special issue of *Psychoanalytic Dialogues* 12.3 (2002).

[13] See Talal Asad, *Genealogies of Religion* (Baltimore: John Hopkins University Press, 1993), Jonathan Z. Smith, 'Religion, religions, religious', in *Critical Terms for Religious Studies*, ed. Mark C. Taylor (Chicago: University of Chicago Press, 1998), 269–84; William E. Arnal, 'Definition', in *Guide to the Study of Religion* (London: Cassell, 2000), 21–34.

[14] Within the sphere of 'disaster studies', technical distinctions are sometimes made between a 'disaster' and a 'catastrophe' for purposes of clarity and nuance when assessing issues of policy making or relief planning. As this book is not focused on such issues, it will use these terms as if they are equivalent. I argue that for the purpose of considering the impact of such events on theological reflection, this is appropriate. For a discussion of the significance of a distinction between such terms, see Havidan Rodriguez, Enrico L. Quarantelli and Russell Dynes, (eds), *Handbook of Disaster Research* (New York: Springer, 2006); Lori A. Peek and Jeannette N. Sutton, 'An Exploratory Comparison of Disasters', *Disasters* 27.4 (2003), 319–35.

Chapter 1

In the Wake of Lisbon, Katrina and Haiti: On the Limits of Theodicy

The aftermath of what is frequently called a 'natural disaster' often includes considerable commentary that is either overtly or indirectly 'theological'. Survivors of the devastation may ask questions like, 'Why did God let this happen? How can I believe in God when the world is full of such suffering?' In the absence of direct references to concepts like 'God', it is not uncommon for individuals to ask 'What did I do to deserve this?' implying that somehow the way they live their lives has caused their present difficulty. Others may simply express their feelings at such times as follows: 'My life will never be the same!' or 'This changes where I place my priorities.' Of course, it is also common for people to fall into deep despair or depression in reaction to discovering that the world was not as safe or secure as they once thought.

This chapter explores such reactions to natural disasters. It does so by focusing particularly on a disaster that not only impacted on the lives of the people who experienced it directly, but that also shocked the cultural ethos of Europe as a whole: the Lisbon earthquake of 1755. Following this event, the lives of many would no longer be the same, including some who only heard about the disaster from pamphlets and letters they read. Some of the most famous philosophers of the period were compelled to respond to the implications of the earthquake, which resulted in considerable theological controversy and debate. In what was perhaps the first great 'cultural shock' of the modern age, a new distinction emerged between 'natural' and 'moral' evil. This impacted on how the nature of suffering was conceived, and the way in which new articulations of 'theodicy' were formulated. The discussion here illustrates some of this debate by analysing an exchange that developed in the aftermath of Lisbon between the philosophers Voltaire and Rousseau.

Beyond demonstrating some of the standard elements of theological explanations for suffering (known as 'theodicy'), the analysis in this chapter demonstrates that theodicies are not simply abstract theological discussions, but are frequently shaped by political and social concerns and agendas. There is nothing purely theoretical or abstract about theodicy; rather, it is a form of response to a disaster that is shaped by the events it tries to explain and by how that event has impacted on the person constructing the theodicy. This is shown with reference to disasters closer to our own time than that of Lisbon: the Asian Pacific Tsunami of 2004, Hurricane Katrina in 2005 and the Haitian earthquake of 2010. The entwinement of theodicy and politics, as well as the very painful challenge of human suffering, illuminate the profoundly problematic nature of theodicy as both an intellectual and emotional exercise. The chapter will conclude, however, that the dynamics of seeking an explanation for suffering are not so easily avoidable despite these problems, even in more 'secular' forms of discourse.

The Lisbon Earthquake

Shortly before ten o'clock in the morning on November 1, 1755, a major earthquake struck the Portuguese capital city of Lisbon. The first shock wave caused great destruction, followed by a second and then a third great tremor. As it was All Saints' Day, churches and chapels were filled with an abundance of lit candles. Furthermore, most people heated their homes and cooked by way of an open fire. Thus, in the chaos and confusion, many fires broke out, and soon the whole city was aflame. It burned for five days. Many of the residents of the city fled to the waterfront, but again tragedy met them. The seismic shock wave of the earthquake caused a tsunami to hit the city, which washed away many of the people seeking refuge at the harbour. Scholars continue to find it difficult to accurately estimate the number of people who died. Some reports from the period go as high as 70,000 people dead, but most researchers today think the number was more likely around 15,000. Of the estimated 20,000 dwellings in the city, it is thought that only about 3,000 were left standing afterwards.[1]

It would be difficult to exaggerate the shock that this terrible event spread across Europe. It was not that earthquakes were unheard of or unfamiliar to Europeans in this period – there had been major earth-quakes recorded in Jamaica in 1692, and in Sicily and Catania in 1693. But Lisbon at the time was the fourth largest city in Europe (after London, Paris and Naples). Its 275,000 residents were wealthy and educated, and many were devout Roman Catholics. The city was known for its gold (from its colonies in Brazil) and for its many impressive churches. Witnesses of the event were, therefore, very shocked to see one of Europe's wealthiest and most beautiful cities being destroyed. One Portuguese officer, writing to a friend, summarized the ruins of the city as 'one of the wide Gates of the vast Empire of Death'.[2] A merchant's letter to a friend in England captures the tone of those terrible days:

> It would be a vain attempt to endeavour describing the numberless miseries and terrible distresses of all kinds occasioned by this dread-ful calamity, as well as the shocking effects that it had on the minds of all people. Infinite were the numbers of poor broken limbed per-sons, who were forced to be deserted even by those who love them best and left to the miserable torture of being burnt alive . . . In passing about the boundaries of the city, for some days after the destruction of it, 'twas extremely affecting to receive the congratu-lations on my escape from those who know me, and to observe those others. For the first few days the natives seemed entirely taken up with acts of devotion and repentance: every road and every field were filled with people at prayers or in processions . . . I have past through the ruins of the principal parts of the city and they are dreadful indeed to behold. I believe so complete a destruction has hardly befallen any place on earth since the overflow of Sodom and Gomorrah.[3]

This eye-witness report highlights one of the reasons that the event captured the imagination of Europe. Beyond being disturbed by the immediate tragedy and destruction, people began to debate the pos-sible reasons for the event. Questions regarding the meaning of the disaster soon had far more significance to observers than did the ter-rible consequences the destruction had on the residents of the city. Set in the context of the 'Enlightenment' or 'Age of Reason', many saw in the effort to understand the Lisbon disaster a great tension between religion and human reason. Some argued that the terrible earthquake should be understood as a 'natural occurrence' without any supernat-ural cause. This was a new idea for many people of the period, given the scientific community's uncertainty at the time over the cause of earthquakes.

Many of the philosophers and scientists of the day, as well as the principal ruler of Lisbon, Sebastian José de Carvalho e Mello (commonly known as the Marques de Pombal), insisted that the cause of the event lay solely in the forces of nature. There was little agreement as to the precise reasons for the earthquake, but such individuals were confident that someday science would bring them to light. Others, however, including Gabriel Malagrida, a Jesuit missionary in Lisbon, argued that the cause of the earthquake was divine punishment for the sinful lives of the people of Lisbon. The tension between these different interpretations within the city grew very heated. Malagrida's position served to discredit the work of other Christian leaders to comfort those left injured and homeless in the city, many of whom were applauded for their efforts.[4]

The dispute became very heated. The authorities sought to focus the efforts and attention of the survivors on rebuilding the city and restoring as much order to society as possible. For preachers like Malagrida, this was entirely wrong-headed. What was required, he argued, was to turn to God in repentance, to go on pilgrimages and to avoid being distracted by worldly concerns. The anxiety level of the general population was not helped by the fact that over 30 small tremors continued to be felt around Lisbon in the week following 1 November.[5] Pombal grew increasingly intolerant of such preaching. He first had the Papal Nuncio banish Malagrida, and when that proved insufficient to silence him, he had the Jesuit preacher imprisoned. Four years later Malagrida was executed.

Disputes over the cause and meaning of the earthquake were found not only within Portugal, but quickly became heated throughout Europe. In Spain, for example, a fierce theological dispute developed as priests like Agustín Sanchez emphasized that 'God uses the creatures to infuse fear in sinners and to move them to repentance.' In opposition to such positions, José de Cevallos insisted that 'the earthquake has been entirely natural, caused by natural and proportioned second causes.'[6] In England, a similar debate developed, although it is clear that the theological discussion was frequently infused with national and political biases. To the question, 'Why Lisbon rather than London', English preachers were prepared to offer some clear answers: because Portugal was Roman Catholic and had failed to follow the path of the Reformation; because the Inquisition was strong within Lisbon; or because God had clearly shown greater favour for the political system of England. One clergyman wrote to ask the survivors, 'Is there a scene of lewdness or debauchery that was ever practised which hath not been daily repeated in your religious houses?'[7] John Wesley wrote with considerable vehemence in a similar fashion: 'Is there indeed a God that judges the world, and is he now making an Inquisition for Blood? If so, it is not surprising that he should begin there (Lisbon) where so much blood has been poured on the ground like water.'[8]

Although such views were common among English theologians and clergy, not all observers were prepared to agree. A poem by John Biddulph would only go so far as to remark, 'but why to them 'twas giv'n, remains among the Mysteries of Heaven.'[9] One satirist angrily dismissed the popular tendency to suggest that Lisbon was being punished for its sins: 'the Pamphleteers, common print-sellers, and Journalists, have been labouring incessantly for some months pasts, not only to keep awake and augment our sympathetic anguish of mind, but (what is still more base) to rob us of the credit and merit of that generosity which inspires it.'[10]

Theodicy and the Book of Job

Such attempts to explain the existence of pain and imperfection in human history are known as exercises in 'theodicy'. Clearly the disaster that happened at Lisbon had a considerable impact on how people thought about the world in which they lived and their place within it. This pattern of theorizing over the possible meaning of such an event, particularly with reference to blaming either the victims of the tragedy themselves for the disaster, or some other political or ideological opponent, is one that remains a common response to catastrophes to this day. It is practically taken for granted that Christian theology and the reflections of other religious traditions inevitably involve such forms of theodicy. When religious adherents confess a belief in a loving and powerful divine being, it is assumed that such faith must inherently involve a theoretical explanation for the existence of tragedy and suffering in the world. Many critics of religion are quick to highlight logical errors or gaps in such forms of reasoning, but few focus on the fact that such theoretical practices are frequently plagued by bias, fear and even political agendas.

It cannot be denied that theodicy has had a central place in Christian thought for many centuries. In the medieval worldview, many understood Christianity to offer a full and complete explanation for how the universe worked. God created the world, and, therefore, it was assumed that everything that happened in the world occurred because God willed it that way. This seems like a simple enough idea, but, of course, things are not so straightforward once one begins to apply this view of God and the world to the realities of human suffering.

The book of Genesis states that after Creation, God saw that the world 'was very good' (1.31).[11] Yet human beings within it sometimes suffer terribly from illness, accidents, violence, poverty and injustice. Christian theology has struggled to try to understand how the Christian idea of a good and powerful creator God can be reconciled with the realities of pain and suffering in the world. Some have argued that when bad things happen, it is because God has willed them – that God wanted them to happen for some reason. Such an understanding suggests that nothing is an 'accident', but that all things have a hidden, divine purpose. Not infrequently, the explanation given for this is that those who suffer do so because they have sinned. This is exactly what many Christian preachers like Malagrida proclaimed in the wake of the Lisbon earthquake.

Although individual passages in the Christian Bible can be cited to support positions like that of Malagrida, they are usually quite brief and fall short of offering a systematic theodicy. For example, in the Gospel of John (9.1–3), Jesus of Nazareth is asked whether a man's blindness is the result of his own sin or is due to the sins of his parents. Jesus replies, 'Neither this man nor his parents sinned.' This answer is rather vague. Does it suggest that Jesus simply did not answer the question, or might it be a subtle criticism of the very premises and concerns which seek to develop a coherent divine explanation for human limitations and problems?

In both the Christian and Jewish Bibles, the book of Job offers the most sustained discussion of the experience of unjust suffering. The book is the story of a man named Job, who was known to be a blameless and upright man. He was seen by others to be kind and just. Job cared for his family and lived according to the ways of God. He and his family prospered for many years, but then adversity strikes. His people are attacked by invaders, and many of his family are killed. A disaster devastates his land, and much of his property is destroyed. His children are killed when their house collapses during a great windstorm. And then Job himself catches a terrible disease and terrible sores break out all over his body.

Three of Job's friends hear of his troubles and set out to comfort and console him. But when Eliphaz, Bildad and Zophar come upon their friend, they hardly even recognize him, as he is completely covered with loathsome sores. The text describes their reaction: 'they raised their voices and wept aloud' (2.12) and sat with him for seven days and seven nights without speaking a word.

Suddenly Job begins to voice a loud cry of protest, insisting upon the depth of the injustice he is suffering. He cries, 'Why did I not die at birth!' His friends can be silent no longer. They are scandalized by this outburst of anger and despair. No doubt shaken by the state of their friend, whom they can hardly recognize beneath his wounds, they scramble to defend God against Job's accusations. The three men rush to engage in what modern philosophy and theology will call 'theodicy'. But after each of the three takes a turn scolding Job and affirming that God must have a purpose for what is occurring to their friend, Job lets them know what he thinks of this exercise of theodicy: 'I have heard many such things, miserable comforters are you all. Have windy words no limit? Or what provokes you that you keep on talking' (16.1–2).

From Job's perspective, the scrambled and panicked religious statements of his friends are of no comfort. He calls them mere 'windy words', and he questions what actually motivates his friends to say what they are saying. Are they actually speaking with the hope of comforting and supporting Job in his suffering? Or do their words have a different purpose? Are they really trying to comfort themselves, seeking to reassure themselves that their understanding of God and the world need not be challenged by what is going on?

Job's questioning of the 'windy words' of his friends continues to challenge all efforts to proscribe divine meaning to human suffering. In the aftermath of the Lisbon earthquake, disagreement over the appropriateness of certain theodicies would come between two other friends, who also happened to be among the most famous philosophers in Europe during that period.

Theodicy after Lisbon: Voltaire and Rousseau

In the eighteenth century, there were well-established theological and philosophical explanations for the reality of suffering in the world. But after the devastating shock of Lisbon, the capacity of such arguments to satisfy the questions raised by the tragedy would be severely weakened. Some people rejected these traditional explanations for human suffering in the world. For many philosophers and political leaders, if such events were to be understood as having any meaning at all, such purpose could not be found in the cause of the event. The earthquake, they argued was a natural event – something that happened for no single or direct reason. The only place such thinkers could locate talk about the meaning of the event was in wrestling over the best way to respond to the tragedy. Before exploring these rejections of theodicy, it is instructive to recall the arguments employed by such philosophical explanations for the reality of suffering.

Within philosophy, the most influential approach to theodicy was articulated by Gottfried Leibniz (1646–1716). Leibniz, who coined the term 'theodicy', sought to defend the concept of a good and loving God against accusations that such a God was irreconcilable with the existence of suffering in the world. Leibniz's defence of a divine Creator rests on two principles. First, he argues that God could not have made a better world than the one that exists. God was limited by the constraints of what sort of 'worlds' could possibly be created. Secondly, Leibniz claims that God acts for the best, since that is part of the very nature of a good divine being. Together these principles imply that the world as it exists is the best of all possible worlds. Any other world that God could have made, Leibniz argues, would have been worse. Why, then, does suffering exist in the world? Leibniz's response is to suggest that it is not the Creator who introduces pain and suffering, but finite creations. By exercising free will, human beings and other creatures sometimes make misguided choices and engage in unfortunate practices, so that 'Man is the Origin of Evil'.[12] Although Leibniz's concepts and his manner of argumentation are very much in the mode of philosophical reasoning, note how well his position corresponds with those versions of Christian theology which explain human suffering as a consequence of sin. What Leibniz calls 'natural evil' (the pain and suffering human beings experience in the world) is inherently linked to 'moral evil' (the crimes and failures committed by human action).

These issues were debated among the many intellectual responses to the Lisbon earthquake. Away from the city of Lisbon itself, one such exchange is particularly notable, for within it two different theodicies were developed, both of which rejected the position of Leibniz and the link between moral and natural evil that he established.

The French philosopher Voltaire (1694–1778), perhaps the most famous and influential thinker in Europe at the time, was horrified by reports from Lisbon. It shattered his worldview, making him doubt his previous trust in human progress and reason. It also impacted on his attitude towards the church and Christianity. He wrote a poem in response to the tragedy, which not only offered a powerful lament against the event, but also challenged the ideas of the English poet Alexander Pope, who wrote a religious poem in 1734 entitled 'An Essay on Man'. To understand Voltaire's position, it is useful to be familiar with Pope's basic approach to theodicy.

Pope's poem intended to vindicate the ways of God to human beings and to warn them against thinking that humans are the centre of all things. In Leibnizian fashion, it sets out to demonstrate that, no matter how imperfect or incomprehensible the world may appear to be, in actuality, the universe follows hidden natural laws, as established by God. It is a defence of the idea of divine 'Providence'. Pope taught that, although the world appears imperfect to human beings, this is only because their perceptions are limited by their feeble moral and intellectual capacities. God, in this view, might be described as a great watchmaker, who has designed a perfect universe that now runs like a well-made clock. Every part works together for the common good. This is essentially a common position among eighteenth-century intellectuals known as 'deism'. Deists largely rejected much of traditional Christianity, especially the authority of the church, but they believed that a divine Creator set up the universe to run according to eternal laws. This creator-God then withdrew to let things run as they ought. It was the task of philosophy to uncover these laws so that people could act accordingly.

Alexander Pope concludes his poem by suggesting that human beings must learn to accept their position as humble creatures in a mysterious world whose ultimate and perfect purpose is not always clear. In one famous section of the poem, he writes,

> All Nature is but Art unknown to thee;
> All chance direction, which thou canst not see;
> All discord, harmony not understood;
> All partial evil, universal good:
> And spite of Pride, in erring Reason's spite,
> One truth is clear, *Whatever is, is right.*[13]

It is this trust in the ultimate goodness of the world that Voltaire rejects after the Lisbon earthquake. He can no longer accept the idea that the world runs like a clock, according to divine laws. For him, the horrors of human suffering make such a position irrational and morally inconceivable. In response to Pope, Voltaire's own poem asks,

When you hear their piteous, half-formed cries,
Or from their ashes see the smoke arise,
Say, will you then eternal laws maintain,
Which God to cruelties like these constrain?
Whilst you these facts replete with horror view,
Will you maintain death to their crimes was due?
And can you then impute a sinful deed
To babes who on their mothers' bosoms bleed?[14]

Voltaire cannot accept the view that the tragedy of Lisbon had a hidden purpose established by some eternal law. Nor can he accept the suggestion that the victims of the destruction were being punished for their sins. And so Voltaire challenges Pope's idea that 'whatever is, is right':

Yet in this direful chaos you'd compose
A general bliss from individuals' woes?
Oh worthless bliss! In injured reason's sight,
With faltering voice you cry, 'Whatever is, is right'?
The universe confutes your boasting vain.[15]

Voltaire's dismay over the destruction, and his anger at an explanation like that of Pope, led him to be increasingly critical of Christianity and religious explanations for human tragedy.

Another philosopher of the period who received the news from Lisbon with horror did not appreciate the tone of Voltaire's poem. Jean Jacques Rousseau (1712–1778) was a prominent intellectual known throughout Europe, and he was a regular enthusiastic correspondent with Voltaire. But in a letter from 18 August 1756, Rousseau criticized Voltaire's response to the earthquake:

All my complaints are . . . against your poem on the Lisbon disaster, because I expected from it more worthy evidence of the humanity that apparently inspired you to write it . . . You so burden the list of our miseries that you further disparage our condition. Instead of the consolations that I expected, you only afflict me further. It might be said that you fear I don't feel my unhappiness enough, and that you are trying to soothe me by proving that all is bad.[16]

Rousseau thought that Voltaire's poem was cold and heartless, leaving little to hope for in this world. He suggests that Voltaire left human beings without meaning or understanding. He also rejects Voltaire's view that the tragedy refutes the idea of divine providence in the world. Rather than blaming God – or the non-existence of God – for the event, Rousseau finds the source of evil 'in man's freedom and perfection – which is also his corruption'. He explains,

> Most of our physical pains, except death . . . are also our own work. Without leaving your Lisbon subject, concede, for example, that it was hardly nature who assembled there twenty-thousand houses of six or seven stories. If the residents of this large city had been more evenly dispersed and less densely housed, the losses would have been fewer or perhaps none at all. Everyone would have fled at the first shock, and would have been seen two days later, twenty leagues away and as happy as if nothing has happened. But we have to stay and expose ourselves to further tremors, many obstinately insisted, because what we would have to leave behind is worth more than we could carry away. How many unfortunates perished in this disaster for wanting to take – one his clothing, another his papers, a third his money?[17]

Rousseau interprets the extent of the disaster with attention to how people made the consequences worse than they might have been. For him, the earthquake was not caused by sin, but by natural occurrences. But human error and limitations – what might be called human 'sin' – contributed to making the natural occurrence much more terrible than it would otherwise have been. If houses were more solidly built and were less cramped together; if people had fled at the first sign of danger, rather than trying to guard their possessions or ignore the warning signs, thousands more would have survived. And so Rousseau's position falls in between a complete dismissal of God and an explanation that blames Lisbon's residents for the occurrence of the earthquake. After outlining this nuanced view, Rousseau ends with a critical passing remark to his friend Voltaire,

> Satiated with glory and disabused of vanity, you live free in the midst of affluence. Certain of your immortality, you peacefully philosophize on the nature of the soul and, if your body should suffer, you have Tronchin as doctor and friend. You however find only evil on earth . . . You enjoy, but I hope.[18]

Here is perhaps the most cutting element of Rousseau's criticism of Voltaire. In effect, he says to the great philosopher: it is all well and good for you to sit at your writing desk and cynically criticize everyone who tries to find some sense of meaning after the tragedy, but you have the luxury of being able to be cynical at a distance, in the comfort of your safe home in Paris. All your cynicism does is deprive people who are left poor and homeless, who have lost loved ones, and who lie injured or maimed, of hope, of comfort, of resources to rebuild meaning in their lives. For this reason, Rousseau rejects the message of Voltaire's poem and continues trying to search for a way to understand the Lisbon disaster in a way that clings to hope.

This may seem both an attractive position and also pragmatically useful, but it involves some difficult issues of its own. Effectively, Rousseau's argument implies that natural disasters are completely neutral. They are meaningless and have no moral significance. At the same time, however, as his criticisms of the behaviour of the citizens of Lisbon reveal, responsibility for the terrible results of the earthquake are transferred to the actions of human beings. Such an observation leads Susan Nieman to argue that, 'while Rousseau underlined the modern separation between natural and moral evil, he did so in a way that seemed to blame us for both.'[19]

Theodicy and Politics: The Asian Pacific Tsunami, Hurricane Katrina and Haiti

Subsequent chapters will explore differing versions of theodicy in more detail. What the remainder of the present chapter will illustrate is that the responses to the Lisbon earthquake of 1755 were by no means unique. Similar religious reactions were common to more recent tragedies, such as the tsunami in the Asian Pacific region in 2004, the devastation caused by Hurricane Katrina to the Gulf of Mexico coast in 2005, and in the aftermath of the 2010 earthquake in Haiti. Making this connection serves not only to highlight the fact that religious theodicies are still very much part of reactions to contemporary disasters; it also helps bring into clearer view the way in which the tendency to blame human beings for such tragedies is by no means limited to theologians and religious practitioners. The modern separation between natural and moral evil that Rousseau popularized continues to develop in a way that blames human beings for both.

With a frequency and vehemence that rivals both the intensity and shock of the great Lisbon earthquake of 1755, these three recent 'natural disasters' have received a considerable amount of attention and commentary. On 26 December 2004, a massive earthquake under the Indian Ocean (measuring over 9.0 on the Richter scale) triggering a series of cataclysmic tsunamis that struck the perimeters of Indonesia, Sri Lanka, India, Thailand and elsewhere. Hundreds of coastal communities were hit, with estimated casualties of 186,983 dead and 42,883 missing, for a total of 229,886.[20]

On 29 August 2005, 'Hurricane Katrina', one of the strongest hurricanes ever recorded in the Gulf of Mexico, made landfall in southeastern Louisiana. The storm surge caused major and catastrophic damage along the coasts Louisiana, Mississippi and Alabama, including several major cities. Levees separating Lake Pontchartrain from New Orleans were breached by the surge, flooding approximately 80% of the city and neighbouring areas. The hurricane is estimated to have caused $75 billion (USD) in damages and to have killed at least 1,599 people.[21]

The Haitian earthquake of 2010 began at 16:43 on 12 January, and measured 7.0 on the Richter scale. It involved at least 52 aftershocks and impacted on the lives of three million people. The Haitian Government reports that an estimated 230,000 people died, 300,000 were injured and 1,000,000 made homeless.[22] Thousands of homes and buildings were destroyed, particularly in Port-au-Prince.

These terrible tragedies were global media events, capturing the attention of millions around the world. People watched news footage in horror, frequently stunned into muted silence, much like the three 'friends' of Job. But once the impact of the spectacle began to subside and the cries and protests of the victims began to be heard, the responses of some religious leaders were much like that of Job's 'miserable comforters'.

Following the Asian Tsunami, for example, spokespeople from a variety of religious traditions offered versions of a theodicy which explained the event as being God's punishment for human sin. For example, Shlomo Amar, an Israeli Rabbi, suggested that 'This is an expression of God's great ire with the world.'[23] Pandit Harikrishna Shastri, a priest of New Delhi's Birla Temple, argued that the disaster was caused by 'a huge amount of pent-up man-made evil on earth, and driven by the position of the planets.'[24] A Muslim cleric and vice president of the opposition party in Malaysia remarked that the disaster was a reminder from God 'that he created the world and can destroy the world.'[25] Finally, Martyn S. Carless, of the Christian group 'Moriel Ministries', wrote,

> Indonesia, the nation worst hit by the Tsunami, had an increasingly extremist Islamic influence. The other countries also affected have likewise in large measure departed from true biblical Christianity and are now embracing radical Islam in its stead. There is no doubt that this is a judgment from God upon such idolatrous practices. Yet, these were by no means extremes for many of the nations affected . . . Likewise there was the sin of rampant child sexual exploitation, where paedophilia, especially from western countries, had been an escalating problem for some time now. Just to what extent this proved to be the case was illustrated when, within no time of the Tsunami actually devastating a certain number of those countries, incredible reports were emerging of criminal gangs marauding around seeking vulnerable children bereaved of families in order to traffic them off into the ever-burgeoning sex trade . . . For the Church to be aghast at the possibility of God judging such wickedness just goes to show how far we have departed from core, biblical Christianity.[26]

All of these theological responses to the terrible tragedy seek to blame human failings for what happened. This trend was not limited to only a few religious traditions. Many religious leaders, representing a variety of different traditions, used the occasion of the Tsunami to try to score rhetorical points in support of some of their views of the world.

Theological responses to Hurricane Katrina were often no more sophisticated. David Crowe of the Oregon-based organization, 'Restore America' wrote,

> Katrina was an act of God upon a sin-loving and rebellious nation, a warning to all who foolishly and arrogantly believe there is no God, and that if He did exist, 'would not have done such a thing!' It is also a serious call to repent, to turn away from our wicked ways, from the heart of a loving Father.[27]

Bill Shanks, pastor of New Covenant Fellowship of New Orleans, said that Christian organizations

> warned people that unless Christians in New Orleans took a strong stand against such things as local abortion clinics, the yearly

Mardi Gras celebrations, and the annual event known as 'Southern Decadence' – an annual six-day 'gay pride' event scheduled to be hosted by the city this week – God's judgment would be felt. [28]

Shanks thus actually gave thanks for Hurricane Katrina:

New Orleans now is abortion free. New Orleans now is Mardi Gras free. New Orleans now is free of Southern Decadence and the sodomites, the witchcraft workers, false religion – it's free of all of those things now . . . God simply, I believe, in His mercy purged all of that stuff out of there.

The most publicized version of such a theodicy after the Haitian earthquake was the television interview with American politician Pat Robertson, who suggested that the Haitian people had 'made a deal with the devil' during their struggle against the colonial rule of France, which only a great 'turning to God' could rectify. Until such a return to Christianity was undertaken, he implied, Haiti's sufferings would continue. [29]

Such statements scandalized many non-Christian and non-religious people, and have been referred to by secular critics as evidence of the dangerous and violent nature of religion as such. In *The God Delusion*, for example, Richard Dawkins points to quotations such as those above and writes,

Their whole education has led them to view natural disasters as bound up with human affairs, paybacks for human misdemeanours rather than anything so impersonal as plate tectonics. By the way, what presumptuous egocentricity to believe that earth-shaking events, on the scale at which a god (or a tectonic plate) might operate, must always have a human connection. Why should a divine being, with creation and eternity on his mind, care a fig for petty human malefactions? [30]

Christopher Hitchens offers a similar view:

Earthquakes and tsunamis are to be expected and can even to some degree be anticipated. It's idiotic to ask whose fault it is. The Earth's thin shell was quaking and cracking millions of years before human sinners evolved, and it will still be wrenched and convulsed long after we are gone. These geological dislocations have no human-behavioral cause. The believers should relax; no educated person is going to ask their numerous gods 'why' such disasters occur. A fault is not the same as a sin. However, the believers can resist anything except temptation. Where would they be if such important and frightening things had natural and rational explanations? They *want* the gods to be blamed.[31]

As was the case in the aftermath of the Lisbon earthquake, in the wake of contemporary disasters, religious leaders and their secular critics frequently trade rhetorical blows against each other in newspapers, during radio and television interviews, and increasingly, through blogs and other electronic media. On both sides, it is frequently clear that the commentator intends to associate the disaster with a particular political position or moral view, or simply seeks to link an opponent to the terrible consequences of the catastrophe. There is reason to ask such voices the same question Job asks of his friends: 'what provokes you that you keep on talking?' What motivates the vast amount of commentators – religious, political and moral – who flood contemporary media in all its forms following a natural disaster? From the examples already illustrated in this chapter, there is sufficient evidence to suggest that it is more than simply concern and compassion towards the tragedy's victims. This alone is reason to approach theodicies with suspicion.

To pick but one example, the ideological nature of the post–Asian Tsunami statement by Martyn Carless is particularly clear.[32] He argues that the Tsunami was caused by God, who used it to punish human beings for the tourist sex trade in the Asian Pacific region – particularly the exploitation of women and children by rich western men. But the logic of this position is clearly flawed. Carless is suggesting that God was punishing humanity for the sexual sins of Western tourists – by killing the victims of these tourists – not the tourists themselves! If Carless's explanation for the cause of the disaster was actually correct, the Tsunami should have wiped out the homes and families of North Americans and Europeans, not the poverty-stricken villages that are exploited by the sort of tourists Carless is concerned about. It is much easier to point the finger of blame on other people and distant lands – and not on things that touch closer to home.

The same dynamic is present in the post-Katrina sermon by Bill Shanks. Once again the suffering of innocent victims is described as being inflicted by an act of God. But the victims themselves have nothing to do with the so-called sins that the religious leader preaches against. The thousands of affluent white college students who flock to the Mardi Gras, 'Girls Gone Wild' and 'Southern Comfort' events in New Orleans that Bill Shanks fumes against, *were not in the city* to face the onslaught of Katrina. Instead, it was primarily poor, black, working-class people who suffered the consequences of the storm and the ruptured levees. If God is indeed seeking to punish those people whom Shanks dislikes, is it possible that God could have missed the god's target to such an astonishing degree? Can divine vengeance so frequently become an accidental act of 'friendly fire'?

As was the case in the aftermath of the Lisbon earthquake, such blatantly self-serving and ideological uses of the suffering of victims has done much to discredit the response of religious people in general to the tragedies. Thus, although many religious organizations have raised millions of dollars in relief support, and many religious organizations have helped bring considerable assistance to those in need, sceptics have been left with the impression that religion has been nothing but a problem in the context of these disasters.

Never a 'Miserable Comforter'

Following the Asian Tsunami, the theologian (and Archbishop of Canterbury) Rowan Williams composed a very different kind of commentary for a London newspaper. He wrote,

> Every single random, accidental death is something that should upset a faith bound up with comfort and ready answers. Faced with the paralysing magnitude of a disaster like this, we naturally feel more deeply outraged – and also more deeply helpless. We can't see how this is going to be dealt with, we can't see how to make it better. We know, with a rather sick feeling, that we shall have to go on facing it and we can't make it go away or make ourselves feel good.[33]

Williams was severely criticized for what he wrote in this newspaper article. For many Christians, the title of his submission, 'Of course this makes us doubt God's existence', was considered offensive and inappropriate for a Christian leader to utter. Such critics thought any sign of lamentation or protest against what had happened threatened to undermine religious faith. Many thus sought to challenge his words, much in the same way that Job's friends scrambled to silence Job's cries of protest.

What Williams offers in this short editorial, however, is an important check on the temptation to rush from discomfort in the face of the terrible suffering of events such as the Asian Tsunami and Hurricane Katrina. He writes,

> The traditional answers will get us only so far. God, we are told, is not a puppet-master in regard either to human actions or to the processes of the world ... If some religious genius did come up with an explanation of exactly why all these deaths made sense, would we feel happier or safer or more confident in God? Wouldn't we feel something of a chill at the prospect of a God who deliberately plans a programme that involves a certain level of casualties?

For Williams, admitting that the suffering caused by natural disasters challenges religious faith is not a sign of weakness or heresy; rather, it is an acknowledgement of the depth of human suffering that confronts human beings. When human beings are confronted with the question of 'Why them and not us?' they are faced with the uncomfortable reality that there is usually no adequate answer available. But such uncertainty, as well as this lack of clear answers, is often difficult to accept. The troubling abuses of religious language quoted earlier in this chapter demonstrate how some people respond to the emotional anger and confusion that human tragedies cause by projecting their inner turmoil outwards onto some scapegoat they can target and blame.

This is perhaps one of the most difficult things for people to accept in the face of events like the Tsunami and Katrina: sometimes there really is not anyone to blame for the tragedies in our world. This not only seems unjust, it is also very difficult to resolve, emotionally. It is a very natural reflex to look for someone to blame when something bad happens. When Job starts to complain, his friends panic, because it sounds to them like he is blaming God. Since, they argue, God cannot be at fault, then it must be Job who is to blame. In their worldview, someone has to bear responsibility for what has happened.

Secular Theodicy?

Thus far the discussion has focused on challenging the propensity of Christian theology to respond to disasters by developing theodicies, but there are many different types of theodicies besides the Christian versions. Non-religious perspectives sometimes develop what could be called a theodicy, as people attempt to explain or rationalize the existence of suffering without any reference to a divine being. Contemporary culture still looks for someone to blame for the 'natural' events that occur. It is still assumed that responsibility for a tragedy can be assigned; only, as in the case of Rousseau's position against Voltaire, the cause of the event is not considered to be God, but human behaviour.

Consider, for example, how Hurricane Katrina became a focus of considerable controversy and debate. Soon after the disaster, a wave of criticism developed over how the aftermath was dealt with by the authorities, emphasizing how human error and moral failings made this disaster much worse than it might have been with better planning and organization.[34] But such explanations and accusations against the Bush administration do not, of course, identify the original cause of the hurricane itself.

Wes Granberg-Michaelson develops a perspective that moves to the level of causality when he asks,

> Just how 'natural' was this disaster? Consider this, for instance. When Katrina left the Florida coast, it was classified as a 'tropical storm' – not even a hurricane. It picked up tremendous power as it passed through the Gulf of Mexico, in part, experts think, because the waters of the Gulf were two degrees warmer than normal. So by the time it reached New Orleans, it was a category four hurricane.[35]

The article furthers this position by suggesting that human neglect of the environment is to blame for the temperature of the Gulf waters, so that human beings are to blame for the hurricane. Such an argument frequently involves identifying those people who are considered particularly to blame for the state of the environment, be they oil companies, energy corporations or car owners. Although no divine being is invoked in such accounts of the disaster, the natural 'evil' of the event continues to be explained with reference to 'moral evils' committed by particular 'sinners'. Again, the basic structure of Rousseau's letter to Voltaire is repeated. Just as he blamed the state of housing construction in Lisbon for the earthquake's devastation (and, by implication, those who built these houses), some sociologists, for example, suggest that neglect of the particular hazards found in the physical landscapes of cities like New Orleans is to a large degree responsible for the high degree of damage the city suffered.[36]

The causal factors that studies such as these illuminate are important contributions to the study of natural disasters, but there is also a tendency among such responses to tragedy to comfortably and quickly move towards a 'secular' form of theodicy, in which blame and responsibility can to be assigned for all the disasters that confront human society. As the journalist Edward Rothstein notes, such secular responses to natural catastrophe 'so readily become political'.[37] Although the search for scientific explanations for such events are significant and urgently needed, at the same time, the fear and trauma that is often attached to these important efforts do little to mediate or constrain reactions which repeat the problematic elements of religious theodicies in a secular form. Clear answers are seldom obvious or immediately available, and often the 'blame game' simply gets reduced to another opportunity to score ideological points. Theodicy – even in secular terms – easily slides into the sort of 'miserable comfort' offered by Job's friends.

Disaster Research on Trauma

Disaster research in disciplines such as sociology and psychiatry are increasingly enhancing understanding of the impact that historical tragedies have on communities and individual human beings. Such knowledge represents substantial contributions to the care of victims, the diminishing of human suffering and the prevention, or at least minimalizing, of future disasters. At the same time, it is noteworthy that the tendency for reactions involving theodicy to be entwined with personal bias or political agendas is frequently overlooked in such literature, particularly when the role of religion is being discussed. For example, when in *In the Wake of Disaster* the psychiatrist Harold Koenig identifies ways in which religion helps people to cope after a disaster, his list of ten reasons includes the following: religion provides a 'positive worldview'; it offers the individual a sense of meaning and purpose; it offers a confidence that God is in control of what otherwise would appear to be a chaotic situation.[38] These are no doubt structures of emotional or psychological support that many human beings find comforting and helpful. The concern to be raised here is not the accuracy of Koenig's findings; rather, it is to note that when religion is conceived of simply as serving an instrumental function – that is, when its role is considered only as a way of making people feel better – then there is considerable risk that religion may serve an ideological role in the wake of a disaster. This is to say that using religion to make oneself feel better may not always be healthy or helpful, particularly when this is accomplished at the expense of someone else or at the price of supporting inaccurate opinions and biases.

Recall the example of Bill Shanks once again. As he is based in New Orleans, it is not difficult to conceive that his Christian faith brought him some comfort, since it 'explains things and provides answers', and allows him to integrate a negative experience by setting it in a worldview that may 'be seen as stable, safe, and predictable.'[39] While Shank's version of Christianity may be psychologically 'useful' to him in this pragmatic sense, this does not necessarily mean that his worldview is healthy, moral or true. Koenig is likely aware of this, but accounts such as his of the utility of religion in the context of disasters often give little attention to this problem. There remains little analysis of this tension between religion's psychological benefits and its ideological potential in disaster research literature, nor is there much in the way of theological reflection on this problem. Wrestling with this issue will be the primary concern of subsequent chapters.

The Challenge of Atheism?

Before proceeding further with such a criticism of religion's ideological function, however, it should be made clear that this problem is not unique to religion as such. Retreat into a familiar and comforting worldview is also a common reflex among secularist observers touched by the impact of a disaster. One example of this is Martin Kettle's article for the British newspaper *The Guardian*, entitled, 'How can religious people explain something like this?' The column offers a direct challenge to religious adherents following the 2004 Tsunamis.

Kettle invokes the legacy of Voltaire to support his point, arguing that, 'Earthquakes and the belief in the judgment of God are . . . very hard to reconcile.' One feels the power of his outrage at the terrible human tragedy when he continues,

> A non-scientific belief system, especially one that is based on any kind of notion of a divine order, has some explaining to do, however. What God sanctions an earthquake? What God protects against it? Why does the quake strike these places and these peoples and not others? What kind of order is it that decrees that a person who went to sleep by the edge of the ocean on Christmas night should wake up the next morning engulfed by the waves, struggling for life?[40]

This is a powerful rhetorical challenge to any religious response to disasters like the Asian Tsunami, but it is also one that is based on a rather limited portrait of Christianity. It cannot be denied that many Christians describe the causes of earthquakes in the manner Kettle describes – this chapter has referred to a number of such examples – but this by no means represents how all Christians conceive of such disasters. David Bentley Hart, for example, challenges the above quotation by Kettle because he does not think that the Christian gospel intends to reconcile earthquakes and divine judgment. Like Rowan Williams, Hart denies that God wills all the events that occur in human history. He argues that the God whom Kettle is challenging, like the God that Voltaire's Lisbon poem criticizes, is not the Christian understanding of God. Rather, the image of God they reject is the deist concept of God – a divine clock-maker who has designed the world as a perfect system. In his book *The Doors of the Sea*, Hart suggests that Christians have a different understanding of Creation: 'Nowhere does Voltaire address the Christian belief in an ancient alienation from God that has wounded creation.' In Hart's view, the world as it exists for us now is only 'a shadowy vestige of the world God truly intends'.[41]

Hart admits that many Christians imagine God as a great Crafts-person, who designed the world to be exactly like it is, natural disasters and all. But he argues that nature is far from being a perfect system that points to a perfect and loving designer. Instead, he insists that nature is purposeless striving. Noting the forces of evolution and the food chain among animals, he writes, 'All life feeds on life,' so that, 'It is as if the entire cosmos were somehow predatory.'[42] If nature sometimes appears to be such a 'cycle of sacrifice', then, Hart continues,

Christians will view nature as being less a sign of a divine Designer, and more a source of mystery and challenge.

The result of such a view is, in Hart's opinion, the realization that there is nothing 'remotely resembling theodicy's attempted moral justification of the present cosmic order' in the Christian Bible.[43] For Hart, God's providence remains beyond the current order of things and the cycles of nature. The sufferings of this world do not serve God's Kingdom, which is to come. And so, confronted with the terrible human suffering caused by the Asian Tsunami, Hart writes, 'when I see the death of a child I do not see the face of God, but the face of his enemy.'[44]

Kettle would no doubt disagree with the Christian eschatological assumptions that support Hart's position, but the point here is simply to illustrate that his angry remarks against Christianity in his editorial are curious for two reasons: first, he offers only a caricature of how Christian theology conceives of such a natural disaster; secondly, it is unclear why he has chosen to write with such passion and anger against theistic belief in God on this occasion. Might it be that his own emotional reaction to the terrible events of the Asian Pacific Tsunami reinforced already held opinions, which, not unlike in the pattern described by Koenig, provided him with a coherent and meaningful worldview with which to feel confirmed and reassured?

Abandoning Theodicy?

Perhaps it is due to at least a subtle recognition of this dynamic that some contemporary Christian theologians are expressing considerable reluctance to advance a theodicy to explain suffering. Neither Rowan Williams nor David Bentley Hart, for example, accept that the Tsunami or Hurricane Katrina were 'Acts of God'. They insist that God does not use such events to punish human beings or to test them. In their view, the challenge that confronts Christians in the face of such tragedies is not, 'Why did God do this?' but only, 'How will God's people respond to this terrible tragedy?' Both theologians imply that Christians should spend less time trying to determine how a natural disaster fits into a systematic theological worldview, and should focus their energy on responding in practical and concrete ways to help and support rescue and recovery efforts that reduce the level of human suffering.

Such is the message of John Swinton's book *Raging with Compassion*. Swinton's thesis is that traditional Christian theodicies do not 'work' (in a logical and philosophical sense), but 'can also be dangerous and have the potential to become sources of evil in and of themselves'.[45] As an alternative to theodicy, Swinton proposes that Christians focus on the communal practices that the church has historically employed as appropriate responses to suffering and loss. These include prayers of lament, acts of forgiveness and nurturing hospitality. Such practices serve as resources for Christian as they try to process the impact that a tragedy has on them. They also shape the church's practical activity as it seeks to assist the victims of such events.

There is much to appreciate in the emphases of each of these three theologians as they criticize theodicy and seek to avoid the trap of employing the anxieties and fears experienced in the midst of a tragedy as fuel for retrenching one's pre-existing ideological biases and agendas. It is sometimes suggested, however, that it is somewhat disingenuous to suggest that one can avoid theodicy altogether. As Susan Nieman observes, 'Every time we make the judgment *this ought not to have happened*, we are stepping onto a path that leads straight to the problem of evil.'[46] Many argue that such moral judgements imply assumptions about the proper order of things, which returns a seemingly practical proposal to the realm of metaphysics and ontology. Thus the positions of Williams, Hart and Swinton all draw upon specific approaches to Christology, as well as upon views relating to the nature and function of the church and its practices. Nieman's perceptive critique is often true of positions which claim to avoid theodicy in any sense whatsoever, although it is perhaps less true of Swinton in this case than of Williams, and most certainly of Hart.

Such an observation suggests that the problem of theodicy cannot be set aside too quickly or straightforwardly. The question of whether it is possible to articulate a coherent 'anti-theology' will re-emerge in Chapter Three and related issues will be discussed more substantially in Chapter Seven. For the present discussion, suffice it to say that, although this chapter has demonstrated that traditional strategies for explaining the existence of suffering are problematic – logically, theologically and practically – at the same time, there is clinical evidence which suggests that there are pragmatically 'useful', as well as philosophical, reasons for exploring the metaphysical implications of the ways in which human beings respond to historical tragedies. Prior to exploring the theoretical issues that these questions raise in greater depth, the following two chapters will first explore the complexity of the relationship between theodicy and politics in more detail by turning to two other historical events which had a traumatic and lasting impact on Western culture: Chapter Two explores how the First World War was experienced by two Christian army chaplains, while Chapter Three wrestles with the terrible legacy of the Holocaust on Jewish thought. These discussions demonstrate that, as one moves from a concern with 'natural disasters' to catastrophes of human making, such as war and genocide, the issues under discussion only get more complex, as well as more troubling.

Notes

[1] T. D. Kendrick discusses the details of the devastation in *The Lisbon Earthquake* (London: Methuen, 1956) 32ff.; Luis A. Mendes-Victor, Carlos Sousa Oliveira and João Azevedo, (eds) *The 1755 Lisbon Earthquake: Revisited* (New York and Berlin: Springer, 2009).

[2] *A Letter from a Portuguese Officer to a Friend in Paris Giving an Account of the Late Dreadful Earthquake* (London: M. Cooper, 1755), 2.

[3] Anonymous, *An Account of the Late Dreadful Earthquake and Fire, which Destroyed the City of Lisbon* (London: J. Payne, 1755), 35, 38–9.

[4] See the account, for example, of Antony Pereria, *A Narrative of the Earthquake and Fire of Lisbon* (London: G. Hawkins, 1756).

[5] Kendrick, 41.

[6] Mendes-Victor, et al. (eds), *The 1755 Lisbon Earthquake: Revisited* (New York and Berlin: Springer, 2009), 9.

[7] *A Letter from a Clergyman at London to the Remaining Disconsolate Inhabitants of Lisbon Occasioned by the Late Dreadfull Earthquake* (London: R. Griffiths, 1756), 11.

[8] John Wesley, *Serious thoughts occasioned by the earthquake at Lisbon* (London, 1756), 4.

[9] John Biddulph, *A Poem on the Earthquake at Lisbon* (London: W. Owen, 1755), 8.

[10] *A Satirical Review of the Manifold Falsehoods and Absurdities Hitherto Publish'd Concerning the Earthquake* (London: A. and C. Corbett, 1756), 2.

[11] All biblical references are from the *New Revised Standard Version*.

[12] G. W. Leibniz, *Theodicy*, trans. E. M. Huggard (La Salle, IL: Open Court, 1985), 123ff.

[13] Alexander Pope, *An Essay on Man and Other Poems* (Mineola, NY: Dover Publications, 1994), 52.

[14] Voltaire, *The Portable Voltaire*, ed. Ben Ray Redman, trans. Tobias Smollett et al. (New York: The Viking Press, 1949), 560.

[15] Ibid., 565.

[16] Jean-Jacques Rousseau, *Correspondence complete de Jean Jacques Rousseau*, vol. 4, ed. J. A. Leigh (Geneva: Institut et Musée Voltaire, 1964), 37–8. Translated by R. Spang.

[17] Ibid., 40.

[18] Ibid., 56–7.

[19] Susan Nieman, *Evil: An Alternative History of Philosophy* (Princeton and Oxford: Princeton University Press, 2002), 39.

[20] UN Office of the Special Envoy for Tsunami Recovery, 'The Human Toll'. Available at: http://www.tsunamispecialenvoy.org/country/humantoll.asp [last accessed 19 April 2011].

21 Lindsay, Robert, 'Katrina Death Explodes to 1,599,' (20 March 2006). Available at: http://robertlindsay.blogspot.com/2006/03/katrina-death-toll-explodes-to-1599.html [last accessed 9 January 2011].

22 'Haiti raises earthquake toll to 230,000', *Washington Post* 10 February 2010.

23 'To God, an age-old question', *The Telegraph* (Calcutta, India) 31 December 2004.

24 Ibid.

25 Ibid.

26 Martyn S. Carless, 'Tsunami: God's Anger Revealed', http://www.moriel.org/articles/discernment/church_issues/tsunami_gods_anger_revealed.htm# [last accessed 10 April 2011].

27 David Crowe, 'Why Katrina?' http://www.restoreamerica.org/content/why_katrina.pdf (last accessed 12 December 2010).

28 J. Brown and A. Martin, 'New Orleans Residents: God's Mercy Evident in Katrina's Wake', *AgapePress* (2005).http://headlines.agapepress.org/archive/9/22005b.asp (accessed 14 December 2005).

29 Ryan Smith, 'Pat Robertson: Haiti "Cursed" After "Pact to the Devil",' *CBS News* 13 January 2010. http://www.cbsnews.com/8301-504083_162-12017-504083.html (accessed 10 December 2010).

30 Richard Dawkins, *The God Delusion* (New York: First Mariner Books, 2008), 270.

31 Christopher Hitchens, 'A Fault Is Not a Sin', *Slate Magazine* 17 Jan. 2010.

32 The concept of 'ideology' will be discussed in detail in Chapter Five.

33 Rowan Williams, 'Of course this makes us doubt God's existence', *Daily Telegraph* (London, 2 January 2005).

34 For a study of the impact of such criticism, see William L. Waugh, Jr., 'The Political Costs of Failure in the Katrina and Rita Disasters', *The Annals of the American Academy of Political and Social Science* 604 (2006), 10–25.

35 Wes Granberg-Michaelson, 'Acts of God or Sins of Humanity?' *Sojourners Magazine* 9 August 2005.

36 DeMond Shondell Miller and Jason David Rivera, *Hurricane Katrina and the Redefinition of Landscape* (Lanham, MD: Lexington Books, 2008).

37 Edward Rothstein, 'Seeking Justice, of God or the Politicians', *New York Times* 8 September 2005.

38 Harold G. Koenig, *In the Wake of Disaster: Religious Responses to Terrorism & Catastrophe* (Philadelphia and London: Templeton Foundation Press, 2006), 29ff.

39 Ibid., 39.

40 Martin Kettle, 'How can religious people explain something like this?' *The Guardian* 28 December 2004.

41 David Bentley Hart, *The Doors of the Sea: Where was God in the Tsunami?* (Grand Rapids, MI: William B. Eerdmans, 2005), 22.

42 Ibid., 48–9.

43 Ibid., 66.

44 Ibid., 9.

45 John Swinton, *Raging with Compassion: Pastoral Responses to the Problem of Evil* (Grand Rapids, MI: William B. Eerdmans, 2007), 3–4.

46 Nieman, 5.

Chapter 2

The 'War to End All Wars': Religion in the Trenches of the Great War

The close of the nineteenth century and the beginning of the twentieth was an age of great confidence and enthusiasm. Much like the mid-eighteenth-century culture of Voltaire's time, the turn-of-the-century period was one full of faith in the idea of progress. Witnessing incredible advances in technology, science and medicine, most people in Europe and North America believed that the world was getting progressively better. With a little effort and patience, they assumed that human beings could accomplish anything they put their minds to. Much of this confidence in the future course of humanity would be shattered in the trenches of World War One.

This chapter explores another event that significantly challenged Western culture and Christian thought: the so-called War to End All Wars of 1914–1918. The generation who came of age prior the First World War often approached Christianity and their national identity with the idea that 'God is on our side.' Before the war, many assumed that what happens in the world is part of God's providence. But after this generation witnessed the terrible reality of the battlefield, such a view would no longer be acceptable to most people.

The discussion in this chapter focuses on two elements of the impact that the First World War had on the culture and religion of its generation: an awareness of the entwinement of religion and politics, and a widespread questioning of traditional theodicy. After a general introduction to the ways in which the war shocked this generation, this chapter analyses the attitude of British and German theologians towards the outbreak of the war. It demonstrates the extent to which, on both sides of the conflict, Christian theologians were quick to equate their nation's cause in the war with the Christian faith itself.

As this equation became increasingly obvious to Christians at the time, a troubling question emerged: to what extent is religion merely an ideological product of the wider culture? This chapter will discuss this concern as it explores ways in which the shock that many experienced in the face of the destruction caused by the conflict resulted in a deep re-evaluation of their attitudes towards God. Particular attention is given to the writings of two army chaplains, G. A. Studdert Kennedy and Paul Tillich. An analysis of their approaches to theodicy, and of their own re-evaluation of the relationship between Christianity and politics, demonstrates how their theologies shift from a focus on the transcendence of God towards an emphasis on divine immanence, and how both of them develop a deep suspicion of the ideological potential of religion.

The Outbreak of the 'Great War'

The causes of what that generation would call the 'Great War' or the 'War to End All Wars' are beyond the scope of this discussion, but the immediate event that caused the outbreak – the assassination of the Austrian Archduke Franz Ferdinand by a separatist in Serbia on 28 June 1914 – serves to illustrate that, in the end, it did not take much to get things going.[1] In hindsight, it is striking to recall that, in almost every nation that became caught up in the war (with the possible exception of the United States), the declaration of war was initially met with a considerable amount of popular enthusiasm. For a number of years, many politicians and journalists had anticipated an outbreak of conflict, and they observed the clear presence of rising tensions and unresolved grievances between a number of the major European nations.

In Germany, the declaration of the war was greeted by newspapers in Berlin with the headline 'It's On!' Great crowds had urged the Kaiser to declare war. It is significant to recall that, at this point in its history, unified Germany was actually a young nation. The many different German states and provinces had only been joined into a single country in 1870. Since that time, German science and industry had become the most advanced and successful in the world. Its manufacturing power now surpassed that of England, and the German navy was beginning to rival that of the British. German culture at the turn of the century was confident and future oriented. The German people had a sense that, although the nineteenth century had belonged to England, the twentieth century was to be theirs. And if other countries wanted to restrain Germany's self-emergence, then Germany had to find the will to assert itself. If that meant a war, then most people accepted that such a price would have to be paid. Germany had beaten France in a short war in 1870, and so most Germans assumed they would win the next 'short' war.[2]

England and France had somewhat different motivations for the conflict, but the people of these countries also greeted the news of war with enthusiasm. In France, many citizens resented Germany's new-found success. They longed to revenge the defeat of 1870 and remind the upstart nation to the east that France's cultural heritage was still superior to the ultra-modern German identity. The war offered the opportunity to teach their neighbour a lesson, and many in the French population met it with excitement. More concretely, after the Franco-Prussian war of 1870, the Germans had annexed Alsace-Lorraine, which aggrieved the French deeply.

To the British, a war represented the chance to defend their ideas of tradition and empire. Like the French, the British resented Germany's rising prominence and wanted to humble the Germans by reminding them that 'Britannia rules the waves.' Thus, although the outbreak of the war may have been met with slightly more English reserve, the British people generally welcomed the war as a chance to do their duty, to serve king and country, and to win honour for themselves and their nation.

In colonial nations like Australia and Canada, the young countries were enthralled with hope for the future, filled with a new confidence that they had matured enough to begin to be independent of their colonial identity and to develop their own destinies without the guidance of Great Britain. Business and agriculture were experiencing a period of great prosperity and growth. The future seemed to offer endless opportunity and possibility. For many young men, volunteering for the war effort appeared to offer a chance to participate in the excitement of a bigger world.

All sides quickly began to try to rally support and focus the excitement of their populations. Great propaganda efforts were initiated, creating posters and advertisements to encourage young people to volunteer for the conflict, and volunteer they did: in the millions. Even in distant Canada, recruiters were able to find thousands of volunteers (except in Quebec and some other francophone areas where the conflict was seen as an 'English' war). Throughout this great propaganda effort, it is noteworthy that nationalism was quite intimately linked with religion. On all sides, the outbreak of war was greeted as a religious challenge and a religious duty.

Germany's declaration of war was issued on 6 August 1914 by Kaiser Wilhelm II. It soon became widely known that the text was composed by one of Germany's most esteemed Protestant theologians, Adolf Harnack. Part of that declaration read,

> To the German Nation:
> We will fight to the last breath of man and beast. We will win this battle even if we must fight against a world of enemies. Never before has Germany been defeated when it is united. Forward with God who will be with us as he was with our Fathers![3]

This public support of the war effort by Germany's most influential theologian was enhanced by a public declaration by ninety-three of the nation's leading intellectuals on 4 October 1914. Among those who signed were twelve leading Christian theologians, including figures from the liberal, conservative and moderate camps. The document, 'Appeal to the Civilized World', denied that Germany was to blame for the outbreak of the war, and that the 'militarism' that the German cause was accused of was both a matter of self-defence and also an expression of the richness of its national 'spirit'.

After the war, the Swiss Reformed theologian Karl Barth would frequently lament this appeal and suggest that it demonstrated the bankrupt state of German liberal theology:

> ninety-three German intellectuals issued a terrible manifesto, identifying themselves before all the world with the war policy of Kaiser Wilhelm II. . . . To me they seemed to have been hopelessly compromised by what I regarded as their failure in the face of the ideology of war.[4]

This would be a lament echoed by many after 1918: how had Christian leaders allowed Christianity to be so closely aligned with nationalism and ideology? Why did their faith not provide greater insight and wisdom? For in the declaration of war, the cause of Germany is seen as being both supported and blessed by God. God was on Germany's side, it was assumed, and so divine providence would see to it that Germany was victorious. But in England and France, the same was also true. 'For God and Country' was a common slogan on British posters, and many Christian preachers urged their congregations to support the struggle. Ministers, priests and chaplains connected the war effort to the Christian duty of 'self-sacrifice' and suggested that it led to opportunities to courageously witness to Christ. Civilians and soldiers on all sides often embraced the war as something glorious, seeing it as an opportunity for both personal and national honour. Many also saw it not only as part of their civic duty, but also as part of their Christian duty. The understanding of God and what it meant to be loyal citizens were closely identified. Serving one was much the same as serving the other. As the declarations of war were made, people in all the nations of Europe looked forward to great success and glory, which God – since God was unquestionably on their side – would reward by keeping them safe and ensuring victory.

Theologians and the 'Ideology of War'

Barth's accusation that Harnack and the other German theologians had been seduced by the war ideology of their nation is frequently taken to be a uniquely German problem. Fritz Fischer, for example, argues that Germany's failure to accommodate the political climate of the other Western liberal nations was due to the influence of Lutheranism on the Prussian state. He argues that Luther's pessimism regarding the capacity of human effort, as well as his dualistic 'two kingdoms' split between the spiritual role of the Church and the independent authority of the state, shaped Germany's politics and culture along a very different path from those nations influenced by either Catholicism or Calvinism.[5] Karl Hammer, Charles Bailey and John Moses all largely support the view that Germany was responsible for the war and highlight the role of German Christian theologians in supporting it, although each historian offers excuses for this failure. Hammer argues that the theologians were ignorant of the true aims and activities of the German government, while Bailey suggests more cultural trends, such as Hegelianism and Social Darwinism, influenced the worldview of Christian leaders.[6] Moses, by contrast, emphasizes how internal social concerns shaped external foreign policy, as fear of social revolution resulted in an overenthusiastic embrace of the communal unity that the war effort brought.[7]

These differing accounts illuminate how it might be that German Christian theologians succumbed to the 'ideology of war' in 1914; however, Barth's lament against his own teachers should not leave the impression that the Germans were somehow uniquely vulnerable to this dynamic. It is instructive to compare the attitude that French and British Christians held towards Germany and the possibility of war in 1913, with the way in which their views changed soon after the outbreak of hostilities in 1914. In the decade prior to the outbreak of the war, the international ecumenical movement had made intensive efforts to unite Christians around the cause of peace. French Christians took some real leadership in these efforts, and close bonds developed between British and German theologians.[8] A highly successful World Missionary Conference was held in Edinburgh in 1910, and representatives of an increasingly strong ecumenical peace movement were to meet in Constance, Germany, in August of 1914, but the war broke out one day before it was to begin.

In reaction to the public support of Harnack and other German theologians for the German war effort, British and French theologians were quick to register vigorous protest and shock.[9] But although these church leaders were less enthusiastic about the initial outbreak of the war than their German counterparts, once the conflict began, many were as prone to equate the cause of their country to that of the Christian Gospel itself.

Some prominent voices, while conceding the necessity of entering the war and sure of Germany's guilt for initiating the conflict, sought to maintain a clear distinction between patriotism and Christian faith. The Archbishop of Canterbury, Randall Davidson, for example, opposed Anglican clergy volunteering to serve as combatants and resisted 'identifying ourselves with the Divine Will to such an extent as to claim that God is simply on our side'.[10] Edward Hicks, the Bishop of Lincoln, warned that when a nation enters into war, it can 'seldom escape the Nemesis of spiritual deterioration'. He cautioned against the dangers of developing a callous hate of the enemy, and the temptation to glorify the drama of war.[11]

Such reserve was not common, however, once hostilities began in earnest. Bishop Winnington-Ingram articulated perhaps the most blatant equation of the British cause with that of Christianity, when he asserted that

> I think the Church can best help the nation first of all by making it realise that it is engaged in a Holy War, and not be afraid of saying so. Christ died on Good Friday for Freedom, Honour and Chivalry, and our boys are dying for the same things. . . . MOBILIZE THE NATION FOR A HOLY WAR![12]

John Adams, a United Free Church army chaplain from Aberdeen, did not hesitate to call the British forces 'God's instruments' fighting in a 'Holy Crusade'.[13]

Henry Gwatkin, a conservative low-church Anglican, compared the Germans to 'demoniacs' and equated the Kaiser to the 'Antichrist'. For such an enemy, there could be 'no room for mercy'.[14] The Roman Catholic politician Emil Prüm, writing from Luxembourg, arrived at a similar conclusion. 'Pan-Germanism', he argues, amounts to 'Neo-Paganism', idolatry and an anti-clerical attack on the Catholic Church. As such, Prüm urges his audience to view Germany as a threat to the Christian faith and civilization itself.[15]

In a scathing post war critique, Julien Benda laments the xenophobia of the French clergy in 1914. He accuses French theologians of miming the example of their German counterparts and of being guilty of a patriotic fanaticism that betrayed their true vocation and social function.[16] Charles Bailey concurs with such a view, arguing that there was very little difference among French citizens in their view of the war: 'on the major demands – German repentance, reparations and the restoration of Alsace – Protestants stood shoulder to shoulder with one another and with their Catholic, Jewish and nonreligious compatriots.'[17]

On both sides of the conflict, most theologians and church leaders were quick not only to offer whole-hearted support for the military cause of their nations, but also to bless and identify the conflict with the Christian faith itself. The German practice of issuing soldiers with belt buckles inscribed with '*Gott mit uns*' ('God with us') may not have been as blatantly matched by the British and French forces, but there was little hesitation on all sides to proclaim that 'God is on our side.' Although such reassurances may have helped support morale on the home front, once soldiers met the reality of modern warfare in the trenches, those who advocated such an equation of divine providence with the conflict were in for quite a shock.

The Impact of the War

The outset of the conflict that was so eagerly and enthusiastically welcomed very quickly turned into a nightmare that few had ever imagined. Europe had never witnessed a conflict of such scale. The new technologies and machinery that were celebrated prior to the war did not prove to accomplish great progress or an efficient expediting of victory, but only unanticipated destruction. Most soldiers marched off to war expecting that it would be short, exciting and victorious. What combatants on all sides met was a long, monotonous and bloody stalemate in muddy and disease-infested trenches. Any confidence in human 'progress' would soon vanish in the face of the great products of human 'ingenuity': mustard gas, tanks and artillery able to hit targets miles and miles away.

Timothy Findley's novel *The Wars* offers a vivid portrait of the experiences of the soldiers at the front. It is the story of Robert Ross, a young Canadian man who volunteers for the army in 1915 and is sent to France to fight. On the day he ships out to England, he attends church with his parents. Throughout the service, Findley portrays Robert's mother as fearful and nervous, as the congregation sings this hymn,

Know that the Lord is God indeed;
Without our aid he doth us make
We are his flock, he doth us feed,
And for his sheep he doth us take.[18]

The scene offers a glimpse of the connection that many made between religion and the conflict in Europe: God is in control of what is going on in the world; the nation is protected by God; and so, as God's flock, one must serve the nation with courage and honour, and pray to be protected.

But then the troops meet the reality of war. Young Robert is sent to the front, where his experience in the trenches is highlighted by one thing in particular: the mud. He also faces another of the infamous elements experienced by soldiers on the battlefield: chlorine gas, which in some places was used in such concentrations that it had soaked into the mud. Findley describes the situation vividly:

The mud. There are no good similes. Mud must be a Flemish word. Mud was invented here . . . The ground is the colour of steel. Over most of the plain there isn't a trace of topsoil: only sand and clay . . . When it rains (which is almost constantly from early September through to March) the water rises at you out of the ground. It rises from your footprints – and an army marching over a field can cause a flood. In 1916, it was said that you 'waded to the front'. Men and horses sank from sight. They drowned in the mud. Their graves, it seemed, just dug themselves and pulled them down . . . Houses, trees and fields of flax once flourished here . . . Now it was a shallow sea of stinking grey from end to end. And this is where you fought the war.[19]

In this portrait, one has a sense of the extent to which the war so quickly destroyed all the ideals that it had begun with. They sank into the filthy mud. Gone was the faith in progress and human potential, along with the idea that it would be a quick and glorious war. Gone were the ideals of serving a great cause for one's country. It was increasingly difficult to imagine that all of the destruction and suffering were serving a higher cause: the honour of one's nation or the will of God. When one of the soldiers in the novel offers to play a song on the trumpet, another snaps, '*Just don't play abide with me.*' Instead, they sing songs like, 'We're here because we're here'. The soldiers are unable to give any more meaning or reason to explain what it is they are living through.[20]

In one scene, the company comes across broken Christian statues in a bombed-out church: an image of the destructiveness that the conflict would have on Christian faith of this generation. While wandering around the ruined church, one man asks, 'Are you religious?'[21] The other soldier denies any such belief, and he adds that he finds it easier to believe in 'fragility'. Fragility and brokenness are all that seem certain in the violent world he must inhabit.

Findley's novel provides a sense of what soldiers experienced at the front While, the extensive war poetry left behing by soldier who fought in the trenches offers even more striking accounts of the impact that war had on those who experienced it directly. Two promine examples serve to illustrate this phenomenon.

Wilfred Owen (1893–1918) was a British poet, Christian and soldier. He was awarded the Military Cross for bravery in September of 1918, only to be killed on the battlefield a few days before the Armistice was signed in November. Owen had been caught up in the patriotism of 1914 and wrote with enthusiasm over the coming conflict:

O meet it is and passing sweet
To live in peace with others,
But sweeter still and far more meet
To die in war for brothers.[22]

To the disapproval of contemporary critics, the tone of Owen's writing made a radical shift after he had served at the front. The poem 'Dulce et Decorum Est' is his most famous. The Latin title of the poem means, 'It is sweet and right'. This is the first line of a saying commonly used in England at the outbreak of the war: *Dulce et decorum est pro patria mori* ('It is sweet and right to die for your country'). If this was the spirit that many British men embraced in 1914, it is clear that, by 1917, it had become something ironic and dark:

> Men marched asleep. Many had lost their boots
> But limped on, blood-shod. All went lame; all blind;
> Drunk with fatigue; deaf even to the hoots.[23]

Owen's description of the horrors of chlorine gas is particularly striking, and it is such a terrible witness that leaves him disillusioned and bitter:

> If you could hear, at every jolt, the blood
> Come gargling from the froth-corrupted lungs,
> Obscene as cancer, bitter as the cud
> Of vile, incurable sores on innocent tongues,–
> My friend, you would not tell with such high zest
> To children ardent for some desperate glory,
> The old Lie: Dulce et decorum est
> Pro patria mori.

T. S. Eliott's poem 'The Hollow Men' is the most famous testimony to postwar disillusionment written in English. Rather than describing the horrors of the war, Eliott describes the effect of the terrible conflict on its survivors: those who lived on after the end of the war. He refers to them as 'hollow men'. This generation is disillusioned, without meaning and without hope:

> We are the hollow men
> We are the stuffed men
> Leaning together
> Headpiece filled with straw. Alas!
> Our dried voices, when
> We whisper together

Are quiet and meaningless
As wind in dry grass[24]

The tone illustrates the impact the war had on the people who witnessed it. The war, indeed, was a terrible 'cultural shock'. Perhaps the poem also points to the difficulty of being a survivor in a generation of which so many died. For the author of the poem, everything has been devastated, except that he lives on for some inexplicable reason. His world had come crashing down in ruins; only he himself has not been destroyed:

This is the way the world ends
This is the way the world ends
This is the way the world ends
Not with a bang but a whimper.

Although this poem has a despairing tone to it, some are inclined to also see in it a sense of reaching, or searching, for some kind of meaning. The narrative voice cannot quite pray, because everything it knows and has believed in has been shattered. But the voice appears to continue to try to pray – to try to find meaning – even if all he can muster is a 'whimper'. And so the poem incorporates some fragments of the words of the Lord's Prayer, although the prayer – like the faith it points to – is now in pieces and fragments:

Between the essence
And the descent
Falls the Shadow
For Thine is the Kingdom
For Thine is
Life is
For Thine is the

These literary reactions to the Great War serve to set the context of this chapter's examination of religious responses to the conflict. They help provide some sense of what religious leaders and theologians were facing during the period. As should be quite obvious at this point, those who sought to speak of God during this terrible conflict faced a very difficult task.

Military Chaplains

An effective way to look at the effect of the First World War on religion is to examine its impact on military chaplains, who, as Christian leaders, entered the war with the same confidence in their faith and nation, but whose experience of the devastation often forced them to rethink their assumptions about God and religion.

As already discussed, many Christians – including Christian leaders – embraced the war effort. Religious rhetoric was often used as propaganda support for the national cause, often at the cost of mature and faithful theological reflection. The various armed forces of Europe saw an important role for chaplaincy during the conflict. In Britain, the novel dependence on non-professional soldiers meant that considerable attention had to be given to the motivations and morale of the civilian soldiers, many of whom were conscripted as the war went on. As such, the role of religious leaders and agencies for supporting the morale of British combatants was considered vital.[25]

Chaplains faced the great difficulty of walking a fine line between consoling soldiers facing death, caring for the injured, and the task of inspiring soldiers to fight. When they allowed their role to become reduced to motivating soldiers in battle, they could effectively become agents of political propaganda. Such was the temptation of chaplains on both sides of the Great War. For example, these words by A. F. Winnington-Ingram, Bishop of London, are all too chilling:

> Kill Germans! Kill them! . . . Not for the sake of killing, but to save the world. . . . kill the good as well as the bad . . . kill the young men as well as the old . . . kill those who have shown kindness. . . . As I have said a thousand times, I look upon it as a war for purity, I look upon everybody who dies in it a martyr.[26]

As troubling as these words are, they should be understood as spoken in the heat of a terrible war. As historian Doris Bergen has noted, chaplains in the armed forces often find themselves in an 'ironic position'.[27] They are called upon to witness to religious faith and to comfort those who are suffering, but at the same time this effort also supports the violence of war by helping soldiers to find the strength to keep fighting. It is no easy task to deal with this tension, nor with the tension of being a non-combatant in an aggressive and hyper-masculine environment.

The memoirs of Frederick G. Scott, Senior Canadian Chaplain of the First Canadian Division, offer a sense of how easy it would be for a chaplain to get caught up in the events he was living through. Recalling his service in the trenches of France, Scott writes,

> The men whom I knew so well, young, strong and full of hope and life . . . were now up in that poisoned atmosphere and under the hideous hail of bullets and shells. The thought almost drove a chaplain to madness. One felt so powerless and longed to be up and doing. Not once or twice in the Great war, have I longed to be a combatant officer with enemy scalps to my credit.[28]

Obviously, the heat of battle, national ideology and the intensity of shared experiences had a considerable impact on how chaplains understood the world and the enemy combatant, as well as their own faith. Looking in greater depth at the lives of two chaplains on separate sides of the war offers us further insight into these issues.

Paul Tillich: 'It's a Catastrophe, What I Have Seen'

Paul Tillich (1886–1965) fled Germany in 1933 after being dismissed from his teaching position for his socialist politics when Hitler became Chancellor. He immigrated to the United States and taught theology in New York and Chicago, and at Harvard, becoming one of the more prominent liberal Protestant theologians of the twentieth century.

As a young man, however, Tillich's life was caught up in the Great War. He had only just completed his theological studies when the war broke out. Like so many others, he volunteered for military service and was a chaplain from 1914 until 1919, serving with the Fourth Artillery Regiment. On 3 December 1914, he was awarded the Iron Cross for bravery under enemy fire. He participated fully in the culture of his day and served his country with distinction.

The German experience of the war was no more glamorous for the Germans than it was for the British and French. Tillich soon became a gravedigger as well as a pastor. During these years, he recalls trying to comfort the men by praising their courage and by preaching sermons like this one:

> Why this murder day after day, why this nameless suffering. . . . yet we must remain responsible to ourselves and to all others: for the sake of love for and devotion to our homeland, for the sake of pride, pride in being Germans, and for the sake of the bond of community, which ties our spirit to the spirit of the nation, for the sake of the glory of the German fatherland.[29]

In these words one sees how his work serves to support the war effort by identifying the struggle and suffering of the soldiers with a divine and eternal purpose, which is closely linked to the identity of the nation. He begins most of his battlefield sermons in 1914 with a patriotic invocation, 'War Comrades!' and his messages are on themes that include 'living means dying for a cause', giving one's life for the Fatherland, protecting one's homeland [Heimat] from 'evil', and the belief that the spiritual struggle and the struggle of the war are one and the same.[30]

Looking back on the war afterwards, Tillich recalls how this association was so deeply and simplistically made by many Germans:

> Together with my whole generation I was grasped by the overwhelming experience of a nationwide community – the end of a merely individualistic and predominantly theoretical existence. . . . The first weeks had not passed before my original enthusiasm disappeared.[31]

He continues elsewhere,

> When the German soldiers went into the First World War most of them shared the popular belief in a nice God who would make everything work out for the best. Actually everything worked out for the worst, for the nation and for almost everyone in it. In the trenches of the war, the popular belief in personal providence was gradually broken down and in the fifth year of war nothing was left of it.[32]

Tillich himself broke down over the course of the war. His confidence in the purity of the war effort began to fade, as did his belief that God was supporting the war aims of Germany. He grows cynical towards his preaching in support of the fight. In August of 1916 he was disciplined by his brigadier general and then forcibly transferred to another unit after arguing with his superior over the power of prayer. The general insisted that Tillich preach that prayer could protect a soldier from enemy fire. Tillich argued against this and refused. In October, he found himself transformed to the frontlines and in the heat of battle. After a close friend died, he suffered a nervous breakdown. Writing from hospital, he wrote to friend,

> I have constantly the most immediate and very strong feeling that I am no longer alive. Therefore I don't take life seriously. . . . I am experiencing the actual death of this our time. I preach almost exclusively 'the end'.[33]

By 1917, during the first Sunday in Advent, he admits in his sermon, that his audience is feeling 'more bitterness than joy, more grief than hope' as they approach the fourth Christmas of the war. He no longer refers to specific details from the war effort, as was a habit earlier in the conflict, but asserts that the Christian's hope in God is one that does not look for signs in events of the world, but can only be found within one's heart: 'Eternity is yours already today.'[34]

One observes a striking transition in Tillich's experiences over the course of the war. He moves from being a young and confident man, full of patriotism and immediate Christian faith, ready to preach that Germany's cause in the war is just and supported by God, to a broken and depressed shell of his former self. In a letter to the theologian Emanuel Hirsch, in November 1917, he laments, 'It is a catastrophe, what I have seen!... The war has only had destructive effects!'[35] His previous image of God lies dead on the battlefield, and he must begin to rethink his former theological convictions. Looking back, he will later write that 'Neither the personal nor the historical belief in providence had depth or real foundation. These beliefs were products of wishful thinking and not of faith.'[36]

G. A. Studdert Kennedy: The Death of God 'Almighty'

Geoffrey Anketell Studdert Kennedy fought on the opposite side of the war from that of Tillich. An Anglican parish priest in the slums of Leeds when the war broke out, Studdert Kennedy volunteered for duty as a chaplain in the British Royal Army. He was sent to France in 1915, where he was soon moved to the trenches of the front lines. He developed the nickname 'Woodbine Willie' for his practice of distributing cigarettes to soldiers and was awarded the Military Cross in 1917 for bravery under fire. In many ways, then, Studdert Kennedy's life paralleled that of Tillich. Like his German counterpart, he would find that his prior image of God was drastically shaken by his experiences in the trenches.

Studdert Kennedy's book *The Hardest Part* appeared in 1918, shocking some by its apparent irreverence. A number of readers were perhaps disturbed by the angry tone of the preface, in which he criticizes the use of religion for political purposes during the war:

> The soldiers never treated Christ with the cynical brutality of the politicians. Political scheming for narrow ends is the most inhuman and disgusting form of violence, and behind it there is more soulless unbelief than there is behind the ferocity of war . . . [T]he doctrine of the sovereign Kaiser-God was impossible to hold on the battle-fields of Flanders and of France, it is even more impossible in the Europe of today. That God is dead, as dead as cold mutton, and even deader, because He can no longer be used as food even for the poor.[37]

Much of what Studdert Kennedy writes in these pages is a criticism of standard pre-war Christian piety and talk about God. As he worked among wounded soldiers, he began to realize that his previous ways of speaking about God were not working. The old slogans and clichés did not connect with the victims of the trenches; and the tired chaplain began to realize that they did not work for him anymore, either. His training had not prepared him very well for what awaited him. At the outset of the war, as Alan Wilkinson recalls, most clergy had little experience of warfare (or even the urban working class), so that 'the majority of clerical reactions to the war came from people far removed from its daily actuality.'[38]

Studdert Kennedy realizes how much religion had been used by the military as an ideological tool. Christianity had been employed to motivate people for sacrifice and duty, but as it served such propaganda, in his view, it also lost its truthfulness and power. He writes,

Christ could not conquer war. He gave us chivalry, and produced the sporting soldier; but even that seems dead, Chivalry and poison gas don't go well together. Christ Himself was turned into a warrior and led men out to war.[39]

In his view, the churches had largely failed society during the pre-war years and were unable to preach a meaningful message during the time of war. And so, when he and his fellow soldiers met the horror of the trenches, their faith and their idealism were shattered. As he laments, 'This world is not a Sunday School; it is a slaughterhouse.'[40]

Slowly and painfully, Studdert Kennedy begins to take apart his former beliefs. He rebels against what he calls the 'doctrine of the glorified policeman', or the concept of 'God Almighty', who controls everything in the world and wills all things to happen. He cannot accept that God is behind the events of the war. And so he angrily rejects this image of God, in words that scandalized many of his readers at the time. He writes,

God himself seems non-existent – the Almighty Ruler Whom all things obey. He seems to have gone to sleep and allowed all things to run amuck. I don't believe there is an Almighty Ruler. I don't see how anyone can believe it. If it were a choice between that God and no God, I would be an atheist.[41]

In these words, one observes an anger and despair similar to that evident in the poems of Owen and Eliot. Also visible is a fatigue and sense of being overwhelmed similar to that which appeared in Tillich's description of life in the trenches as a chaplain. Studdert Kennedy continues, 'War is evil. It is a cruel and insane waste of energy and life. If God wills war, then I am morally mad and life has no meaning. I hate war, and if God wills it then I hate God.'[42]

But although his Christian faith is tattered and torn by his experiences, it is not destroyed altogether. Still, Studdert Kennedy cannot believe everything he used to believe. His former idea that God was an Englishman, who sat on a heavenly throne and controlled the universe, was completely shattered. But he begins to focus on the person of Jesus of Nazareth and his crucifixion. He finds in the image of the suffering Jesus a figure to whom he can powerfully relate. He finds it comforting to imagine that God is not far away on a throne in heaven, but that

God is with him, in the trenches, suffering from the trials and evils of the world at war. He writes, 'How near the God Whom Christ revealed comes at a time like this: nearer than breathing, nearer than hands and feet.' He continues, 'It's funny how it is always Christ upon the cross that comforts; never God upon a throne.'[43]

Studdert Kennedy begins to articulate a different understanding of God – one that he finds more meaningful given his experiences in the trenches. This new vision has implications for how he thinks about theodicy. He can no longer believe that God plans everything that happens in the world or that God's providence caused the war. Nor can he accept the idea of 'progress' or that somehow the war will serve a greater good. Instead, Studdert Kennedy insists that, 'Human strife is not God's method, but His problem.' He continues, 'Strife and warfare arise from the limitation which the God of Love had to submit to in order to create spiritual personalities worthy to be called His sons. War is the crucifixion of God, not the working of His will.'[44]

This approach links theodicy to human free will. Why does God permit a world of pain and suffering? The answer suggested here is that the only way God could make war and violence impossible would be to deny human beings free will. Because God loves human beings, and wanted them to be able to *choose* love and to *choose* to respond to God, then God had to give human beings the freedom to decide for themselves. War and violence arise, according to Studdert Kennedy, when human beings make the wrong decisions and choose to give into anger, jealousy and fear, rather than to hold fast to love, hope and faith. This suggests to him that, 'War is the crucifixion of God, not the working of His will. The cross is not past, but present.'[45] This leads him to conclude, 'God, the Father God of Love, is everywhere in history, but nowhere is He Almighty.'[46]

In the postscript to his book, Studdert Kennedy admits that many he had shared such views with found the rejection of this image of God quite threatening. They worried that it left God seemingly rather powerless. Some wondered whether this meant that God couldn't stop the war from happening. If God is not 'Almighty', they ask, doesn't this mean that God is powerless?

Studdert Kennedy thought about this problem somewhat differently. For behind these worries about God's 'Almighty' power is an assumption about what it means to be 'powerful'. The idea that God is almighty is usually thought of in terms of God manipulating all things, that God's will is a force that rules and governs. The tendency is to conceive of God's power as resembling that of kings and armies. This is to imagine that God is like the powerful rulers of the world, only multiplied on a cosmic scale.

But here is the radical nature (for his time) of Studdert Kennedy's emerging faith in the trenches. He asks, what if God's power is not anything like our human understanding of power? What if God's 'almightiness' has nothing to do with control? He starts to think of God's power not as strength or force, but as love. If God's perfection and power are understood through the concept of love, rather than through the idea of control, then perhaps God is almighty, but only in the sense of all-powerful love. God is almighty love: perfect and unlimited divine compassion. Studdert Kennedy writes, 'If the Christian religion means anything, it means that God is suffering Love, and that all real progress is caused by the working of Suffering Love in the World.'[47] Thus, he begins to try to preach this message to the soldiers he works with. And his basic message becomes

> It's always the Cross in the end – God, not Almighty, but God the Father with a Father's sorrow and a Father's weakness, which is the strength of love; God splendid, suffering, crucified – Christ.[48]

The Suffering of God

This idea that God's power is expressed as suffering love challenges many ideas and images of God to which many of his generation clung. For some, it seemed to make God less all-powerful: less in control, less exciting, less protecting. For Studdert Kennedy, though, this was the only way he could make sense of his Christian faith. He had become disillusioned with the old images of God, which he thought had been manipulated and abused by the leaders of the nations to convince people to fight.

Intriguingly, his counterpart on the opposing side of the trenches came to a similar position late in the war. By 1918, Tillich's sermons make a subtle shift, from an abstract hope in an internal spiritual eternity, to a more concrete focus on God's suffering presence, as made visible in Christ. He writes, 'God suffers with us all in our affliction. He does not come to us as an enraged God to increase our suffering, but comes to us to carry us as Friend, as Father, as our God.'[49]

This turn away from an image of God as all-controlling and as in any way connected to the waging of the terrible conflict found in the trenches of Europe would become a prominent trend following the war. Traditional theodicy, as least for many Christians touched by the conflict, had been shattered. As Wilkinson observes, 'in the post-war world, few were able to hold transcendence and immanence together.'[50] One sees such a split developing in the thought of both Tillich and Studdert Kennedy. Having both been initially caught up in the patriotism and excitement surrounding the outbreak of the war, both enthusiastically enlisted, confident that God was with them. When this theological naïveté was shattered by the reality they met in the muddy trenches, the only trace they could find of the divine remained in the image of the suffering on the cross, which they saw made immanent in the misery and self-sacrifice of their fellow soldiers.[51]

In *The Hardest Part*, however, there is some evidence that Studdert Kennedy's emerging theodicy has some limitations to it. While he is visiting a field hospital, a wounded soldier asks him, 'What is God like?'[52] Studdert Kennedy points to a crucifix on the wall as a way to express his new vision of a suffering God, which he thinks might comfort the suffering soldier. It is noteworthy, though, that this answer does no such thing:

> That is a battered, wounded and bleeding figure, nailed to a cross and helpless, defeated by the world and broken in all but spirit. That is not God . . . I tell you that cross does not help me a bit; it makes things worse. I admire Jesus of Nazareth; I think he was splendid like my friends at the front are splendid – splendid in their courage, patience, and unbroken spirit. But I asked you not what Jesus was like, but what God is like.

Although Kennedy focuses on the way in which this soldier continues to seek after an image of an 'Almighty' God, a problem with his own view of God, which he does not address, begins to emerge in this conversation. Why does he assume that the fact that God suffers with human beings make human suffering any more bearable or acceptable? As the soldier's lament in the hospital implies, the fact that Jesus suffered and died, just like his friends in the trenches suffered and died, does not eliminate the reality that his friends have died.

As understandable as the orientation towards an image of a suffering God is, it is important to recognize the dilemma it opens up for Christian theology. For is there no way to hold together both divine transcendence and immanence? Without such a combination, theology is left with a choice between two problematic options. A choice to emphasize the exclusivity of transcendence results in a theology that can become elitist or escapist, with little to say directly to contemporary life. Limiting theological reflection to immanence, however, risks reducing theology to a sentimental, or even tyrannical, embrace of present life. For all the difference in tone to the 'war theology' embraced by both sides in 1914 from the writing of these chaplains, the structure of their arguments could jointly be accused of amounting to a sacralizing of contemporary cultural trends. If that risk is indeed present, then, despite the shift in theological content, the wartime theologies of Tillich and Studdert Kennedy still do not offer sufficient resources to interrupt the slide into to the problem of 'ideology' with which this chapter began. They have certainly had their previous understanding of God shattered, and they have distanced their new vision of God from the ruling authorities of their nations. But is it not also the case that the God they now describe begins to look a lot like themselves, insofar as the God they describe is a God who experiences exactly the same traumas as they have just undergone?

This a problem to be explored more deeply in the next chapter, as the discussion turns to the devastation suffered by the Jewish peoples of Europe during the Second World War. Prior to focusing on the problem of the ideological nature of theology, however, the chapter will begin with a discussion that problematizes the very theological orientation that gives comfort to both Tillich and Studdert Kennedy. As the German Jewish philosopher Emil Fackenheim passionately argues, there are considerable problems remaining in a theodicy that reduces all suffering to the fallibility of the human will, while asserting the suffering and present nature of God. For the 'War to End All Wars' did nothing of the kind. Twenty years after the guns of August were finally silenced, they would begin firing once again. This time, however, speaking of the presence of the suffering Christ would bring little comfort to the millions of non-Christian victims of the Nazi 'Final Solution': the Jews of Europe.

Notes

[1]   For views on the war's origins, see, Annika Mombauer, *The Origins of the First World War: Controversies and Consensus* (London: Longman, 2002); David Fromkin, *Europe's Last Summer: Who Started the Great War in 1914?* (New York: Knopf, 2004); Ruth B. Henig, *The Origins of the First World War* (London: Routledge, 1992).

[2] For a useful cultural portrait of the major European powers at the outbreak of the war, see, Modris Eksteins, *The Rites of Spring: The Great War and the Birth of the Modern Age* (Toronto: Lester & Orpen Dennys, 1989).

[3] Eksteins, 61.

[4] Eberhard Busch, *Karl Barth: His Life from Letters and Autobiographical Texts* (Minneapolis, MN: Fortress Press, 1976), 81.

[5] Fritz Fischer, *Germany's Aims in the First World War*, trans. James Joll (London: Chatto & Windus, 1967). For a discussion of this thesis, see, Julian Jenkins, 'War Theology, 1914, and Germany's *Sonderweg*: Luther's Heirs and Patriotism', *The Journal of Religious History* 15.3 (1989), 292–310.

[6] Karl Hammer, *Deutsche Kriegstheologie, 1870–1918* (Munich: Kösel Verlag, 1972); Charles E. Bailey, 'The British Protestant Theologians in the First World War: Germanophobia Unleashed', *Harvard Theological Review* 77.2 (1984), 195–221.

[7] John A. Moses, 'State, War, Revolution and the German Evangelical Church, 1914–18', *Journal of Religious History* 17.1 (1992), 55.

[8] Nils Karlström, 'Movements for International Friendship and Life and Work: 1910–1925', *A History of the Ecumenical Movement: 1517–1948*, ed. Ruth Rouse and Stephen Charles Neill (London: SPCK, 1967), 511.

[9] See, for example, H. S. Holland et al., *To the Christian Scholars of Europe and America: A Reply from Oxford to the German Address to Evangelical Christians* (London: Oxford University Press, 1914).

[10] Alan Wilkinson, *The Church of England and the First World War* (London: SCM Press, 1996), 40, 29.

[11] Edward Lee Hicks, *The Church and the War* (London: Oxford University Press, 1914), 10–12.

[12] Quoted in Albert Marrin, *The Last Crusade: The Church of England in the First World War* (Durham, NC: Duke University Press, 1974), 139.

[13] John Esselmont Adams, *The Chaplain and the War* (Edinburgh: T&T Clark, 1915), 11.

[14] Quoted in Bailey, 'The British Protestant Theologians', 207, 211.

[15] René Johannet (ed.), *Pan-Germanism versus Christendom: The Conversion of a Neutral* (London, New York, Toronto: Hodder and Stoughton, 1916), 29, 179.

[16] Julien Brenda, *La Trahison des Clercs* (Paris: Bernard Grasset, 1927), 69–70.

[17] Charles E. Bailey, 'The Verdict of French Protestantism Against Germany in the First World War', *Church History* 58.1 (1989), 77.

[18] Timothy Findley, *The Wars* (London: Macmillian, 1978), 55.

[19] Ibid., 71–2.

[20] Ibid., 91, 83.

[21] Ibid., 87.

[22] Quoted in Jon Stallworthy, *Wilfred Owen* (London: Oxford University Press, 1974), 104.

[23] Jon Stallworthy (ed.), *The Oxford Book of War Poetry* (Oxford: University of Oxford Press, 2008), 140.

[24] T. S. Elliott, *The Complete Plays and Poetry: 1909–1950*, (London and New York: HarcourtBrace & Co., 1980), 56–9.

[25] Michael Snape, *God and the British Soldier: Religion and the British Army in the First and Second World Wars* (London and New York: Routledge, 2005), 17.

[26] Quoted in Eksteins, *Rites of Spring*, 236.

[27] Doris L. Bergen (ed.), *The Sword of the Lord: Military Chaplains from the First to the Twenty-First Century* (Notre Dame: University of Notre Dame Press, 2004), 8.

[28] Frederick George Scott, *The Great War as I Saw it* (Vancouver: The Clarke & Stuart Co, 1934), 64.

[29] Quoted in Wilhelm and Marion Pauck (eds), *Paul Tillich: His Life and Thought*, vol. 1 (New York: Harper & Row, 1976), 45.

[30] Paul Tillich, *Frühe Predigten (1909–1918)*, ed. Erdmann Sturm (Berlin: Walter de Gruyter,1994), 357–9, 371.

[31] Paul Tillich, *My Search for Absolutes* (New York: Simon & Schuster, 1967), 38–9.

[32] Paul Tillich, *The New Being* (New York: Charles Scribner's Sons, 1955), 52.

[33] Pauck, *Paul Tillich*, 51.

[34] Tillich, *Frühe Predigten*, 621–4.

[35] Paul Tillich, *Briefwechsel und Streifschriften*, ed. Walter Schmidt (Frankfurt am Main: Evangelische Verlagwerk, 1983), 97.

[36] Tillich, *The New Being*, 53.

[37] G. A. Studdert Kennedy, *The Hardest Part* (New York: George H. Doran Company, 1918), viii.

[38] Wilkinson, *The Church of England and the First World War*, 230.

[39] Studdent Kennedy, *The Hardest Part*, 31.

[40] Ibid., 35.

[41] Ibid., 11.

[42] Ibid., 33.

[43] Ibid., 11, 9.

[44] Ibid., 41–2.

[45] Ibid., 42.

[46] Ibid., 39.

[47] Ibid., 41.

[48] Ibid., 13.

[49] Tillich, *Frühe Predigten*, 637.

[50] Wilkinson, *The Church of England and the First World War*, 246.

[51] For contemporary examples of theologies which emphasize the suffering of God, see Paul S. Fiddes, *The Creative Suffering of God* (Oxford: Oxford University Press, 1988); Jürgen Moltmann, *The Crucified God: The Cross of Christ as the Foundation and Criticism of Christian Theology*, trans. R. A. Wilson and John Bowden (London: SCM Press, 1974). The concept of God as suffering is challenged in Chapter Three, and Moltmann's position in particular will be critiqued in Chapter Seven.

[52] Studdert Kennedy, *The Hardest Part*, ix.

Chapter 3

Jewish Theological Responses to the Shoah

Desolation
(p. 68)

It would be difficult to exaggerate the shock and the trauma wrought by the systematic murder of six million European Jews by the German National Socialists and their allies during the Second World War. The novelist and survivor of Auschwitz Elie Wiesel describes the impact of the Shoah as follows: 'In the beginning there was the Holocaust. We must start all over again.'[1] For Imre Kertész, the 2002 laureate of the Nobel Prize for Literature, 'the zero point that is Auschwitz' is not a 'one-time aberration', but 'the end point of a great adventure', which is the human race.[2] The rabbi and theologian Richard Rubenstein laments, 'We have lost all hope, consolation, and illusion.'[3] Given the depth of such lamentation, Susan Neiman argues that, while humankind lost faith in the natural world following the Lisbon earthquake, after Auschwitz, human beings lost faith in themselves.[4]

The previous chapter illustrated that following the shock of the First World War many Europeans despaired of the nature of human beings. For some, this disillusion would linger and remain something from which they would never recover. Many others, however, would begin to rebuild their lives around some new goals, whether it was 'Peace in our Time', a revived internationalism or ecumenicalism, or, as witnessed in the examples of Tillich and Studdert Kennedy, the development of a reworked Christian theodicy based on the concept of the suffering of God.

Tragically, the conflict of 1914–1918 was not to be the 'War to End All Wars'. It is a common assumption that human beings can learn from disaster so that they will not repeat the past, and yet, in just over twenty years, Europe would find itself once again plunged into a war that would reach all corners of the globe. Once again, human ingenuity, creativity and good will ran into the limits of their own power. But although the battlefields of the Second World War would be as bloody and horrifying at those of the First, the scale and destruction of the conflict would not be as shocking to the culture of the period; they had seen it before in living memory. Thus, rather than explore reactions to the Second World War generally, this chapter focuses instead on what would become the most devastating symbol of catastrophe from those terrible years: the attempted destruction of the Jewish people. The traumatic events of the 'Holocaust', along with another shocking event of the War – the atimic bombing of Japan – would have a lasting impact on twentieth-century culture, and it would challenge the previous self-understanding of human society held by many people.

This chapter focuses on the Jewish experience of the Holocaust, particularly on the impact it had on Jewish theology. For after facing such terrible devastation, not only would many Jewish people have difficulty imagining that the God of Israel existed, many would also find it difficult to believe in the goodness of humanity itself. As the discussion will demonstrate, in such an atmosphere the Christian concept of a suffering God, of the sort articulated by Studdert Kennedy, becomes untenable. The chapter then turns to an analysis of the response of the Jewish philosopher Emil Fackenheim to the devastation wrought by Auschwitz, and how his interpretation of the 'Commanding Voice of Auschwitz' results in an 'anti-theodicy' that rejects assigning any meaning to suffering, but one which also forbids him from abandoning his own Judaism and becoming an atheist.

The Holocaust

The 'Holocaust' is the term commonly used to refer to the intentional, determined and systematically organized attempt by the National Socialist regime in Germany (the Nazis) to exterminate the Jews of Europe. The causes of this event, and how it could be possible, are important and complex issues, but these questions are beyond the scope of the present discussion.[5] It is important, however, to recognize the significance and uniqueness of this terrible tragedy.

Although there have been countless tragic slaughters of human beings throughout human history, many scholars argue that the Holocaust was different, perhaps even unique.[6] What was so astonishing and horrifying about this catastrophe was how planned and systematic it was. The Jews were not simply killed out of hatred, but as the result of a carefully constructed ideology. The German population first had to be prepared regarding how to think about the Jewish people, and how to treat them, before the organized processes of the Final Solution could begin. Secondly, the killing of the Jews was such a massive undertaking that a whole economy had to be organized to deal with it. Train schedules and routes had to be developed. Ways to dispose of the biological remains had to be invented. Important war material and industry were reassigned from the business of fighting the war so that the process of exterminating Jewish people could continue. In the Holocaust, the latest science and technology of communications, transportation, organization management, human psychology, demographics and logistical efficiency were applied to the specific purpose of systematically killing Jewish people.[7] Entire bureaucratic systems had to be developed to manage all of this. And so it was a slaughter unlike any other slaughter in terms of its careful planning, organization and thoroughness.

The process began rather gradually. At first minor restrictions and limitations were placed upon the Jewish citizens of Germany. This escalated into a system of new laws governing the status of Jews in the country. When Adolf Hitler became Chancellor in 1933, he proclaimed a one-day boycott against Jewish shops. This was followed by a law against kosher butchering. Then restrictions on Jewish children in public schools were introduced. In 1935, the 'Nuremberg Laws' issued in a large series of new policies, including dissolving German citizenship for Jews (even those who had fought in the war for Germany) and making interfaith marriages illegal. In 1936, all Jews lost the right to vote in Germany. Events began to come to a head in 1938, when on 10 November, 101 synagogues and 7,500 Jewish businesses were burned in the country, and 26,000 Jews were arrested and put into concentration camps. There were many public attacks of Jews in the streets, and 91 people were killed. The night became known as 'Kristallnacht' (or, 'Night of Broken Glass').

The Christian Churches and the Jewish People

The Holocaust is often assumed to have emerged from a unique cultural context, as if to say that German culture history and were to blame for the attitude of Germans towards Jews.[8] But anti-Semitism has been expressed in many cultures and nations throughout the history of the West. Most historians and philosophers, therefore, argue that the origins of the Holocaust are much wider than the borders of Germany. The majority of scholars who share this view also suggest that part of the story directly involves the Christian tradition.

The history of Christian anti-Semitism is almost as long as the history of the Christian church. Many Christians have tended to downplay the fact that Jesus himself was a Jew, and that the disciples and first Christian communities were Jewish. Eventually a division developed between Christian and Jewish communities over the emerging Christian self-understanding, and the writings of the Christian Bible contain some evidence of this when they target or criticize Jewish opponents (for example, in the Gospel of John). Since that time, many Christians have treated Jewish people as traitors or as those responsible for the crucifixion of Jesus (which was actually authorized and executed by the Roman authorities).

The history of Europe is filled with many tragic periods and waves of attacks on Jewish communities, known as 'pogroms'. This legacy of anti-Semitism remained well established even after the Middle Ages. It is an unfortunate fact that in many periods of Christian history, Jewish communities fared much better in Muslim Spain than they did in Protestant Germany, Catholic Poland or Orthodox Russia. Many historians argue that this tragic history of Christian anti-Semitism contributed to preparing Western culture for something like the Holocaust.[9]

As was the case in the First World War, the Christian churches demonstrated considerable vulnerability to being shaped by the culture and ideology of their context during the Second World War. After Adolf Hitler's rise to power, he immediately started to lobby both the Protestant and Catholic churches for support. Hitler had little respect for Christianity, but he understood how influential the churches were in German society, and also sought greater international legitimacy through the support of Christian churches. Just as he required all civil servants to make an oath of loyalty to the *Führer*, Hitler wanted to be assured of the loyalty of Church leadership. He pressured the national Protestant Church to commit itself to the new German Reich. Calling themselves the 'German Christians', the main Protestant organizations argued that loyalty to the nation was part of one's Christian duty – in much the same way that Christians had thought about the relationship between church and state in the lead-up to the First World War.

Of course, not all Christians agreed with the majority. A group of German Protestants disagreed vigorously with the 'German Christian' movement and split off to form what became known as the 'Confessing Church'. This movement, led by Martin Niemöller and Dietrich Bonhoeffer (and influenced by Karl Barth), insisted that the German Christians had surrendered the authority of the church to the state. They articulated an alternative doctrine of the church in their famous statement, the *Barmen Declaration*. Unfortunately, they were very much in the minority of Protestants (and it is noteworthy that their primary opposition to Hitler was not motivated out of a desire to defend German Jews).[10] Dietrich Bonhoeffer would later participate in a plot to assassinate Hitler. When the plot failed, he was arrested and put in a concentration camp outside of Berlin, where he was hung.

Many German Roman Catholics were also content to let the state worry about politics and to associate their Christian identity with German nationalism.[11] Again, a minority of Catholics resisted, including Bernhard Lichtenberg, a priest who began to preach against the persecution of the Jews on *Kristallnacht*, until he was arrested in 1941 and sent to the concentration camp Dachau. He died in transit after becoming ill due to the harsh conditions in which he was kept.

As the different European nations fell under German control, the Christians in the occupied nations tended to behave much like Christians in Germany did. Some Christians helped Jews escape, but most acquiesced to the authority of the Nazis, and many participated in persecuting Jewish people – especially when that appeared to mean that the Germans left other people alone. In France, Belgium, Holland, Poland, Romania, Bulgaria, Hungry, Italy and Czechoslovakia, Jews were rounded up and interned with at least some assistance from the local population.

Speaking About the Unspeakable

It is very difficult to talk in any intelligent way about the impact or meaning of the Holocaust. Explaining how such a thing could be possible is practically inconceivable. For many Jewish people, there can be no meaning after Auschwitz; some have argued that the death camps destroyed all that remained of modern civilization, leaving only a culture of barbarism in its wake. In the face of such a catastrophe, such scholars argue that the only appropriate response is silence. George

Steiner, for example, argues that 'The world of Auschwitz lies out-side speech as it lies outside reason.'[12] Theodor Adorno famously once said that 'to write poetry after Auschwitz is barbaric.'[13] Such views are raised when there is the concern that reactions to the horrors of the death camps will become sentimentalized, or that the rhetorical power of the tragedy will be used to defend a particular political ideology or policy position.[14] Is it, perhaps, more respectful of the victims of such horror to remain silent before its gruesome reality?

Most post-Holocaust scholars, however, argue that to remain mute is to confine the victims of the Nazis to an ongoing silence, which is to effectively remain complicit with the forces that built Auschwitz and with the cynicism and nihilism it represents. Adorno himself was con-vinced of this after his slogan about 'no poetry after Auschwitz' was criticized by the poet Paul Celan, who was himself a Jewish survive. But if the events of the catastrophe are to be spoken of and represented, how to do so in an appropriate manner has remained a controversial problem.

Consider, for example, debates among Jewish scholars over the basic question of how to refer to the Nazi attempt to destroy European Jewry. Some suggest that the term 'Holocaust' is not an appropriate name for the devastation. Although the term is the most common way to refer to the tragedy, and was initially proposed by some Jewish intellectuals, the word has its origins in ancient Greek and is gener-ally translated as 'burnt offering'. It appeared in Middle English in the fourteenth century – particularly in works by Christian authors – and was used to refer to the sacrificial offering of animals to God. Thus the Christian roots of the term are considered by some to be problem-atic. Giorgio Agamben, for example, suggests that the word was often used in polemical attacks against Jews by Christians in the late Middle Ages, and for this reason is an inappropriate name for the murder of Jewish people.[15]

For other Jewish scholars, it is the more precise root meaning of the term 'holocaust' that is problematic. For using a term to describe the Nazi Final Solution which literally means 'burnt offering' would seem to suggest that the destruction of Jewish people served some purpose; that is to say that Jews were being burned as an offering to God. Some Christians have interpreted the event as punishment for the rejection of Christ, while a few Jews have seen the destruction as resembling the story from Genesis 22, in which Abraham is ordered by God to sacrifice his son Isaac. Only during the Holocaust, unlike in the case of the story from Genesis, when Isaac asks 'The fire and wood are here, but where is the lamb for a burnt offering?' no alternative lamb is provided, and God does not act to stop the murder.

Most Jews find such an interpretation of the Holocaust unacceptable. If this is how God relates to the Jewish people, then such a God does not deserve their attention. Some Jews rejected religious belief and became atheists in the wake of the tragedy. Others, struggling for a way remain Jewish after the terrible suffering of their people, suggested that the word 'holocaust' may not be appropriate, given the ancient roots of its meaning and what the word implies. This is the primary reason why more historically precise words like 'Auschwitz' or the 'Final Solution' are frequently employed to refer to the tragedy. This specificity is seen by some to be symbolically powerful and free from implied metaphysically laden meaning. Yet such a solution is far from acceptable to some Jews. In the view of Arthur Cohen, for example, Auschwitz 'is a name which belongs to *them*. It is not a name which commemorates.'[16] Among those who consider the term 'holocaust' inappropriate, therefore, some propose the use of the Hebrew word 'Shoah', which simply means 'desolation'.[17]

The politics of representation surrounding the debate over what to call the events of the 'Final Solution' reflect the disruptive nature of a deeply traumatic event. As numerous theorists studying the Holocaust have suggested, the shock of such a catastrophe often leaves those touched by it unable to assimilate it or fully comprehend its impact. As Dominick LaCapra asks, 'when things of an unimaginable magnitude actually occur . . . what is there for the imagination to do?'[18] His work wrestles with the effect of trauma on memory and representation, highlighting the obstacles and complications which hinder clear and straightforward descriptions of shocking events like the Holocaust.

If such a dynamic disturbs the very terminology used to describe the Jewish experience of 1933–1945, the impact on attempts to speak theologically about the Holocaust is perhaps even more disruptive. For in the midst of shock and trauma, how is one to know what motivates speech about God? What sort of agendas might be sacralized through the implementation of religious language?

Given the controversial and sensitive nature of any discussion of the Shoah in theological terms, it is important to linger on the depth of the catastrophe, so as not to leap sentimentally over its horrors and engage in theological apologetics in haste. Thus, prior to exploring specific theological reactions to the Holocaust, the discussion will first give some brief attention to an author who argues that only survivors of the Shoah are entitled to speak about it. In his novel *Night*, Elie Wiesel, himself a survivor of the infamous death camp Auschwitz, describes the experiences of one of its 'survivors'.

The Impact of the Camps

Early in *Night*, the main character – a young teenage boy – describes his first day in the Birkenau camp, which was a reception centre for Auschwitz. As his family is unloaded from the cramped, hot boxcar of the train that had taken them away from their home, the narrator describes what they saw:

> In front of us flames. In the air that smell of burning flesh . . . An SS non-commissioned officer came to meet us, a truncheon in his hand: 'Men to the left! Women to the right!' . . . I did not know that in that in that place at that moment, I was parting from my mother and [my sister] forever.[19]

The young boy is led away with his father. As he watches the smoke rising out of the crematoriums, Wiesel writes,

> Never shall I forget those flames which consumed my faith forever. Never shall I forget that nocturnal silence which deprived me, for all eternity, of the desire to live. Never shall I forget those moments which murdered my God and my soul and turned my dreams to dust.[20]

In the events that follow, the reader gets a sense of the experiences that lead him to such despair. In the struggle to survive, the inmates of the camps are slowly and systematically robbed of their dignity. Gradually they become more and more animalistic in their desire for the basic necessities of food and shelter. Inmates beat each other in fights over food. They steal from the sick and weak. At first, the young boy is disgusted by this behaviour. He shares his little scraps of food with his sick father. But later he, too, succumbs to the gradual loss of humanity. He watches his father being beaten, and, rather than feeling anger at the *Kapo* who is hitting him, he becomes angry with his own father:

> I watched the whole scene without moving. I kept quiet. In fact I was thinking of how to get farther away so that I would not be hit

myself. What is more, any anger I felt at that moment was directed, not against the *Kapo*, but against my father. I was angry with him, for not knowing how to avoid [the guard's] outbreak. That is what concentration camp life had made of me.[21]

There has been considerable analysis of this phenomenon of dehumanization. The Nazi leaders in the camps quite intentionally sought to reduce the inmates to this level. It helped to create an atmosphere that prevented the prisoners from working together to offer resistance or revolt. It also made them easier to control and manipulate.

In the camps, a term developed to describe people who had reached a complete state of dehumanization – those who had lost their will and consciousness, and existed as hollow shells of their former selves. They were known as the '*Muselmanner*'. Another famous Jewish novelist, Primo Levi, describes this phenomenon:

All the *Muselmanner* who finished in the gas chambers have the same story, or more exactly, have no story; they followed the slope down to the bottom, like streams that run down the sea. On their entry into the camp, through basic incapacity, or by misfortune, or through some banal incident, they are overcome before they can adapt themselves . . . Their life is short but their numbers are endless; they, the *Muselmanner*, the drowned, form the backbone of the camp, an anonymous mass, continuously renewed and always identical, of non-men who march and labor in silence, the divine spark dead within them is already too empty really to suffer. One hesitates to call them living: one hesitates to call their death 'death.'[22]

At the end of *Night*, after having been liberated from the death camp, Wiesel describes himself in this way, 'I wanted to see myself in the mirror hanging on the opposite wall. I had not seen myself since the ghetto. From the depths of the mirror, a corpse gazed back at me. The look in his eyes, as they stared into mine, has never left me.'[23]

Among those who survived the Holocaust, such testimony has been haunting. Some Jews despaired, feeling as if all the good Jews had died, and that only those who had been reduced to *Muselmanner* had been able to survive. One of the struggles among Jewish theologians has been to wrestle with what such experiences suggest about human beings and their nature. Thus Emil Fackenheim asks, 'Who dares assert that, had he been then and there rather than here and now, he would not have been reduced to a *Muselman*'?[24]

The Silence of God

Such a devastating assault on the dignity of the human being has led many to suggest that it is impossible to believe in the existence of a divine being. If this is what happens to those considered to be God's 'Chosen People' then, so the argument goes, clearly the very concept of God must be called into question. For those who believe in God, at the very least, it would seem that God failed to act, was entirely absent or remained silent in the face of the catastrophe. How can God be spoken of or conceived in such a situation?

The dilemma facing Jewish theologians is illustrated by one of the more well-known scenes from Wiesel's novel *Night*. The prisoners are summoned to the centre of the camp to witness the execution of three inmates accused of being connected to an act of sabotage. One of them is a young boy, described as having 'the face of a sad angel'. After watching the child die a slow and agonizing death, one person in the crowd whispers, 'Where is God? Where is He?' The narrator continues, 'I heard a voice within me answer him: 'Where is He? Here He is – He is hanging here on this gallows.'[25]

This disturbing scene has resonated powerfully with many readers. How it is interpreted, however, varies considerably. Does this statement by Wiesel's narrator effectively voice the final death of any belief in God? Is it intended to suggest that God is somehow powerless in the face of such murderous acts and can only helplessly stand by as a witness? Or, as others suggest, is God somehow present in such an event, and suffering along with the victims of the tragedy? Versions of all three readings are implied in the differing approaches to theodicy that post-Holocaust Jewish thinkers develop.

Jewish Theodicy and Anti-Theodicy

There are a wide variety of different Jewish theological responses to the Holocaust. A representative orthodox version of traditional theodicy is articulated by Eliezer Berkovits. Developing a version of the classical 'free will' position, Berkovits argues that the silence of God in the face of historical tragedies is necessary for human beings to act ethically. God must 'absent' godself in order for it to be possible for human beings to have to choose between good and evil.[26] To a degree, then, his response to the Holocaust shares some basic similarities to the theodicy articulated in the previous chapter by Studdert Kennedy. God's failure to act in the face of evil is not due to some character flaw, weakness or disinterestedness, but is rather a choice not to act by God in order to enable human beings to be free creatures. Irving Greenberg suggests a similar position, although, like Berkovits, he does admit that, after the Holocaust, such a mode of being by God in the face of the catastrophe does raise the question of the nature of God's 'covenant' with the Jewish people. Might it be that God's covenantal obligations are more 'voluntary' than traditionally assumed by Jewish thought?[27]

For many Jewish scholars, however, such a position is untenable. Steven Katz, for example, asks, 'Could not God, possessed of omniscience, omnipotence, and absolute goodness, have created a world in which there was human freedom but no evil?' Furthermore, he suggests that God could have created a world where humans possessed moral goodness without having to first confront evil. Finally, Katz laments that it would be better for God to limit human freedom of the will than to allow Auschwitz: 'The price is just too high.'[28] For reasons similar to those presented by Katz, Richard Rubenstein rejects the God of Jewish theology entirely. If a God who is the author of history exists, then the Holocaust had to be willed by God. Seeing few options for theology other than traditional theodicy, Rubenstein pronounces the 'death of God'.[29]

Another approach to theodicy within Jewish thought shares some similarities to the direction plotted by Rousseau, which was discussed in Chapter One. Martin Buber, Abraham Heschel and Mordecai Kaplan each present very different conceptions of God, but they all displace blame for the Holocaust away from God by emphasizing that its terrible acts were performed by human beings.[30]

Zachary Braiterman classifies all such post-Holocaust reflections as operating within the traditional boundaries of theodicy.[31] Even Katz and Rubenstein, while developing quite different positions from each other, still maintain the premise that the concept of God implies an all-powerful and all-knowing divine being who, if he exists, should have and could have stopped a catastrophe like the Shoah. Since no such God acted to defend the Jewish people, both argue that the concept of

God has been painfully but decisively falsified by historical experience. At the same time, theologians like Greenberg and Berkovits, but also Buber and Kaplan, develop explanations for why the traditional concept of God can remain in place despite God's failure to act to defend the Jewish people from the Nazis. As such, all of these thinkers remain within the general orbit of traditional theodicy.

Braiterman identifies another pattern of Jewish theological response to Auschwitz, however, which he suggests represents an 'anti-theodicy'. Such a stance towards the Holocaust refuses to try to justify the catastrophe or establish any direct relationship between evil, suffering and God. Braiterman argues that the Jewish tradition, far from being monolithic, contains numerous counter-narratives and resources, which resist describing God or historical tragedies along the lines of traditional theodicy. Such perspectives 'neither justify, explain, ascribe positive meaning, account for, resolve, understand, accept, or theologically rectify the presence of evil in human affairs.' Rather than silence the cries of human beings in order to defend God (as Job's friends attempt to do), an anti-theodicy 'represents a type of religious thought in which human persons (not God) occupy central attention'.[32]

Such a distinction between traditional theodicy and the nature of the theological responses offered by many Jewish thinkers is an important one. The complex and highly nuanced nature of post-Holocaust theology does not sit well with traditional attempts to connect God and such a terrible event. This emphasis recalls the question that emerged at the end of the first chapter, in the form of Nieman's question of whether any critical judgement always implies a positive assertion about the true order of things. To illustrate how this is so, rather than offer a general summary of this dynamic, the remainder of the chapter focuses on one particular example of a philosopher that Braiterman classifies as developing an 'antitheodicy'. An analysis of the thought of Emil Fackenheim illustrates why some Jewish thinkers are compelled to shun traditional theodicy, while at the same time continue to reflect theologically, rather than abandon Judaism and become atheists. Furthermore, Fackenheim's example will also bring into view some of the perils and limitations that such an anti-theodicy can introduce to reflection on historical tragedies. For indeed, his judgements about the evils of human history contain some subtle, yet significant, judgements about what things should be positively privileged in the world.

Fackenheim and the Commanding Voice of Auschwitz

Emil Fackenheim was born in Halle, Germany, in 1916 and came of age during the interwar period and the rise of the Nazis. He was arrested on *Kristallnacht* and sent to the concentration camp Sachenhausen, where he stayed until he was released in early 1939. He was ordained a rabbi and was then able to escape to Aberdeen, Scotland, where his parents soon joined him. His brother refused to leave Germany and was killed during the Holocaust. After the war broke out, Fackenheim was interred by the British for being an enemy alien. He was then sent to Canada, where he was eventually released. He studied philosophy at the University of Toronto, where he would become a professor and teach for 36 years. When he retired in 1984, Fackenheim immigrated to Israel. He lived there until his death in 2003.

In a challenging and searching essay entitled 'The Commanding Voice of Auschwitz', Fackenheim asks a very basic and blunt question: can the Jewish protest against the Holocaust 'remain within the sphere of faith?'[33] Obviously, for his generation, atheism was a very real possibility and temptation. For after the Shoah, how could a Jew possibly believe that God was with them? Fackenheim is one of those Jewish theologians who, without minimizing in any way the terrible impact of the Shoah, consistently insisted that a theological response was not only possible, but was a necessity.

To illustrate the dilemma facing Jewish people, he refers to another story by Elie Wiesel, in which Jews are hiding from the Nazis and are praying. But then one of them interrupts and declares: 'Do not pray so loud! God will hear you.'[34] This scene captures the great paradox facing many Jewish people at the time: if they do not pray, they are no longer Jews. But the God they pray to appears to have turned against them – allowing their destruction – and so the Jewish person might do well to stay as far away from this God as possible. Caught in this paradox, Fackenheim writes, 'any Jewish prayer at Auschwitz is madness.'[35] Although he admits this terrible dilemma, he refuses to let go of his Jewish identity or his faith. Even if it is madness to pray at Auschwitz, he concludes that it would also be madness to stop. What does he mean by this?

For Fackenheim, the Holocaust has no precedent in Jewish history. It is unlike any other event. Why? In his view, although the Nazi program of the Final Solution killed millions of Jews, it is not the numerical figure that is most significant, but the fact that such killing had no rational basis whatsoever. Killing Jews accomplished nothing for the Nazis. Jews were not an enemy army challenging the German nation. They did not occupy a country that the Nazis wanted to conquer. The Nazis killed Jews because they *were Jews*. It was, Fackenheim says, 'an ideological project'. To make this point even more vivid, Fackenheim observes that Jews were not even killed because of their faith. They did not die as martyrs (as, for example, Jews did under the Roman Empire). Jews were not told to disavow their faith or face death. In fact, many German Jews had already abandoned their faith. Some had even converted to Christianity, but even that was not grounds for the Nazis to spare them. It did not matter if a Jew believed in God or not. How the Nazis defined who was a Jew was whether one of their great-grandparents was Jewish. And so Fackenheim observes that Jews 'died neither because of their faith, nor despite their faith', but 'they were murdered because of the Jewish faith of their great-grandparents.'[36] It was merely 'annihilation for the sake of annihilation'.

For Fackenheim, this reality implies that many traditional answers to the questions of theodicy make no sense when applied to the Holocaust. For example, Jews could not imagine that they were being tested by God in this situation. It is also impossible to conceive that they were being punished for their sins. Neither is logically even possible because, in the eyes of the Nazis, the victims of the Final Solution were not able to determine their own 'Jewishness', and so assigning responsibility to them makes no sense. The only absurdity that could be suggested is that they were being punished for the sins of their great-grandparents, or tested for the sake of their great-grandparents' faith. And so Fackenheim completely rejects making an analogy that some have made between the Shoah and Genesis 22. He dismisses any comparison between the Holocaust and Abraham's sacrifice of his son Isaac in faith, for, 'unlike Abraham, they [the great-grandparents] did not know what they were doing' – they had no idea what sacrifice their faith would require of their great-grandchildren.[37]

Fackenheim also insists that one should not suggest that God was somehow present in the death camps with the Jewish people, suffering with them. To do so, in his view, effectively implies Christian meaning to the event by comparing the suffering of the Jewish people with the suffering of Jesus. For him, 'never in the two thousand years of Jewish-Christian confrontation has it been less possible for a Jew to abandon either his Jewishness or his Judaism and embrace Christianity.'[38] Thus a theodicy of the sort developed by Studdert Kennedy represents a complete anathema to how Fackenheim would interpret the Holocaust.

After illustrating these terrible paradoxes that confront Jewish people after the Shoah, Fackenheim argues, however, that Jews must not give in to atheism. He admits that 'silence would, perhaps, be best now'.[39] But instead, for him, Auschwitz presents a Jewish person with an imposed commandment. This 'commanding voice' confronts Jews with the following message: 'Jews are forbidden to hand Hitler posthumous victories.'[40] If the surviving Jews were to leave behind their Jewish identity by abandoning their faith in God, Fackenheim argues that they would actually be helping to eliminate Judaism from the face of the earth. Jews must become determined to survive as a people – which also means preserving their religious faith – or else, in the end, Hitler's goal will have been accomplished. This command then – to go on in faith to avoid giving Hitler a posthumous victory – is what Fackenheim calls the 614th commandment (there are 613 commandments in the orthodox Jewish tradition).

Challenge to Christianity

Fackenheim's writing often includes moments in which he addresses Christian readers, and some comments are relevant for what will follow in subsequent chapters. His first message has already been eluded to: after Auschwitz, it is impossible for a Jew to consider converting. His other arguments are more theological. The preceding discussion demonstrated his attitude towards the idea that suffering can be redeemed or that some meaning can be found in the experience of suffering: he rejects reading some redemptive message in the powerlessness of divine suffering. He remains uninspired and unconvinced by the Christian image of God and asks, 'at Auschwitz, did the grave not win the victory after all, or, worse than the grave, did the devil himself win?'[41] In his book *To Mend the Word*, he makes this point in even more striking terms:

> At Auschwitz, other free persons were reduced to *Muselmanner*, to the living dead . . . We ask: Could Jesus of Nazareth have been made into a *Muselmann*? . . . If the incarnate Son of God was as fully human as all humanity, then the Trinitarian Christian . . . lest he heap a posthumous insult on all actual *Muselmanner*, must

acknowledge the possibility of an incarnate *Muselmann* . . . However the Christian theologian seeks to understand the Good News that is his heritage, it is ruptured by the Holocaust. One ponders this awesome fact and is shaken.[42]

This is a powerful and challenging remark to Christians, one that should interrupt any easy sentimentality they might cling to in their responses to the Holocaust. To imagine God's presence with human beings, as a human being, in a Nazi death camp, is, for Fackenheim, to allow for the possibility that God could be reduced to a *Muselmann*.

Fackenheim's response to Auschwitz, then, identifies nothing in its events that can be considered meaningful or redemptive. This is what leads someone like Braiterman to describe his position as being an 'antitheodicy'. Fackenheim refuses to make meaning out of suffering. For him, the only possible way he can locate God is to describe God as being in 'exile'. God shares in the exile of the Jewish people. As the world rejects the Jews, God is rejected and shut out. And so Fackenheim arrives at his most basic point. He argues that the only lesson to be drawn from Auschwitz is: NEVER AGAIN! He writes, 'After the death camps, we are left with only one supreme value: existence.'[43] Jews must find a way to continue to exist in a hostile world. And so Fackenheim becomes a determined supporter of the state of Israel.

This turn to the political status of the nation of Israel will be analyzed below. Before leaving behind Fackenheim's more explicit theological work, this summary of his thought remains incomplete without some clarification of his concept of the *Tikkun*, which lies at the heart of his anti-theodicy.

Tikkun ="Mending"

In the Midrash tradition of Judaism, which is a form of exposition or interpretation of the Jewish bible that emerged around the thirteenth century – one that focuses on rabbinic commentary and stories – the concept *Tikkun* is developed. This Hebrew word means 'mending' – a repairing of what is broken. In the Jewish mystical tradition of the Lurianic Kabbalah, the creation of the universe by God is described as involving *Tikkun*. The original creation is presented as being fragile and unstable – like a pottery vessel – which has difficulty containing the holiness of God. Inevitably the fallible material fails, and the vessel is broken. Thus, continues the story, the universe is broken and in need of repair. In Kabbalah spirituality, all human and divine powers are needed to help mend the rupture.

In this re-imaging of the biblical account of creation, God is described as intimately involved with creation. But it is a fragile relationship, for the perfect divine is difficult to contain in imperfect matter. This complication is not only a problem for the universe and all it contains; it is also a problem for God. For because of the divine's intimate connection to the Creation, God also becomes vulnerable and affected by the brokenness of the universe.

Before the world, there was God, and only God. But in the *Tikkun* description of creation, God contracts godself, in order to make space for creation to happen. God – the divine all in all – first had to restrict godself before there would be any place outside of God for Creation to exist. Another way to describe this understanding in this Jewish tradition is to say that God had to 'exile' godself. God had to remove godself from where the divine would normally be, so that something else could come into existence. But such an arrangement is precarious and dangerous. The world's situation is fragile, and God has also made godself vulnerable to the world – by voluntarily opening up this fragility within the divine being. The ultimate goal of God in this vision is to return to the fullness of God being all in all. But this return will not be done simply by eliminating the universe. The achievement of the divine wholeness is to be achieved with creation's participation and cooperation. And so the division between the divine holiness and the fragile creation needs to be mended. *Tikkun* is required.

In this theological imagination, God's 'power' and involvement with the world is described in a way that helps the theologian to articulate how it is that the world is imperfect, and how it is that God exists, without necessarily identifying any value or meaning to suffering. Even though God is in 'exile', this does not mean that God's love is being withheld, or that God's love is impotent. This is because the very reason for the exile, and the very condition for the vulnerability of creation in the first place, is actually based on the love of God. God submitted to self-exile out of love, in order to allow the universe to come into being. The universe would not even exist if God did not decide to risk godself by choosing to go into exile.

Fackenheim moves from this metaphysical discussion to explore the political implications of *Tikkun*. He uses the concept to speak of relationships with Christians. After Auschwitz, he asks, 'Can there be a *Tikkun* between Christians and Jews?' His answer has numerous dimensions to it. First, he suggests that 'Zionism . . . must after Auschwitz be a Christian commitment as well. No less than Jews themselves, Christians must wish Jewish existence to be liberated from dependence of charity.'[44] He insists that Christians now have a responsibility to help insure that the Jewish people can live in security and peace.

Second, he looks back to the witness of the Catholic priest Bernhard Lichtenberg, who, on the day of *Kristallnacht* – the day Fackenheim was himself arrested – returned to his church as the synagogues burned and began to hold public services during which he prayed 'on behalf of the Jews and the poor concentration camp prisoners'. He prayed this prayer in public every day until he was arrested on 23 October 1941. For Fackenheim, this action – because it was done *in public* and in opposition to the Nazi regime – contributed to the work of *Tikkun*. He writes, 'So long as it was on behalf of *Jews* – not merely mankind-in-general or all-oppressed-in-general . . . such a prayer went far toward closing the abyss that had been created between "Aryan" Christians' and the Jewish people; 'The Good News is in the prayer itself, and the Holy Spirit dwells in it.' He concludes, 'It is the rock on which the Christian faith can rebuild the broken church.'[45]

After Auschwitz, Fackenheim argues that the work of *Tikkun* must begin in the daily events of this troubled world: in acts of solidarity between different peoples and different religions. If human beings are able to respond to tragic events like the Shoah in this way, then perhaps they continue to have much to hope for and believe in. A Hassidic tale recalled by the German theologian Dorothee Sölle captures the tone and spirit of Fackenheim's use of the *Tikkun* concept:

> A famous rabbi once asked his students how one could recognize the time when night ends and day begins. 'Is it when, from a great distance, you can tell a dog from a sheep?' one student asked. 'No', said the rabbi. 'Is it when, from a great distance, you can tell a date palm from a fig tree?' another student asked. 'No', replied the rabbi once again. 'Then when is it?' the students asked. In a soft voice, the old rabbi said, 'It is when you look into the face of any human creature and see your sister or brother there. Until then, night is still with us.'[46]

Religion and Politics

There is much to appreciate about the spirit of this theological vision as presented by Fackenheim. There is also a subtle complication that is implied by his position, however, and it is one that is common among such 'anti-theologies'. Recall how his 614th Commandment instructs Jews to never allow themselves to be victimized again. This perspective implies a degree of defensive preparedness on the part of the Jewish people, which is certainly understandable, but note the tone it takes in Fackenheim's argument: he writes, 'After the death camps, we are left with only one supreme value: existence.'[47] For him, Jewish survival is a 'holy duty'. Given this position, Fackenheim expresses approval for the view that, 'rather than be shot, he [the Jew] will shoot first when there is no third alternative. But he will shoot with tears in his eyes.'[48]

While the reasons that Fackenheim – or any Jewish person for that matter – would think it necessary to stress self-defence after the Holocaust are perfectly clear and defensible, this position becomes more problematic when set against the painful complexities of the relationship between the contemporary state of Israel and its Palestinian neighbours. There is little nuance in Fackenheim's position of the sort that would assist the Jewish person to balance concerns for the security of Israel with the grievances and sufferings of Muslim Palestinians. The primary theological response to Auschwitz that he articulates has taken on a concrete political form: the existence of a Jewish state in Palestine. This is not only a 'holy duty' for Jews, according to Fackenheim, but, he argues, it is also a moral obligation for Christians. At this point, is it not possible that his anti-theodicy has collapsed theology into politics, leaving little critical distance between the two? If so, his theological position, though for many reasons understandable, remains vulnerable to manipulation by ideology and contemporary culture. To a lesser but significant degree, there is some structural similarity between the supremacy he grants to Jewish survival and the way in which German Christians were unable to distinguish between Nazi ideology and their own faith. To be absolutely clear: this is not to suggest at all that there is any similarity at the level of content between Fackenheim and the 'German Christians'; the issue is simply that Fackenheim does not offer many resources to assist his theology to resist the temptation to follow the movement of custom and ideology in the confusion and trauma that emerges during difficult historical crises. His anti-theology is supported by some implied judgements about the world, and there is little evidence in his work of wrestling with this tension.

In his own analysis of Fackenheim and other Jewish anti-theodicies, Braiterman suggests that in this new theological discourse, 'the memory of Auschwitz and the State of Israel virtually displace God and Torah.'[49] This is to say that the symbol of Auschwitz and the political entity of Israel are, in a way, being sacralized. Braiterman himself implies a degree of approval for this shift when he quotes the following statement by Michael Wyschogrod: 'If there is no need for sacrament in Judaism, it is because the people of Israel in whose flesh the presence of God makes itself felt in the world becomes the sacrament.'[50] Note that there is a level of irony here: although God is deemed to be silent and absent during the Holocaust, the state of Israel is considered to offer immediate access to the divine. Fackenheim does not go this far himself, but his theology offers little to resist such a drift, and it can be found in some other versions of post-Holocaust theology.

In an analysis of Holocaust literature, Michael Steele observes that a pattern often exists in literature of atrocity, which 'reveals an almost total lack of moral order'. Contemporary literary responses to catastrophes often shun theodicy entirely, and this chapter has illustrated powerful reasons for doing so; but the price of such a decision is often the abandonment of any real form of transcendence.[51] This initially appears understandable and attractive when viewed from a strictly theological or philosophical perspective; the limitations and potential vulgarities of theodicy in the face of a gruesome tragedy like the Shoah are powerful and humbling. But when viewed from a more practical and political perspective, the evasion of any position from which some form of reflexive critical leverage can be brought to bear on one's own theoretical position – theological or otherwise – is potentially problematic. Ruth Linn has explored the ways in which aesthetic and rhetorical responses to the Holocaust have sometimes blinded Israelis to the plight of Palestinian Arabs.[52] Ronit Lentin has similarly sought to uncouple Jewish protests against – and memorials of – the Shoah from nationalist rhetoric and ideological politics.[53]

It is from the perspective of the messiness of post-Holocaust Israeli politics, then, that some concerns can be raised about the anti-theodicies of Fackenheim and similarly inclined contemporary Jewish thinkers. The point is not to fault their critical challenge to and protest against the Nazi atrocities; nor is it to undermine their critiques of traditional theodicies for ignoring the depth of the suffering experienced by Jews; rather, the concern is to raise once again how their constructed position takes insufficient note of the problem of ideology. In response to tragedy and trauma, all forms of human thought – theological or anti-theological – can easily succumb the comforts of an ideological position. Chapter One illustrated how this impacted on the debate over the Lisbon Earthquake, Chapter Two explored how a similar problem plagued Christian thought at the outbreak of the First World War. This chapter's exploration of post-Holocaust thought has demonstrated that leaving behind the tangles of theodicy does not render one sufficiently immune to this dilemma.

The challenge this chapter leaves us with, then, is one which resembles the debate over how to represent the terrible events of the Nazi attempt to destroy the Jewish people. Recall the criticism raised by Paul Celan and others against rendering oneself silent before the catastrophe. In Giorgio Agamben's critique of such a move, he argues, 'To say that Auschwitz is "unsayable" or "incomprehensible" is equivalent to *euphmein*, to adoring silence, as one does with a god. Regardless of one's intentions, this contributes to its glory.'[54] In other words, not to speak of the Holocaust is to render it holy and sacred.[55] In much the same way, has the analysis of Fackenheim's theology not suggested that to shun transcendence entirely contributes to sacralizing the present moment or context which presents itself? Not to look for possibilities and ideas that reach beyond the current moment is to restrict thought and imagination to what one already knows. Such is the temptation for people who find themselves caught at the centre of a terrible tragedy. The task of the chapters which follow will be to begin to reflect on forms of thought and practice that may help resist collapsing the real to the immediate tragedy that presents itself, but in a way that avoids the dangerous trappings of traditional theology.

[handwritten margin note: silence does not need to be two-way – one can speak, the other listen]

Notes

[1]   Elie Wiesel, 'Jewish Values in the Post-Holocaust Future', *Judaism* 16.3 (1967), 285.
[2]   Imre Kertész, 'Nobel Lecture – Literature 2002', Nobelprize.org. 5 August 2010 http://nobelprize.org/nobel_prizes/literature/laureates/2002/kertesz-lecture-e.html [accessed 19 April 2011].
[3]   Richard L. Rubenstein, *After Auschwitz: Radical Theology and Contemporary Judaism* (Indianapolis, New York, Kansas City: Bobbs-Merrill Company, 1966), 70.
[4]   Susan Neiman, *Evil: An Alternative History of Philosophy* (Princeton and Oxford: Princeton University Press, 2002), 250.
[5]   See Raul Hilberg, *The Destruction of the European Jews*, 3 vols (New York: Holmes & Meier, 1985); Michael R. Marrus, *The Holocaust in History* (London: Penguin Books, 1987); Lucy S. Dawidowicz, *The War Against the Jews* (Toronto, New York, London: Bantam Books, 1976).

6 There is some debate over the possibility that the Turkish slaughter of Armenians immediately after World War One may qualify as a similar event. Contemporary acts of genocide, such as those in Rwanda and the former Yugoslavia, are sometimes comparatively described as 'holocausts'.

7 It is well established that other minority groups within Europe also suffered terribly during the Holocaust, including gays and lesbians, Jehovah Witnesses, Gypsies/Roma and the mentally disabled. While such groups were victims of the Nazi death camps, it is also the case that they were not the primary reason for the existence of the camps, nor was their persecution as determined, systematic or thoroughly implemented as the campaign against the Jewish people.

8 A controversial example of such an argument is Daniel J. Goldhagen, *Hitler's Willing Executioners: Ordinary Germans and the Holocaust* (New York: A. Knopf, 1995).

9 See Rosemary Radford Ruether, *Faith and Fratricide: The Theological Roots of Anti-Semitism* (New York: Seabury Press, 1974); Robert Michael, *Holy Hatred: Christianity, Antisemitism, and the Holocaust* (New York: Palgrave Macmillan, 2006).

10 For more on the 'Church Struggle' in Germany, see Matthew D. Hockenos, *A Church Divided: German Protestants Confront the Nazi Past* (Bloomington: Indiana University Press, 2004).

11 John Cornwell, *Hitler's Pope: The Secret History of Pius XII* (London: Penguin, 2000).

12 George Steiner, *Language and Silence: Essays on Language, Literature, and the Inhuman* (New York: Atheneum, 1967), 123.

13 Theodor W. Adorno, *Prisms*, trans. Samuel and Shierry Weber (Cambridge, MA: The MIT Press, 1981), 34.

14 For further discussion of such issues, see Norman G. Finkelstein, *The Holocaust Industry: Reflections on the Exploitation of Jewish Suffering* (London: Verso, 2003); Tim Cole, *Selling the Holocaust* (London: Routledge, 1999).

15 Giorgio Agamben, *Remnants of Auschwitz*, trans. Daniel Heller-Roazen (New York: Zone Books, 1999), 30.

16 Arthur Cohen, *The Cohen Reader*, ed. David Stern and Paul Mendes-Flohr (Detroit: Wayne State University Press, 1998), 240.

17 For a discussion of these issues, see James E. Young, *Writing and Re-Writing the Holocaust: Narrative and the Consequences of Interpretation* (Bloomington, IN: Indiana University Press, 1990), 87; Joe Petrie, 'The Secular Word HOLOCAUST: Scholarly Myths, History, and 20th Century Meanings', *Journal of Genocide Research* 2.1 (2000), 31–63.

18 Dominick LaCapra, *History and Memory After Auschwitz* (Ithaca and London: Cornell University Press, 1998), 181.

19 Elie Wiesel, *Night*, trans. Stella Rodway (Toronto, New York, London: Bantam Books, 1982), 27.

20 Ibid., 32.

21 Ibid., 52.

22 Primo Levi, *Survival in Auschwitz: If This is a Man*, trans. Stuart Woolf (New York: The Orion Press, 2007). 64.

23 Wiesel, *Night*, 109.

24 Emil Fackenheim, *To Mend the World* (Bloomington and Indianapolis: Indiana University Press, 1982), 25.

[25] Wiesel, *Night*, 61–2.

[26] Eliezer Berkovits, *Faith after the Holocaust* (Jersey City: Ktav Publishing, 1977).

[27] Irving Greenberg, 'Cloud of Smoke, Pillar of Fire; Judaism, Christianity and Modernity after the Holocaust', *Auschwitz: Beginning a New Era*, ed. E. Fleischner (New York: Ktav, 1977), 7–55.

[28] Steven T. Katz, *The Impact of the Holocaust on Jewish Theology* (New York and London: New York University Press, 2005), 30–3.

[29] Richard Rubenstein, *After Auschwitz: Radical Theology and Contemporary Judaism* (Indianapolis, New York, Kansas City: Bobbs-Merrill Company, 1966).

[30] See Martin Buber, *Eclipse of God: Studies in the Relation between Religion and Philosophy* (New York and Evanston: Harper and Row, 1952); Abraham Joshua Heschel, *Man Is Not Alone: A Philosophy of Religion* (Philadelphia: Jewish Publication Society, 1951); Mordecai Kaplan, *Questions Jews Ask: Reconstructionist Answers* (New York: Reconstructionist Press, 1956).

[31] Zachary Braiterman, *(God) After Auschwitz: Tradition and Change in Post-Holocaust Jewish Thought* (Princeton: Princeton University Press, 1998).

[32] Ibid., 37.

[33] Emil Fackenheim, *God's Presence in History* (New York, Evanston, London: Harper & Row, 1972), 76.

[34] Ibid., 67.

[35] Ibid., 69.

[36] Ibid., 70.

[37] Ibid., 71.

[38] Ibid., 77–8.

[39] Ibid., 72.

[40] Ibid., 84.

[41] Ibid., 75.

[42] Fackenheim, *To Mend the World*, 286–8.

[43] Fackenheim, *God's Presence in History*, 87.

[44] Fackenheim, *To Mend the World*, 285.

[45] Ibid., 291–3.

[46] Dorothee Sölle, *The Strength of the Weak*, trans. Robert and Rita Kimber (Philadelphia: Westminster Press, 1984), 41.

[47] Fackenheim, *God's Presence in History*, 87.

[48] Ibid., 91

[49] Braiterman, *(God) After Auschwitz*, 162.

[50] Ibid., 176.

[51] Michael R. Steele, *Christianity, Tragedy, and Holocaust Literature* (Westport, CT and London: Greenwood Press 1995), 151.

[52] Ruth Linn, 'In the Name of the Holocaust: Fears and Hopes Among Israeli Soldiers and Palestinians', *Journal of Genocide Research* 1.3 (1999), 439–53.

[53] Ronit Lentin, *Israel and the Daughters of the Shoah: Reoccupying the Territories of Silence* (New York and Oxford: Gerghahn Books, 2000).

[54] Agamben, *Remnants of Auschwitz*, 32.

[55] Such is the effect of Arthur Cohen's decision to describe the Shoah as 'the Tremendum', See Arthur A. Cohen, *The Tremendum* (New York: Crossroad, 1981).

Chapter 4

September 11, 2001: Religion Reviled and Revived

The Impact of 9/11

In Don Delillo's novel *Falling Man*, an estranged couple, living in New York during the immediate aftermath of the 9/11 terrorist attacks, meet to discuss some troubling behaviour displayed by their seven-year-old son Justin. They have learned that during visits to the neighbour's apartment, Justin and his friends spend all their time at the window of one of the bedrooms, speaking in a strange sort of gibberish. The parents of the children become concerned when the behaviour persists, particularly when one parent overhears them whisper a man's name: 'Bill Lawton'. The discomfort of the adults increases when they discover that the children are frequently carrying a pair of binoculars with them. This is exacerbated as the group begin speaking only in monosyllables when the adults are around. Finally, Justin confides the secret nature of their activities to his father. As the children huddle in the bedroom with the binoculars, they are searching the sky for planes, in case one might fly into their building. They watch the skies for a man named 'Bill Lawton', who they believe is out to get them. In their mythological imaginings, this dangerous man has a long beard, wears a robe and intends to poison what they eat, but only certain food. And so the children are developing a list of what is not safe to consume. With chilling recognition, the parents realize that the mysterious male name being whispered is a seven-year-old's rendering of 'bin Laden'.[1]

There are many powerful and evocative images and stories one could refer to in order to illustrate the impact of the terrorist attacks of September 11, 2001 on the cultural ethos of the United States, but this portrait of very young children taking it upon themselves to keep vigilant watch of the skies, due to their interpretation of the adult conversations they overhear, is a powerful and prescient example. It brings to mind Peter Sloterdijk's suggestion that terrorism 'voids the distinction between violence against people and violence against things: it comprises a form of violence against the very human-ambient "things" without which people cannot remain people.'[2] In this statement, Sloterdijk describes the shock of the introduction of mustard gas into the trenches of World War One, whereby violence was conducted against the very air that human beings require to breathe. With characteristic flair, he adds, 'the air totally lost its innocence.'[3] Such is the tone of the scene from *Falling Man*; for these seven-year-old children, after 9/11 the sky had lost its innocence.[4]

There are a number of ways in which the terrorist attacks of 11 September in the United States defy the innocence of simple categorization. In scholarly debates within 'disaster studies', for example, it is common practice to distinguish between catastrophes brought on by natural causes or technological failings (e.g. earthquakes, failures of a safety system in a power plant) and those caused by human conflict (war). According to E. L. Quarantelli, from a public policy perspective, natural disasters are 'consensus-type' events, in that they frequently result in widespread solidarity, shared communal response and a focus on re-establishing normalcy. 'Conflict-type' disasters, by contrast (which include terrorist attacks), are considered to be typified by widespread anti-social behaviour, such as looting or rioting.[5] But as Peek and Sutton observe, the September 11, terrorist attacks do not fit exclusively into either of these paradigms. Instead, the 'culture of disaster' in the United States following the tragedy exhibited elements of both consensus and conflict type events.[6] In the wake of the attacks, there was very little looting or vandalism in New York City or Washington, DC, and many individuals report experiencing a positive sense of the community coming together. At the same time, the aftermath included an atmosphere in which many sought to focus blame for the attacks, which occasionally resulted in conflict and violence (e.g. attacks on mosques and individual Muslims, wars in Afghanistan and Iraq). Thus, the public reaction in the United States to 9/11 does not fit neatly in to common categories of disaster response.

Philosophers have also wrestled over how to describe the nature of the aftermath of 9/11. For example, while Susan Nieman argues that the Lisbon earthquake revealed how remote the world is from the human, and that Auschwitz demonstrated the remoteness of humans from themselves, she suggests that contemporary terrorism does not represent a new form of evil.[7] Lisbon encouraged a distinction between nature and morality, so that 'evil' could now only refer to a moral deficit. Auschwitz, by contrast, demonstrated the embodiment of 'radical evil' *within* human beings, even in the absence of a clear and direct 'intention' on the part of the perpetrators to commit such terrible evil. For Nieman, the example of Adolf Eichmann's distant and bureaucratic role in administering the 'Final Solution' weakens any clear connection between the explicit perpetrators' intention to commit evil and acts of moral evil themselves.

As to categorizing the nature of the terrorist attacks of September 11, however, Nieman offers a more tentative and inconclusive reading. Rather than signifying a new form of evil, September 11 is more 'old-fashioned in structure', in that it was an instance of 'awesomely intentional' destruction.[8] As such, the 9/11 terrorist attacks blend dimensions of moral and natural evil, which had become philosophically distinguished after Lisbon. In their impersonal unpredictability, terrorist strikes resemble the arbitrariness of a natural disaster; but in their calculated destruction, such attacks incorporate what she calls moral evil. For Nieman, such a 'blend of moral and natural evil is so appalling that we seemed doomed to despair'.[9]

The scholarly difficulty over how to classify the impact of 9/11 on individual persons, but also on the general cultural atmosphere of the United States, is suggestive of both the complexity of the geopolitical situation in the contemporary world and also the disorienting nature of the shock caused by the attacks. The dis-ease experienced by many people is not limited to children like Justin in *Falling Man*, however, nor to residents of the United States. A scene from the novel *Saturday* by British writer Ian McEwan illustrates this point.

The novel opens as Henry Perowne, a neurosurgeon living in London, awakes in the middle of the night and looks out the window, only to see an airplane streaking across the sky with its engines in flames. Horrified and transfixed by the sight, his mind races with conflicting ideas and fears:

> If Perowne were inclined to religious feeling, to supernatural explanations, he would play with the idea that he's been summoned; that having woken up in an unusual state of mind, and gone to the window for no reason, he should acknowledge a hidden order, and external intelligence which wants to show or tell him something of significance.[10]

Perowne tries to dismiss such feelings as primitive and childish, but his discomfort with his own 'religious' musings is not simply the result of his atheism, for his subsequent thoughts are of the religious belief that might have compelled 'a man of sound faith with a bomb' to be the cause of the immanent disaster before his eyes. He then imagines terrified passengers on the plane praying to their God for assistance, about which he thinks, cynically, 'if there are deaths, the very god who ordained them will soon be funereally petitioned for comfort.'[11] Adding one further dimension to the complexity of Perowne's troubled state, McEwan captures the doctor's anxiety as the scene continues: 'The noise of the engine's distress is fading. Is the undercarriage down? As he wonders, he also wishes it, or wills it. A kind of praying?'

Perowne eventually learns that the flaming plane he saw was a Russian cargo jet with engine trouble, and the two-man crew was able to land safely. But the reaction the sight causes is symbolic of the effect that the 9/11 terrorist attacks have had on this British doctor (the London 7/7 bombings of 2005 had yet to occur). Every unusual or troubling event he encounters is taken as a possible sign of imminent terrorist atrocity. In a manner not unlike Delillo's character Justin, Perowne's attention to his environment has changed since 9/11. He describes this transformation in himself: 'There is no going back. The Nineties are looking like an innocent decade, and who would have thought that at the time? Now we breathe a different air.'[12]

This emphasis recalls Sloterdijk's remark, as Perowne's experience resonates with the observation that terrorism 'exploits the fact that ordinary inhabitants have a user relationship to their environment.'[13] The reliance of human beings upon their context, indeed the very fact that they must inhabit an environment, is experienced as an ominous vulnerability. Translating this into Nieman's terms, one can say that this phenomenon represents not so much a reversal of Lisbon's separation between the natural and moral evil, but rather a radical extension of the connection marked by Auschwitz between human beings and moral evil. Modernity's conceptualization of evil has come full circle, as potentially anything – an aircraft in trouble, an abandoned briefcase, a public trash bin, even the sky one lives under – might serve as an agent of moral evil. The very environment that Perowne inhabits has become a potential hazard.

This chapter explores two ways in which the post-9/11 atmosphere captured by fictional accounts like those of Delillo and McEwan is connected to the idea of 'religion'. The reactions modelled by the characters of Perowne and Justin resonate with the claims of the many people and media services who have suggested that, after September 11, 'the world will never be the same'.[14]

Before Chapter Five picks up the more abstract nature of the impact of 9/11 on the 'ideological' imagination of Western culture, two more immediate and obvious ways that the attacks have impacted on discourse about religion will be explored. First, this chapter analyses how 'religion' has become an object of suspicion and potential danger, as many citizens of the West associate it with the motivations and intentions of the hijackers of 9/11. After September 11, religion as such (although, more frequently, Islam in particular) has become something to be reviled. A second cultural response to the attacks, however, has been a revival of interest in what used to be thought of as 'religious' concerns: the desire for a meaningful life, for purpose and value beyond the daily struggles for security and success, and the search for existential security and trust in an insecure world. Perowne fights the tendency of his own such longings to find expression in any specific religious tradition, and yet at the same time these concerns resonate within him. In the immediate aftermath of the attacks, churches and synagogues in North America reported a sudden surge in attendance at worship services. Such a phenomenon requires analysis, as does the fact that this surge gradually disappeared, when people seemingly did not find what they were seeking in traditional religious institutions, or else no longer felt the same urgency to connect their lives to religion as they did immediately after the shock of 9/11.

Religion Reviled

The attacks on September 11, 2001, by hijackers using passenger planes as weapons of terror, were shocking both for the extent of the destruction they caused, and also for the level of calculated organization they displayed. United Airlines Flight 11 struck the north tower of the World Trade Center at 8:45 am. Flight 175 struck the south tower at 9:05, while Flight 77 hit the Pentagon in Washington, DC, at 9:45 am. The south tower of the World Trade Centre started to collapse at 9:55 am. At 10:20, another plane (Flight 93) crashed into a field 80 miles outside of Pittsburgh. Finally, at 10:28 am, the north tower of the World Trade Centre collapsed. In under two hours, four commercial airlines had been hijacked, and the planes turned into weapons of mass destruction. The official count records 2,986 deaths in the attacks, including the nineteen hijackers.

The initial media response to the attacks was one of shock and confusion. Commentators watched a screen filled with the image of the burning towers of the World Trade Centre and speculated over whether it was the result of an accident or a purposeful attack. Reporters on the street scrambled to make sense of the chaos. Soon, however, most were concluding that the first plane crash was no accident, and that the United States was the victim of a coordinated terrorist attack. As this realization became widespread, numerous New Yorkers wondered aloud on television, 'Why do they hate us?' In his speech on national television shortly after 11 am, President Bush said of the attacks, 'Today, our nation saw evil, the very worst of human nature.'[15] Numerous newspapers through the United States and across the world ran similar headlines: 'Pure Evil'.[16]

There is much that is of interest in these initial responses to the tragic events of the day, but for the moment it is significant to recognize how many observers soon identified religion as being the culprit for the event. In his book *Terror in the Mind of God* (published one year before the attack), Mark Juergensmeyer explores the emergence of religious terrorism in many of its forms: abortion clinic bombings, the Tokyo subway bombings, Timothy McVeigh's attack on Oklahoma City, and Osama bin Laden. Juergensmeyer argues that, 'A strain of violence . . . may be found at the deepest levels of religious imagination.'[17] By this he means that religion often brings with it unwillingness to compromise. Religious people, he suggests, frequently display an aggressive attitude towards the wider world. In their devotion to a higher power, they refuse to make concessions on the expression of their ideals and values within society, which results in a hostile attitude towards those things which fall short of their standards and expectations. When this occurs, religion might be said to contain within it an impulse towards violence.

After September 11, this would be a way that many people would respond to the event – arguing that it was religion's fault and warning that there something about 'religion' and 'religious people' that makes them more prone to acts of extreme violence. Juergensmeyer put his position in the form of a question: 'What puzzles me is not why bad things are done by bad people, but rather why bad things are done by people who otherwise appear to be good – in cases of religious terrorism, by pious people dedicated to a moral vision of the world.'[18] Other more well-known intellectuals took a similar message to television broadcasts and newspaper columns, warning that 'religion' was showing once again how dangerous and intolerant it could become. Contemplating how it is possible for a human being to fly a plane into a building with intent to kill, Richard Dawkins writes,

> Feed them a complete and self-consistent background mythology to make the big lie sound plausible when it comes. Give them a holy book and make them learn it by heart. Do you know, I really think it might work. As luck would have it, we have just the thing to hand: a ready-made system of mind-control which has been honed over centuries, handed down through generations. Millions of people have been brought up in it. It is called religion and, for reasons which one day we may understand, most people fall for it (nowhere more so than America itself, though the irony passes unnoticed). Now all we need is to round up a few of these faith-heads and give them flying lessons.[19]

Christopher Hitchens wrote similarly passionate and heated columns in the wake of the attacks, and later expanded his critical remarks against Islam into an accusation against religion as such, arguing that organized religion is 'the main source of hatred in the world.'[20] For secularist atheists like Martin Amis, because 'religion itself is an eggshell' due to the fact that 'there are no good excuses for religious belief' in the contemporary world, religious adherents are prone to excessive violence when the unsecure foundations of their 'ignorant' and 'sentimental' ideas are challenged by modernity.[21] The novelist John Updike adds sexual repression to his version of an armchair diagnosis of the cause of Islamic terrorism. In *Terrorist*, eighteen-year-old Ahmad, living in New Jersey, reacts against the casual sexuality of his mother, and his own discomfort with his attraction to a promiscuous young woman at his school, by fleeing into the protective security of an authoritarian Imam and a an extremist form of Islam.[22]

Despite the fact that most scholarly analysis of the roots of Islamic terrorism is concerned to emphasize the history of political and economic grievances between the Middle East and the West,[23] it has been writings such as those just mentioned which have popularized the association of the 9/11 terrorist attacks with religion as such. To a considerable degree, rather than helping people to understand the complexity of the factors involved in motivating such actions, many newscasts and newspapers only repeated and reinforced these stereotypes and simplistic assumptions. Of such a trend, the social theorist

Susan Buck-Morss writes, 'One might have hoped that in the "democratic" United States the media would have educated audiences regarding Islamist discourses in all of their political variations and historical complexities. But in the heavy atmosphere of patriotism and military preparedness that was generated after the September 11 attacks, indepth understanding was not on the national agenda.'[24]

Lack of rigour in the analysis of the relationship between religion and violence in the post-9/11 environment is not unique to columnists on the right wing of the political spectrum. While commenting on the idea that 'these attacks won't offer us new political scenery, but that they confirm the existence of a problem inside the [American] "Empire",' Noam Chomsky emphasizes George Bush's reference to the 'war on terrorism' as a 'crusade' in his presidential address of 16 September 2001.[25] While Chomsky is quite right to emphasize what a public relations disaster this choice of words was, particularly in relation to Muslim nations and citizens, his intent is to suggest that the president's evangelical Christian belief was shaping the American response to the emergency situation. Such accusations are not difficult to encounter in the more popular press,[26] but they also appear in academic venues as well. Bruce Lincoln suggests that, in his speech to the nation of 7 October 2001, Bush's references to terrorists seeking to evade American retaliation by trying to 'burrow deeper into caves' is intended to evoke the biblical passage in Revelation 6.15–17, in which the kings of the earth 'hid in caves' at the appearance of the Lamb of God.[27] Although there is much to appreciate about Lincoln's book, his reduction of the motivations and rhetoric of Bush's speech to coded allusions to biblical texts aimed at his evangelical Christian supporters is more than a little far-fetched (e.g. the characterization of the terrorists as 'killers of innocents' being a subtle reference to Herod's slaughter of innocent children in Matthew 2).

Although this interpretation of President Bush's speech might exaggerate the 'religious' undertones of his message, there is no question of overreaction when Lincoln turns to an analysis of a letter left behind by the airline hijackers. In the luggage abandoned in a hotel by one of the terrorists, the FBI found a letter containing final instructions. The contents of the document are chilling: a step-by-step outline of what to do and how to behave on the day of the attack. The letter reads like a manual for a religious ritual to be followed while preparing for the attack. Here is a sample of the instructions:

Purify your soul from all unclean things. Completely forget something called 'this world.' The time for play is over and the serious time is upon us . . . Do not seem confused or show signs of nervous tension. Be happy, optimistic, calm because you are heading for a deed that God loves and will accept . . .

If God decrees that any of you are to slaughter, dedicate the slaughter to your fathers . . . because you have obligations toward them. Do not disagree, and obey . . . When you ride the [airplane], before your foot steps in it, and before you enter it, you make a prayer and supplications. Remember that this is a battle for the sake of God.[28]

This text is particularly noteworthy for the way in which the hijackers invoke their obedience to God's will, as it is God 'who controls everything', and how they describe the act of killing in terms of religious ritual 'slaughter'. This is a vision of a God who is Almighty Power, and of a God who is angry with the state of the world. When the text of this list of instructions was made public, it is not difficult to see why some identified religion, or at least Islam in particular, as the root cause for the terrible events of September 11. Here is a portrait of the kind of hijacker Perowne fears is on the plane he is watching at the beginning of McEwan's novel *Saturday*. Such a text is a blueprint for Updike's crazed young man in *Terrorist*. In the face of such a chilling document, however, the question to be asked is whether the explanation for the cold-blooded attitudes it expresses, and the actions it inspired, can be easily reduced to the fact that these men were 'religious' or 'Muslim'?

Lincoln on 'Maximalist' and 'Minimalist' Religion

Lincoln himself brings a level of nuance to his analysis of this letter, as he explores how the 'religious' element of the text might be more clearly described. He observes that the document reveals how the entire terrorist operation was 'decomposed into a series of minute actions, each of which is invested with religious significance'.[29] This suggests to Lincoln that how one understands 'religion' should attend not only to ideas, but to the level of practice and action. The form of religion in this text, he notes, welds 'practice to discourse: providing each grubby, banal, or lethal act with authoritative speech that ennobles and redefines it'.[30] There are thus many different dimensions to the phenomenon of this letter that could lead one to describe it as 'religious': there is the text itself, and the authority that those who wrote have in the eyes of those to whom it was given (the 'community' of the hijackers). This is complemented by the prayers and ritual action ('practice') that connects the hijackers in an intimate way to the divine referent of the letter; and the letter quotes from the Quran (a 'privileged discourse'). Lincoln's intention in breaking down the different elements of the letter is to develop an understanding of the concept of 'religion' that avoids reducing it to the level of metaphysical ideas about the divine or to some unique form of interior experience. Rather, for Lincoln, a 'religion' is the complex historical and cultural product that generally combines four domains: a privileged discourse that claims authoritative and transcendent authority, a set of practices to which it is connected, a community that defines its identity in relation to these elements, and an institutional framework that proves coherent over time and across space.[31]

Lincoln describes this four-fold dimension of 'religion' in response to debates within the academic study of religion, as well as in anthropology, which argue that there cannot be a universal definition of 'religion' due to the diversity of beliefs and practices across human cultures, but also because religions change over time.[32] This multi-dimensional perspective on religion also permits him to develop a distinction between different expressions of religion, which relate differently to the question of violence. The particular ways in which religions combine their particular discourses, communities, practices and institutions can vary in different times and places, so that very different expressions of the same religious tradition emerge.

A distinction Lincoln wants to make here is between expressions of religion that are prone to violence and those forms of religious expression which are not dangerous or aggressive. If different historical forms of a religion can take on distinct characteristics, then Lincoln can argue that it is not religion as such that is violent, but only some particular manifestations of religion. The political import of such a theoretical move is clear: it supports the argument that it is not the religion of Islam which is inherently dangerous and violent, but only particular expressions of Islam.

Lincoln thus establishes two ideal types of formations of religious expression in the contemporary world: 'minimalism' and 'maximalism'. 'Minimalist' religion is the position taken by many religious adherents and communities in modernity, in which their religious practice and belief is restricted 'to an important set of (chiefly metaphysical) concerns'.[33] Minimalist religion occupies the space delegated to it by the Enlightenment and by philosophers like Kant or Locke. It is separate from affairs of the state and is largely confined to the private sphere of domestic life, such as Sunday mornings, bedtime prayers and the religious holiday seasons. Religion is thus marginalized within society, because it is no longer able to claim authority over the general values and practices of the population. In exchange, the state agrees to allow a religion to operate without interference within its own limited realm of activity.

'Maximalist' religion, however, breaks this truce between religious faith and modernity. Lincoln prefers this term to 'fundamentalism', as for him, the central problem with this model of religion is not the nature of its beliefs, but rather its attitude to the society external to the religious community. The issue with 'maximalism' is that it asserts that 'religion ought to permeate all aspects of social, indeed of human existence.'[34] The maximalist cannot accept the modern separation of spheres in society. The prototype for Lincoln's conceptualization of this model of religion is Sayyid Qutb, an Egyptian Islamist author and founder of the Muslim Brotherhood in the 1950s. In Qutb, Lincoln perceives a determined withdrawal from modern social and political norms, in order to defend an authoritative and self-enclosed version of Islam that refuses to compromise with the world external to it. But because this external society threatens to interrupt or confine what is felt to be the purity of a sacred and absolute way of life, it is viewed as threatening and corrupting.

It is this aggressive rejection of the society external to the religious community, and this refusal to compromise with and agree to conform one's religious norms to a more privatized sphere of life, that, in Lincoln's view, leads to violence. Thus, in his interpretation, the dangerous thing about the letter left behind by the hijackers is not that it is written by Muslims, but that it is written by maximalists. In this way, the critique of religion's connection to violence is distanced from any one particular tradition and focused on a particular model of religious expression that can be found in all historical religions.

To a considerable degree, Lincoln's distinction between minimalist and maximalist religion offers a more sophisticated way to interpret the role of religion in the terrorist attacks of 9/11 than do critics like Hitchens, Dawkins and Amis. It also goes some way to respond to critics of Juergensmeyer and other social scientific approaches to religious violence, such as the Christian theologian William Cavanaugh. In *The Myth of Religious Violence*, Cavanaugh responds rather vigorously against the accusation that religion possesses some inherent propensity towards violence.[35] One object of his criticism is Juergensmeyer's distinction between acts of violence undertaken with clear instrumental purpose and those with a more 'symbolic' intention. For example, the takeover of a television broadcasting station would represent an action with a clear strategic purpose and function: it allows the group to broadcast their message in the media. A symbolic act, however, does not achieve any concrete objective, but rather intends to point to something beyond itself. Juergensmeyer's example is the releasing of nerve gas in the Tokyo subway, which, while causing considerable panic, did not result in any utilitarian gain on the part of the terrorists. As Juergensmeyer present it, 'religious violence' is 'symbolic', while political violence has more concrete strategic ends.[36] In this regard, it is noteworthy that Lincoln implies something similar when he distinguishes between 9/11 and the attack on Pearl Harbour in 1941. The latter was a strategic act of war intended to cripple the American navy, whereas the 'Islamists designed their assault more for sign value than use value.'[37]

Cavanaugh argues that Juergensmeyer undercuts such a distinction when the latter admits that symbolic acts can actually weaken the power and influence of a political government: 'Because power is largely a matter of perception, symbolic statements can lead to real results.'[38] Cavanaugh develops this point to claim that the distinction between religious and political violence is largely unsustainable, so that the accusation that religion has some unique connection to violence falls apart.

This critique of a clear distinction between 'religious' and other forms of violence complicates Lincoln's somewhat simplistic suggestion that violence committed by members of a religious tradition is generally the result of their 'maximalist' identity. One might ask, for example, why 'maximalism' is being used as a descriptive category of forms of *religion*, as opposed to models of political, national or psychological attitudes? Do not individuals without any connection to a religious tradition of any kind on occasion also lash out in violence against the external society when it fails to conform to their expectations? What the structure of Lincoln's argument actually describes is the resentment some people feel to difference and lack of control; what is essentially 'religious' about this problem, however, is far from clear.

A second complication Lincoln's schema faces is the fact that many religious adherents who, according to his definitions, could only be classified as 'maximalists', fail to exhibit any interest in exercising violence at all. Radical Christian sects like the Amish certainly challenge the distinction drawn by liberal political theory between public and private spheres of life, and they live as though their faith ought to inform all of their personal choices and permeate all aspects of their cultural life. The fact that the vast majority of people outside of their communities live very differently, however, has not led them to vent any resentment or anger at this world outside their own norms in the form of 'religious' violence. Thus, if Lincoln's distinction between 'minimalism' and 'maximalism' is to have any value, it will be at the level of *describing* some expressions of religious identity, but it does not represent an *explanation* for violence on the part of religious adherents.

The 'Clash of Civilizations'

Despite the compelling evidence that it is not religion *as such* that causes terrorist violence, but rather a more complicated constellation of social, political, economic and historical factors (as well as psychological considerations), there persists a strong tendency among reactions to 9/11 in North Atlantic societies to revile religion for being dangerous and backward. This reaction has frequently been associated with an interpretation of the geopolitical situation in the world that predated the attacks of September 11: the 'Clash of Civilizations' thesis. This formulation was made famous in an article by Samuel Huntington that appeared in the American journal *Foreign Affairs*. In his essay, Huntington argues,

> World politics is entering a new phase, in which the great divisions among humankind and the dominating source of international conflict will be cultural. Nation states will remain the most powerful actors in world affairs, but the principal conflicts of global politics will occur between nations and groups of different civilizations. The clash of civilizations will dominate global politics. The fault lines between civilizations will be the battle lines of the future.[39]

Huntington argues that the great political divisions of the Cold War are now out of date. Instead of clashes between different nation states on ideological grounds, conflicts will now occur between different 'civilizations'. By 'civilization', he means 'a cultural entity. Villages, regions, ethnic groups, nationalities, religious groups, all have distinct cultures.'[40] This is a controversial and rather odd conclusion. It assumes that different civilizations and religions are complete and unique cultures of their own. People who inhabit them, it is suggested, all think and act in similar ways. All members of such a group would construct their world in exactly the same manner, so that there are not fundamental disagreements within a civilization over values, morals and opinions. 'Civilizations' are portrayed as large groupings of individuals who share the same values and basic ideas about the world, and it is membership in such a civilization that is treated as the driver of history. Belonging to a civilization, therefore, is a prime determinant of behaviour.

This is a difficult thesis to accept. As critics of Huntington have observed, the so-called principal civilizations often identified (the West, Asia, the Muslim world, etc.) do not often appear so monolithic when examined closely.[41] The Islamic 'Civilization' is rent by numerous internal divisions – ethnic, regional, economic, historic and religious. One need only mention a few other examples – the tensions between India and Pakistan, Iran and Iraq – to illustrate that one has to zoom one's theoretical lens quite far out from events on the ground before entire regions of the world might be seen as a harmonious collectives of shared 'values'.

According to Huntington, though, there are critical disagreements between different 'civilizations'. In his view, the culture of the West is incompatible with the religion and culture of Islam; therefore, the world is confronted by an inevitable 'clash of civilizations'. There can be no reconciliation or peaceful coexistence in this worldview. Inevitably, the opposing value systems of different civilizations will result in a conflict that will last until one worldview is defeated. Democracy in the West, it is suggested, is incompatible with how Muslim society understands the world. In this view, it is not religion in general that is the cause of violence, but a certain form of religion: Islam.

It is not difficult to identify examples of this way of conceiving of the global situation following 9/11. The rhetoric of two of the main players in the drama – Osama bin Laden and George W. Bush – both describe the world in such terms. In his speech of 16 September, for example, President Bush states,

> On this day of faith, I've never had more faith in America than I have right now . . . But we need to be alert to the fact that these evil-doers still exist. We haven't seen this kind of barbarism in a long period of time . . . This is a new kind of – a new kind of evil. And we

understand. And the American people are beginning to understand. This crusade, this war on terrorism is going to take a while.[41]

The Bush administration quickly dropped this kind of language after being harshly criticized for it, recognizing that it might be taken as identifying Islamic culture as a general threat to 'the West'. But the general tendency to divide the world into two distinct and inherently opposed groups persists in his speeches. Bruce Lincoln's analysis of Bush's address to the nation on 7 October makes this clear. Given in response to the airing of Osama bin Laden's videotape that same day, the speech is made as air strikes are initiated in Afghanistan. As this conflict begins, the president describes what is involved: 'We are joined in this operation by our staunch friend, Great Britain. Other close friends, including Canada, Australia, Germany and France, have pledged forces ... We are supported by the collective will of the world.' To this list, he is careful to add 'the friends of almost a billion worldwide who practice the Islamic faith' and those who wish to 'raise their children free from fear'. The opponents he names are 'the terrorists' and the 'Taliban', 'Evil doers', and those who oppose freedom. And God, it is said, is clearly on one side, for the president ends his speech with 'May God continue to bless America.'[42]

As Lincoln observes, the speech divides the world up into two distinct groups: America and its allies, and the terrorists and their supporters. There is no middle ground. The president himself acknowledges this when he adds,

> Every nation has a choice to make. In this conflict, there is no neutral ground. If any government sponsors the outlaws and killers of innocents, they have become outlaws and murderers, themselves. And they will take that lonely path at their own peril.

Lincoln's analysis compares the basic structure of this portrait of the world with that implied by the videotaped speech by Osama bin Laden, which also aired on 7 October 2001. In this recorded broadcast, bin Laden asserts that 'American was struck by God Almighty in one of its vital organs, so that its greatest buildings are destroyed.' He adds, 'God has blessed a group of vanguard Muslims, the forefront of Islam, to destroy America.'[44] Clearly, for him, the acts of terrorism in which he is involved are intended to initiate a war with a religious rationale, for it is said to not only be sanctioned by God, but inspired by God. He asserts that God is on his side.

In the course of the speech, bin Laden also focuses on two other groups of people. First, he says that these acts are done in defence of 'weak children'. He suggests that, 'A million innocent children are dying at this time as we speak, killed in Iraq without any guilt.' And so these actions are said to be justified, because they are defending the vulnerable and oppressed. The second group he describes are his opponents: 'those hypocrites . . . and apostates who followed the wrong path'. Anyone who opposes his understanding of God, including any Muslims who disagree with his interpretation of Allah's intentions, 'will get what they deserve'.

After describing the world as being a division between these two groups, bin Laden argues that all people now must choose which side they are on. He says,

> I tell them all that these events have divided the world into two camps, the camp of the faithful and the camp of infidels. May God shield us and you from them . . . Every Muslim must rise to defend his religion. Bin Laden divides the world into two camps, which are absolutely and inevitably in opposition. In such a confrontation, there can be no in-between space, no neutrality and no compromise. This is indeed a 'maximalist' perspective on world affairs.

Although Lincoln is careful to distinguish between the very different forms of the political authority invoked by the figures of President Bush and Osama bin Laden, and he by no means argues that they 'say the same thing', his analysis is concerned to show how the structure of both of these speeches divide the world into two absolute and opposing camps, so that all people of the world must choose which side they are on. Both speeches, Lincoln argues, describe the world in terms of a 'Manichean struggle'.[45] By this, he means that the struggle can only be understood as a conflict between good and evil, 'Us' and 'Them'. 'Manicheanism' refers to a prominent form of Gnostic religion from the ancient world that conceived of history as a struggle between forces of darkness in the material world and forces of light of the spiritual realm.[46] Lincoln's use of such a term to refer to these speeches thus intends to suggest that both speakers imply that there is no third option, no middle ground, at ground zero.

This rejection of the possibility of neutrality, or for a different perspective on the situation, leaves little room to deal with complexity, for dialogue and debate, or for listening to the voice of the other. Instead, a position which accepts such a version of the 'clash of civilization' thesis often reduces political rhetoric to the level of slogans and to simplistic descriptions of the conflict. This tendency to reduce the issues to an 'Us' versus 'Them' position, where there can be no middle ground or gray areas, gets at the heart of one of the more troubling questions that arise in reactions to the shock of the attacks of September 11 2001 and other similar events. A question for religious adherents to wrestle with is whether religious belief, as critics of religion often argue, encourages this way of looking at the world. Does religious commitment sometimes prevent people from seeking a more 'in-depth' understanding of reality, by promoting a dualistic view of society and politics? Is religion inherently 'Manichean', in the sense of inherently implying an opposition between believers and non-believers? Although Lincoln does not make this explicit claim himself, he does warn that 'conversion of secular political speech into religious discourse invests otherwise merely human events with transcendent significance.'[47]

This issue requires much more attention and analysis than it usually receives in theological discussion, for if there is a danger that religious speech about politics often distorts one's vision of reality, what does this imply about the possibility of the involvement of religious citizens in the political debates of the countries in which they inhabit? Should religion have no place in public life, as some of the 'new Atheists' like Dawkins and Hitchens assert, or might shutting out the concerns of religious citizens be one of the factors causing their resentment of secular society? Such will be a topic of concern in subsequent chapters. For the remainder of this chapter, the discussion will explore reactions to the September 11 terrorist attacks which, rather than protesting against religion, turned towards it in search of support and guidance.

Religion Revived

In the wake of the attacks of September 11, there has been a heightened interest in the nature and activities of religious communities. Some churches and similar institutions have reported an increased level of attendance and membership in response to the attacks, leading them to ask whether 9/11 could actually result in 'revive within religious communities'. The form of post-9/11 'religious revival' that critics of religion focus on resembles the sort of opportunistic assertions by religious leaders like those discussed in Chapter one: those who argue that God has caused a historical disaster in order to punish people who have gone astray.

The form of 'religious revival' that critics of religion focus on resembles the sort of opportunistic assertions by religious leaders like those discussed in Chapter One: those who argue that God has caused a historical disaster in order to punish people who have gone astray. Lincoln himself focuses on this form of revival when he analyses the transcript of a conversation between the American television evangelists Jerry Falwell and Pat Robertson, which occurred on 13 September 2001. Both leaders blatantly advocate the view that tragedies like 9/11 are caused by God as a way to punish human sin. Notably, the way they frame the situation theologically has much in common with the approach to human tragedy expressed by Malagrida after the Lisbon Earthquake.

In the interview, Falwell and Robertson described their opponents in American culture and politics as 'evil' and 'Christ-haters'. Robertson explains the cause of 9/11 as follows:

> Well, why it's happening is that God Almighty is lifting his protection from us. And once that protection is gone, we are all vulnerable because we're a free society . . . We lay naked before these thousands of terrorists who have infiltrated our country . . . And the only thing that's going to sustain us is the umbrella power of the Almighty God.[48]

This statement presents an image of God who is Almighty power and control: God functions like a strategic umbrella, not unlike a force field or the 'Star Wars' missile defence system. As such, one had better ensure that one does nothing to compel the divine umbrella to withdraw his protection. The implied message in this discussion is that terrible things happen in this world because God lets them happen, and God even causes them happen. In his reply to this description of God, Falwell adds that the attacks of 11 September occurred because (some) Americans had sinned:

The abortionists have got to bear some burden for this because God will not be mocked. And when we destroy 40 million little innocent babies, we make God mad. I really believe that pagans, and the abortionists, and the feminists, and the gays and lesbians, who are actively trying to make that an alternative lifestyle . . . I point the finger in their face and say: 'You helped to make this happen.'

In this statement, the responsibility for the terrible tragedy of 11 September is placed on everyone that Falwell does not like. He blames it on the sins of his political opponents and insists that God is on his side. The role of the terrorists themselves actually gets pushed to the side. The terrorists did not really cause the events – God did. God let it happened because God was angry at America, angry at those groups and interests that Falwell disagrees with. The result is that – astonishingly – Falwell shifts responsibility for the destruction *from the terrorists* to God, pagans, feminists, gays and lesbians, and those who perform abortions. Here, as in the speeches of President Bush and bin Laden, the situation the world is experiencing is reduced to a confrontation between two distinct groups: those on the side of God and those who sin – 'Us' and 'Them'.

Before proceeding on to a more general examination of religious responses to 9/11, it is noteworthy that the basic theodicy articulated by Falwell and Robertson has some structural similarities to more 'secular' explanations for the terrorist attacks. Many commentators from the left-wing political spectrum, for example, have argued that, in the terrorist attacks, the United States got what it deserved. Such narratives suggested that, because the powerful and wealthy nation had exploited and marginalized people in the Arab world, America was only reaping what it had sowed. For example, Noam Chomsky wrote, 'we can think of the United States as an "innocent victim" only if we adopt the convenient path of ignoring the record of its actions and those of its allies.'[49] The film director Michael Moore was even more overt: 'We created the monster known as Osama bin Laden . . . That was our work, you and me folks.'[50] These ways of describing the event, although intending very different political agendas from those of both Bush and bin Laden, have a basic structural similarity to the theodicy of Falwell and Robertson: the United States got what it deserved because it had sinned, and those who are responsible for the sinning ought now to be identified and punished.

9/11 as an Opportunity for a 'Spiritual Awakening'

In the weeks and months following the attacks of 11 September, many churches and synagogues in North America reported a sudden increase in attendance at worship services. Most came seeking solace and comfort to soothe their troubled minds and their fears. What were people looking for, exactly? Did their spiritual lives really change?

In a special issue of *Macleans* magazine on this phenomenon, the writer Ron Graham observes how

> In our sorrow, we were convinced that nothing would ever be the same, least of all ourselves . . . And we made vows, as earnest as New Year's resolutions, to rearrange our priorities, reassess our values, become wiser and kinder, because life is brief and leads only to the tomb.[51]

The magazine conducted a survey of 1,200 Canadians in order to try to assess whether the terrorist attacks had indeed had some sort of impact on the spiritual or ethical concerns of people. The results included the following: 72% of respondents said that they have become more appreciative of family life; 26% claimed that they had less interest in material wealth and possessions; 23% felt a stronger need for religious beliefs; and 16% expressed a stronger desire to go to a place of worship.[52] A survey of 1,500 American citizens by the Pew Research Center, however, concludes that 'there is little evidence that many Americans who were not actively religious prior to the attacks have turned to religion in the wake of the crisis.' Many people did suggest that that had become 'more religious' since 9/11, particularly in the form of praying more frequently (69%).[53] This implies that reports of increased levels of attendance at worship services might well be caused by the fact that people who were already religious adherents were attending such ceremonies more frequently than they usually did. Non-religious citizens, therefore, did not seem to suddenly become religious practitioners in any great numbers.

What, then, of the survey results found by *Macleans* magazine? Other than suggesting a possible difference between the initial public reactions in Canada and the United States, the magazine itself suggests that the sudden elevation of religious activity was short-lived. It reports,

Houses of worship have already started to witness some backsliding. Immediately after the attacks, people crowded into churches, synagogues, temples and mosques – many for the first time in years. Since then, attendance has been dropping.[54]

Social scientific research into human responses to disaster suggests some general patterns that resonate with the phenomena these two surveys describe. J. S. Tyhurst proposes a three-phase model of community response to disasters.[55] In phase one, individuals are likely to experience shock and may feel numbed or try to deny the severity of the situation. This is followed by a second 'recoil' phase, in which individuals gradually respond to the situation by trying to make sense of what has happened by turning to their traditional sources of support: family, friends and small groups. The third stage in Tyhurst's schema is the 'recovery' phase, during which members of the community adjust and return to regular patterns of life, with possibly the occasional relapse into earlier phases of reaction.[56]

The reactions to 9/11 observed by the Pew Center and the *Macleans* survey could be understood as being expressions of the 'recoil' phases of disaster response. The reactions of the individuals surveyed are forms of behaviour that seek support from sources of comfort, support and security: family, friends, small community groups and traditional resources for moral and spiritual guidance. For those with some connection to a traditional religious community, it makes sense that they would turn to them during such a time of 'recoil'. As the psychiatrist David Alexander argues while criticizing some of the ways in which trauma counsellors operate following a disaster, victims and witnesses require time to express and process the powerful feelings they experience. In this situation, 'mere ventilation of feelings is rarely enough.'[57] Such individuals frequently require a network of support to help challenge unrealistic ideas of worries they might have or to reassure them against feelings of guilt. A social and cultural 'framework' is often required to help those suffering the emotional impact of a tragedy to work through their emotional reactions and to find the resilience to rebuild their lives. During such a time, a religious community, as a social network, a moral discourse and a set of spiritual practices, can play a useful role. But as individuals move out of this recoil phase, and into what Tyhurst loosely calls the period of 'recovery', the Pew and *Macleans* surveys suggest that many people will require less from their support networks, and so might well return to their prior patterns and routines.

For the purpose of evaluating the relative benefits or dangers of religion for individuals and communities experiencing the traumas of a disaster, the so-called recoil phase – or simply, the time between the initial shock caused by the disaster and the return to any sense of normalcy – is crucial. For this reason, the remainder of the discussion in this chapter, as well as that of the subsequent chapter, will reflect on it at greater length.

Who Is Your 'We'?

In his essay, 'September 11 and the Children of Abraham', Peter Ochs reflects on the events of 9/11 from the perspective of an American Jew. He describes Septembet 11, as being 'a symptom of an Event'.[58] By an 'Event', he means. Something which suddenly interrupts people, wounding them leading them to recoil and fall back on very basic habits and beliefs, An event is, 'what shocks me to turn to the *we* that guides me in times of dislocation.' As a Jewish man, the 'we' he refers to comprises the history and traditions of Judaism, as well as his local Jewish community. By 'symptoms', he means, 'pains and confusions' that at present cannot be mended; 'interruptions in the social fabric of our everyday lives – "big-time wounds" – that cannot be healed without significant changes or reforms in our fundamental institutions'.

The problem confronting the United States, Ochs continues, is that 'the symptoms of such Events cannot even be read properly' by most Americans, 'since such symptoms would contradict, or remain invisible to, what [our] leaders . . . are trained to expect of the world.' For example, if one shows a doctor an illness, the doctor may not be able to recognize it, because it is not in the medical books yet. If 9/11 was such a 'symptom of an Event', for which the precise causes had yet to be 'diagnosed', then Ochs argues that it is no surprise that governments responded to the symptom as they always have and were trained to – much like a doctor is guided by a medical textbook. 'How would they act? Only as they already do!' And so Ochs challenges his reader:

> I fear it is only our task – we whose job it is to observe the not yet visible – to get cracking on our work of observation. What do we see? What hypotheses do we have to offer about how this society's service institutions must change if the society is to adjust to a new world it does not yet see but we must?

Note that in these remarks, Ochs shifts the attention of his reader away from the subjective '*I*' who is shocked by an Event, to a communal '*we*' who respond to the shock collectively.

In his own way, Ochs is describing the sociological and psychological dynamics of what Tyhurst calls the 'recoil' phase. In Ochs's essay, however, he adds a cautionary tone: one can recoil in more or less helpful ways. Some forms of recoil, and some of the places one retreats to, may be less productive and healthy than others. In other words, he is asking: who is the 'we' that helps shape someone's perspective after a disaster? If an Event like 9/11 shocks a society's cultural life, so that it recoils and withdraws into a 'we' that offers comfort and guidance, then who this 'we' is becomes vitally important.

Of course, all citizens are members of many different communities: their immediate families, local municipalities, regions and countries. They have a particular language, gender, race and ethnicity. Then there are numerous other groups people might associate with: social class, profession, religion and so forth. Each individual is influenced and shaped by many different associations and relationships. The question that presents itself to Christians and religious practitioners in the wake of September 11 is: which of these identities has the greatest influence on shaping one's response to the terrible tragedy? What do religious adherents fall back on in times of disruption, confusion and shock, as if by reflex or habit?

Clearly, theologians and religious leaders would hope, like Ochs, that the 'we' that religious people turn to is the religious tradition to which they belong. Theologians would expect the religious perspective ought to play a key role in shaping a healthy, truthful and moral response to historical tragedy. In the course of this chapter, however, at least two different kinds of problems have already emerged with such an approach. The first is the potential that the religious expression that individuals will articulate during a troubled and stressful situation might just as easily become a violent form of aggression. Lincoln's analyses of bin Laden's videotaped address, as well as of the conversation between Falwell and Robertson, illustrate that turning to 'religion' at ground zero is neither an innocent nor a straightforward exercise. As was illustrated in Chapter Two, religion can easily become a tool for ideological and political agendas during times of crises, or even a form of psychological projection in moments of stress and anxiety. It is not simply *that* people turn to religion which ought to concern theologians and religious leaders, but the *way* that they engage with their tradition and their *motivations* for doing so.

Furthermore, as the example of the 'clash of civilizations' thesis demonstrated, and the speeches of both President Bush and Osama bin Laden modelled structurally, political rhetoric in the face of disaster easily becomes reduced to a simplistic opposition between 'Us' and 'Them'. This is a second danger inherent to the call to turn to the support of the 'we' during times of recoil. To make this point is not to challenge the claims of either Tyhurst or Ochs for the value and need of such support; it is only to caution once again that different individuals will engage in this process in different ways. Some reaffirmations of community identity and location come at the cost of being established in opposition to other identities and locations. The tension between 'identity' and 'difference' can become powerful and problematic, particularly in times of crisis.[59]

Ideology and Collective Imagination

This problem is frequently overlooked in theological writing on 9/11 and other disasters. In *Redeeming the Broken Body*, for example, Gabriel A. Santos offers a provocative reflection on the cultural politics of disaster. He explores how different catastrophes have undermined the 'lifeworlds' and support systems of human beings, and how this disrupts the stories and narratives which nurture them. Underneath these rich observations, however, is an agenda that intends to contrast the healing capacities of an ecclesial identity rooted in the church, with a more problematic and ideologically laden collective identity shaped by the interests of the state. Santos describes the reaction of the state to disasters as being driven by a monolithic theopolitics, which narrowly focuses on 'security' and managerial questions, while neglecting local community interests and concerns. The concern to be raised about this approach is not to do with Santos's suggestion that the nation frequently reacts to disasters through the lens of a 'statist political imaginary', for indeed it does. This chapter has already demonstrated how susceptible political leaders are to describing an emergency situation in simplistic and problematic terms. The issue, rather, is with the way in which Santos presents the church as a seamless 'counter liturgy' to the perspective of the state, as if to suggest that the church is considerably less susceptible to the problems of ideology and self-interest than the state is.[60]

Such inherent complexities with the reaffirmation of religious identity, and with efforts to 'revive' religion during times of catastrophe and crisis, will be the concern of Chapter Five. It will focus on an issue which has been lurking under the surface of the discussions in this book since it began: the problem of ideology. The chapter explores this challenge through an analysis of the work of Slavoj Žižek, particularly as he develops his concept of ideology in relation to the events of 9/11. What will be of particular concern, and subjected to critical discussion, is the way in which Žižek's response to September 11 is resourced by attention to the dynamics of religion and belief. This discussion will provide a deeper level of understanding of issues that have come into clearer view over the course of this chapter: the complex relationships between religion and ideology, individual and collective identity, and emotional reactions to traumatic events.

Notes

1 Don Delillo, *Falling Man* (London: Picador, 2007).
2 Peter Sloterdijk, *Terror from the Air* (Los Angeles: Semiotext(e), 2009), 25.
3 Ibid., 109.
4 In a survey conducted five days after September 11, 2001, 35% of children were found to have at least one symptom related to Post Traumatic Stress Disorder (PTSD). Two years after the Oklahoma City bombings in 1995, 16% of children surveyed in the city continued to show signs of PTSD. See David Alan Alexander and Susan Klein, 'Biochemical Terrorism: Too Awful to Contemplate, Too Serious to Ignore', *British Journal of Psychiatry* 183 (2003), 491–7.
5 E. L. Quarantelli, 'Community Crisis', *Journal of Contingencies and Crisis Management* 1.2 (1993), 67–78.
6 Lori A. Peek and Jeannette N. Sutton, 'An Exploratory Comparison of Disasters', *Disasters* 27.4 (2003), 319–35.
7 Susan Nieman, *Evil: An Alternative History of Philosophy* (Princeton and Oxford: Princeton University Press, 2002), 240.
8 Ibid., 283.
9 Ibid., 287.
10 Ian McEwan, *Saturday* (London: Vintage, 2005), 17.
11 Ibid., 18.
12 Ibid., 32.
13 Sloterdijk, 28.
14 For example, Michael Elliot, 'America Will Never Be the Same' *Time Magazine Online* 11 September 2001. www.time.com/time/nation/article/0,8599,174540,00.html [last accessed 19 April 2011.
15 Text of Bush's Speech, CNN.com http://edition.cnn.com/2001/US/09/11/bush.speech. text/ [last accessed 19 April 2011].
16 For example, Australia's *The Herald Sun*, on 12 September 2001, p. 1.
17 Mark Juergensmeyer, *Terror in the Mind of God: The Global Rise of Religious Violence* (Berkeley: University of California Press, 2000), 6.

[18] Ibid., 7.

[19] Richard Dawkins, 'Religion's Misguided Missiles', *The Guardian* (London, 15 September 2001).

[20] Christopher Hitchens, *God is not Great: How Religion Poisons Everything* (New York: Twelve Books, 2007), 283.

[21] Martin Amis, *The Second Plane* (London: Vintage Books, 2008), 49.

[22] John Updike, *Terrorist* (London: Penguin Books, 2006).

[23] John L. Esposito, *Unholy War: Terror in the Name of Islam* (Oxford: Oxford University Press, 2002).

[24] Susan Buck-Morss, *Thinking Past Terror* (London and New York: Verso, 2003), 3.

[25] Noam Chomsky, *9/11* (New York: Open Media/Seven Stories Press, 2001), 12–13.

[26] Hugh B. Urban, *The Secrets of the Kingdom: Religion and Concealment in the Bush Administration* (Lanham, MD: Rowman & Littlefield Publishers, 2007).

[27] Bruce Lincoln, *Holy Terrors: Thinking about Religion after September 11* (Chicago: University of Chicago Press, 2003), 30.

[28] Ibid., 93–8.

[29] Ibid., 10.

[30] Ibid., 11.

[31] Ibid., 1–8.

[32] Lincoln is particularly concerned with the criticisms of Talal Asad. See Asad, *Genealogies of Religion* (Baltimore: John Hopkins University Press, 1993).

[33] Ibid., 5.

[34] Ibid., 5.

[35] William T. Cavanaugh, *The Myth of Religious Violence* (Oxford: Oxford University Press, 2010)

[36] Juergensmeyer, 122–3.

[37] Lincoln, 17.

[38] Cavanaugh, 29; quoting Juergensmeyer, 132–3.

[39] Samuel Huntington, 'The Clash of Civilizations', *Foreign Affairs* 72.3 (1993), 22.

[40] Ibid., 24.

[41] See, for example, Paul Berman, *Terror and Liberalism* (New York and London: W. W. Norton, 2003); Amartya Sen, *Identity and Violence: The Illusion of Destiny* (New York: W. W. Norton, 2006).

[42] http://georgewbush-whitehouse.archives.gov/news/releases/2001/09/20010916-2.html. [last accessed 19 April 2011]

[43] Lincoln, 99–101.

[44] Lincoln, 102–3.

[45] Lincoln, 20.

[46] See, for example, Jason David BeDuhn, *The Manichaean Body: In Discipline and Ritual* (Baltimore: Johns Hopkins University Press, 2002).

[47] Lincoln, 32.

[48] Lincoln, 108.

[49] Chomsky, 9–11, 35.

[50] Michael Moore, 'Death, Downtown' (12 September 2001). www.michaelmoore.com/words/mikes-letter/death-downtown [accessed 15 December 2010].

[51] Ron Graham, 'Death's Gift to Life', *Macleans* (17 December 2001), 16.

[52] Ibid., 24.

53 'Post September 11 Attitudes', The Pew Research Center for the People and the Press, 6 December 2001. http://people-press.org/report/144/post-september-11-attitudes [last accessed 19 April 2011].

54 Graham, *Macleans*, 24.

55 J. S. Tyhurst, 'Individual Reactions to Community Disaster', *American Journal of Psychiatry* 107 (1951), 764–9.

56 For a more contemporary application of Tyhurst's schema to terrorism, see David A. Alexander and Susan Klein, 'The Psychological Aspects of Terrorism: From Denial to hyperbole', *Journal of the Royal Society of Medicine* 98 (December 2005), 557–62. Many criticisms of 'stage' theories relating to processes of grief and shock have been formulated. Swinton, for example, raises significant concerns about the way in which Elisabeth Kübler-Ross's 'five stages of grief' frequently gets employed in formulaic ways, to the detriment of people in mourning whose own experiences do not conform to the stages that the theory insists they follow (see John Swinton, *Raging for Compassion*, (Grand Rapids, MN: Eerdmans, 2007) 119–20). This can be equally a problem when theories like that of Tyhurst are employed rigidly during disaster relief efforts. Nevertheless, it is important to recognize the widespread use of such theoretical models in disaster relief, and of the potential usefulness – when appropriately understood – of theoretical models for providing some contextual framework with which to operate.

57 David Alexander, 'Psychological Intervention for Victims and Helpers after Disasters', *British Journal of General Practice* 40 (August 1990), 346.

58 Peter Ochs, 'September 11 and the Children of Abraham', *Dissent from the Homeland*, ed. Stanley Hauerwas and Frank Lentricchia (Durham, NC: Duke University Press, 2002), 393.

59 See William E. Connolly *Identity/Difference: Democratic Negotiations of Political Paradox* (Minneapolis, MN: University of Minnesota Press, 1991).

60 Gabriel A. Santos, *Redeeming the Broken Body: Church and State After Disaster* (Eugene, OR: Cascade Books, 2009).

Chapter 5

Belief and the Trauma of Catastrophic 'Events'

In Albert Camus's novel *The Plague*, the Algerian city of Oran is suddenly struck with a disease that had supposedly disappeared from the modern world: the bubonic plague. After a month of steadily increasing anxiety in the town, the local Catholic priest, Father Paneloux, organizes a week of prayer, which concludes with a High Mass in the cathedral. To the large crowd that gathers for the service, Paneloux begins his sermon with a theme common to traditional theodicies: 'Calamity has come upon you, my brethren, and, my brethren, you deserved it.'[1] He preaches that God is angry with the evil of the world, and so the plague should be understood as 'the flail of God'. All is not lost, however, for Paneloux promises that the compassionate God will forgive those who use this opportunity to change their way of life.

As the plague rages on, one of the doctors attempts to develop a drug to counter the disease. When it is tested on a young child, the boy suffers a gruesome death, partly due to the fact that the serum actually strengthened his body's capacity to resist the plague. After having witnessed the terrible suffering of this innocent victim, Father Paneloux is again called upon to preach in the cathedral. On this occasion, however, he no longer finds the theodicy of his first sermon compelling. He admits that the former homily 'lacked in charity'.[2] Paneloux notes in his remarks that the plague had left the people of the town 'with our backs to the wall'. Although he had previously sought to explain the reasons for the calamity, he now refrains from doing so, for no such knowledge is available to him; 'for who would dare to assert that eternal happiness can compensate for a single moment's human suffering?'

Paneloux no longer thinks the calamity before him can be explained by a theodicy, but this does not lead him to reject his traditional Christian beliefs. He urges his audience, rather, to make a leap of faith, and to take comfort from the image of the suffering Christ on the cross. The situation, the priest proclaims, demands a choice between the despair of nihilism and the hope of faith. He phrases it this way: 'a time of testing has come for us all. We must believe everything, or deny everything. And who among you, I ask, would dare to deny everything.'[3] Paneloux's appeal for religious faith is not based on a particular line of argumentation or on any empirical evidence available to him; rather it is presented largely on the basis that there is little other choice but to believe or fall into despair. It is the old priest's own version of the common cliché: 'there are no atheists in foxholes.'

This chapter focuses on the writing of a prominent commentator on the events of 11 September 2001, the philosopher and cultural theorist Slavoj Žižek. Žižek's position is intriguing for the way in which, as a materialist atheist, his interpretation of 9/11 leads him to emphasize the significance of belief for progressive politics and philosophy. An analysis of his work demonstrates, however, that his theoretical position shares many parallels with the second sermon of Father Paneloux. Žižek's idea that a 'radical Act' is what enables human beings to challenge post-9/11 ideologies threatens to become, a call for blind faith and zeal for the sake of being zealous. But prior to analysing Žižek's concept of 'belief', the chapter will first discuss his understanding of 'ideology'. The concern that ideological agendas and concerns have tainted theology has been raised on a number of occasions in previous chapters, and so it is necessary to explore the significance and meaning of this complex dynamic directly. For this task, Žižek's writing is insightful and instructive.

Before the chapter focuses on Žižek's thought, it begins by putting his post-9/11 appeal for renewed commitment and political engagement in a wider context. For the terrorists attacks that occurred on September 11, 2001 have led many scholars and politicians to suggest that these events have brought the social and political issues confronting the globe into clearer view. As such, such writers suggest that 9/11 calls for a renewed commitment to the democratic ideals of the Enlightenment. The attacks have also enhanced the attention religion as a concept has received, as well as religious communities as social and political entities, in wider political and theoretical debates.[4] There is a widespread view that 'All of our ready conceptual assurances are confounded by 9/11. The assumption that we have captured the world in our theories has been stalemated by the world itself.'[5] At the same time, numerous intellectuals warn that such a realization cannot be permitted to lead to cynicism or a moral relativism, for the dangers to democratic society, not to mention human lives, are so great as to demand commitment to political, social and – not infrequently – military engagement.[6]

Security as a 'Conservation Stoppers'?

While the discussion in this chapter cannot deal in any adequate manner with the complexities of the debates over international relations, global security and specific policy proposals, it will step back to ask whether the intensity of some urgent calls for action resembles the structural logic of Father Paneloux's sermon in *The Plague*. For the dilemma of the post-9/11 world is frequently described in a manner that resembles the dualistic choice of the 'Us' versus 'Them' dynamic that was examined in Chapter Four. In the contemporary political climate, North Atlantic societies are often told that they must act decisively to confront the new dangers to their security, for failure to act imperils the safety and survival of their citizens. To what extent does this understandable concern, however, risk a similar type of demand stated in a more conceptual register: 'believe everything or deny everything'? Critics of religion sometimes accuse members of religions communities of expressing their beliefs in such esoteric and stubborn ways that it effectively makes productive communications with people who do not share their way of life impossible. Richard Rorty, for example, has on occasion referred to religion as a 'conversation stopper'.[7] Might it be that, in poast 9/11 politics, the demands to ensure the 'security' of citizens against terrorism risks taking on such a rhetorical functions of shutting down critical inquiry? Such will be the question driving the discussion that follows in this chapter. Another way to phrase this concern, which also serves as a summary of the criticism that will be developed against Žižek later in this chapter, is to ask the following: when the Enlightenment is presented as 'endless, ever deepening critique', so that it results in 'an interminable movement of disenchantment', why is it that contemporary responses to 11 September 2001 so frequently engage in projects that seemingly 're-enchant' politics and concepts of moral agency?[9]

9/11 as New Moral Clarity

In her analysis of the development of the concept of 'evil' in Western philosophy, Susan Nieman suggests that the terrorist attacks of 9/11 confronted Western intellectuals, who had become unaccustomed to 'straightforward moral judgments', with a dilemma. The common tendency to presume that 'any conflict between good and evil themselves was nothing but hype', she argues, results in the paralysis of moral reaction. The cynical avoidance of words like 'evil' to describe the hijackers, Nieman continues, effectively relativizes the murders they committed, which is to risk 'a first step towards making them justifiable'.[8]

Versions of such an emphasis can be found in a many reflections on the political or social implications of 9/11 from across the differing sides of the political spectrum. The critical theorist Jürgen Habermas, for example, explains the rise of militant Islam as a reaction against modernity. As the political and economic influence of the West continues to undermine and challenge more local beliefs and customs, what he calls 'fundamentalism' emerges as a 'defensive reaction against a violent uprooting of traditional ways of life'.[10] The problem, as Giovanna Borradori colourfully phrases it, is that 'Western consumerism explodes like a landmine' in non-Western cultures, causing considerable disruption and dislocation.[11] But although Habermas diagnoses the problem of terrorism as a symptom of modernity, his proposed solution is not to abandon modern liberalism, but a renewed commitment to its ideals. He argues that members of religious communities should be encouraged to participate fully in public democratic debates, in order to convince them that the secular democracies of the West are not inherently opposed to religion.

Other calls for a more committed defence of the traditions of the West are not as nuanced or conciliatory as that of Habermas. Paul Berman, for example, making his own reference to Camus, argues that, confronted by the dangers of violent terrorism, 'We are in an absurd situation.'[12] Accepting Huntington's 'clash of civilizations' thesis, Berman argues that the invasions of Afghanistan and Iraq were necessary examples of 'liberal interventionism', which only irresponsible or sentimental thinking will fail to recognize. Liberal democrats must be prepared to stand up to Islamic 'fascism', he states, in order to defend the ideals and security of Western societies.

In an environment in which many scholars and politicians describe the political choices demanded by the terrorist emergency to be clear and obvious, Peter Alexander Meyers asks whether 'the acts of September 11 were an assault on politics itself', so that a citizen's most important task in the aftermath of the attacks 'is to defend politics'.[13] His suggestion is that one of the first victims of 9/11 was politics itself.

By this, he means that the conception of a human being as a 'political animal' is one which presumes that people relate to each other, in order to debate, negotiate, compromise and establish mutual understanding. 'Politics' as such is thus the work of a 'middle space', insofar as it becomes the mediating connection in between differing individuals. Politics demands, therefore, engagement between human beings over time and remains an ongoing process. When politicians cease to engage with others across boundaries that divide them, or when action is no longer conceived of as a process of interaction and negotiation, but becomes self-initiated activity based on personal conviction, in Meyers's view, it is no longer properly 'political'.

If Meyers is correct, there is a sense in which the concept of 9/11 has taken on a symbolic role, as it serves the function of simplifying and defining how different individuals conceive of present existence. Recall the analysis in Chapter Three of the debates over how to represent the Jewish experience of the Nazi Final Solution: in that discussion, the danger of rendering the Holocaust as something 'sacred' or 'holy' was raised. This tendency was shown to correspond to a sacralizing of present experience, so that it becomes easier to limit thought and imagination to what one already knows. Treating the Holocaust as something 'incomprehensible' does not enhance understanding of it or one's capacity to respond effectively to it; rather, it solidifies and congeals emotional and political imagination, preventing one from learning anything new.

In the intensity surrounding the demand to respond to the challenges presented by the attacks of 11 September, there is a degree to which '9/11' has become a symbol which functions in a similar manner. It is such a concern that leads Thomas Brudholm and Thomas Cushman to note that the intensity surrounding official commemorations of contemporary catastrophes like 9/11 'encourages politicians to act like clerics'.[14] Given this complex relationship between political discourse and the representation of catastrophes, the problem of ideology once again presents itself.

The Power of Symbols at Ground Zero

Numerous aspects of the events of September 11 revolve around the power of symbols, as many scholars now acknowledge. Bruce Lincoln observes that September 11 has frequently been compared to the Japanese surprise attack on Pearl Harbor in 1941, but he himself denies the similarity. The Japanese attack was an act of war aiming to 'end the war with a single blow by crippling American military capacities' The attacks of September 11 had a different purpose. Lincoln argues, 'In contrast to the imperial Japanese, the [terrorists] designed their assault more for sign value than use value.' Instead of Pearl Harbor, Lincoln suggests that the attacks 'were meant to be Hiroshima'.[15] He explains what he means when he writes: 'That is to say, a spectacular event in which sign value and use value supported each other and were meant to display power that was not only overwhelming and decisive, but unprecedented and incomparable.'

Lincoln's point is not that the terrorist attacks intended to cause as much destruction and death as a nuclear bomb; rather, he is emphasizing the psychological impact of the strikes on the principal symbolic buildings of America. The power of the attacks was not their level of destruction, but their symbolic power. The aim was not to cripple the military of the United States; it was to shock the culture of the Western world. The goal of the terrorists was to cause a 'cultural shock' or traumatic event. By shattering the images that are central to American self-understanding and community identity, Osama bin Laden hoped to cause a great cultural trauma that would interrupt the lives of all Western people.

This symbolic aspect of the events of 9/11 is important for understanding the intense reactions experienced by so many people to the fear and destruction caused by the terrorist attacks. It is also a major aspect of how religion functioned in the midst of the disaster. This 'symbolic' aspect to responses to catastrophes is what interests the philosopher and cultural critic Slavoj Žižek in his book *Welcome to the Desert of the Real*. The power of symbols and their relation to culture and human behaviour are key issues of analysis in his work. Since the 1990s, Žižek has become one of the more prolific and recognized cultural theorists in the world. A native of Slovenia, Žižek grew up in an authoritarian communist country and then later watched as this nation tore itself apart in a brutal civil war between different ethnic groups. Perhaps as a result, he is very interested in questions of political power and authority, and especially in identity formation of the kind encouraged by nationalism, ethnic background and religion. Although principally a philosopher, Žižek is deeply influenced by psychoanalytic theory. Specifically, he draws a great deal from the work of Jacques Lacan, a French psychoanalytic theorist and analyst, who reinterpreted Sigmund Freud in a unique and complex way. Much of Žižek's writing resembles the work of a fantasies. He likes to question strange human behaviour and habits – particularly more extreme examples – because he thinks the extremes of human actions reveal key information about people in general. Unlike a psychoanalyst, however, Žižek is not trying to treat or analyze individual people. His goal is not to offer therapy to a patient or to interpret someone's dreams. Instead, Žižek intends to interpret Western society in general. His 'patient', so to speak, is Western culture and its strange 'dreams' and 'psychoses'. Rather than focusing on individual psychological problems, his interest is in more general cultural 'psychoses'.

Žižek on Ideology

Žižek argues that many of the events and reactions to 9/11 can be described via the concept of ideology. Although this is a common enough word, his use of it is rather complicated and technical. Sometimes people use the word 'ideology' to mean something like 'an opinion' or 'a way of thinking'.[16] This does not get at what Žižek means. 'Ideology', as Žižek employs the term, refers to the way one understands the world, but this understanding is not something one chooses from a list of different possible views. One does not simply acquire an ideology, for example, by looking at a list of possible theories about the world (Christianity, Communism, Liberalism, etc.) and choosing one to represent one's own 'ideology'. For Žižek, an ideology goes much deeper into one's being and psyche than does an opinion or a conscious choice. The concept of ideology refers to something that actually influences us *before* we form an opinion or make a choice. It is not only about ideas; it can also involve one's emotional life, one's assumptions and what sort of things one prefers and expects. For Žižek, ideology is not a neutral word (like 'opinion' or 'worldview'). The existence of ideology is a problem. It prevents people from seeing the world clearly or from understanding themselves accurately. He warns that it 'mystifies our perception of the situation instead of allowing us to think.'[17] Ideology blurs our vision; it creates 'blind spots' that keep us from noticing certain things; it places a filter over our perception, so that we tend to see the world in a certain way that is not accurate. And the most powerful thing about ideology is that we do not usually notice that it is doing this. An ideology is usually something we are not even aware of. It shapes how we experience the world without us being conscious of it. Psychologically speaking, it is a bit like the 'unconscious' (although it is not exactly the same thing).[18]

Recall for a moment the lament from Chapter Two voiced by Karl Barth at the outbreak of the First World War:

> ninety-three German intellectuals issued a terrible manifesto, identifying themselves before all the world with the war policy of Kaiser Wilhelm II. . . . To me they seemed to have been hopelessly compromised by what I regarded as their failure in the face of the ideology of war.[19]

Barth is dismayed by the fact that many of his theology professors supported the German Declaration of War. He cannot understand how they could have thought that this was the right thing to do, or how they reconciled it with their Christian faith. In his view, they had been seduced by the 'ideology of war'. It was not something they necessarily chose directly – the word 'seduced' helps to capture the psychological aspect to it. How these intellectuals saw the world was shaped in very subtle ways by the culture around them, and hindsight reveals that this was incorrect and highly unfortunate. Here one can see an example of ideology at work on the very ways in which Christians engage in theological reflection. For this reason, the problem of ideology should be a significant concern for theologians.

In the discussion in the previous chapter of the dynamic between 'Us' and 'Them', it was noted that, to a certain extent, one cannot avoid developing categories of people identified as 'Them'. What Žižek means by 'ideology' relates to this phenomenon. An ideology includes the failure to notice this problem of objectifying the other, as well as the ideas and prejudices one projects onto 'Them'. For when someone constructs an identity for themselves based on assumptions about other people and places, such views are often not based on an accurate or complete perception of the world, but rather on clichés and exaggerations. They are false, but people tend to forget this. It is not simply that one's view about other people is wrong, but that one's whole self-understanding is based on an inaccurate or incomplete impression of the world. This is how ideology becomes such a deep and pervasive thing. We construct an understanding of the world, but then forget that we constructed it. Thus an 'ideology' is usually understood to be a form of 'false consciousness' – something that is inaccurate, but at the same time preserves and supports the status quo, with all of its assumptions and power structures.

Žižek offers a chilling example of how ideology can be used to manipulate and control. It comes in the form of a quotation by Hermann

Goering (Hitler's second-in-command during the Nazi Regime) at the Nuremberg war trials in 1946:

> Of course the people don't want war ... But after all, it is the leaders of the country who determine policy, and it's always a simple matter to drag people along ... All you have to do is tell them they are being attacked, and denounce the pacifists for lack of patriotism and exposing the country to danger. It works the same in any country.[20]

One would hope that this statement is not true, and that religion and morality represent resources that help prevent such manipulation. But all too often in human history, as earlier chapters in this book have illustrated, this terrible conclusion by Hermann Goering has had purchase. This is why it is important to wrestle with what ideology is, in order to better resist its seductive power.

Žižek's theory of ideology is closely related to how he thinks about responses to 9/11, and so it is helpful to summarize his theoretical approach to the concept in further detail. In very basic terms, Žižek starts from the assumption that there is no necessary relationship between reality and the way we describe it (or, as a philosopher might write, there is no necessary relation between our experience of the world and its symbolization). The words we employ to describe our world are just tools; they do not capture reality, nor are they absolutely trustworthy. Words are, in Žižek's terminology, only part of the 'Symbolic order'. Language is a tool to help us talk about objects in the world, but these words are not the objects themselves; they only represent them. Although our symbolic descriptions do not necessarily capture how things really are, and so always leave something out, at the same time, people frequently fail to recognize this. Thus objects in our world begin to resemble the description we give to them. How one describes things shapes one's understanding of them. The 'Symbolic order' – the tools we use to shape and build human culture – is actually incomplete and imperfect, and thus serves to limit and influence our understanding of reality.

Another example may to help to clarify the significance of this point. Consider how Western society's understanding of the word 'woman' has changed over the last century. How long has Western culture's description of a 'woman' limited and controlled how women are viewed and treated? Many people operate with a 'Symbolic' description of women that goes something like this: women are the 'weaker sex', they are gentle and passive, driven by emotion as opposed to the mind, more biologically suited to caring for a family than for the complexities of public social life. Due to this way of symbolizing the concept 'woman', this is how many people come to view individual women – not according to their actual abilities and potential – but according to this symbolic description. The same was true for many centuries of relationships between Protestant and Catholics, Jews and Christians, French and English, black- and white-skinned human beings and so forth.

In hindsight, many of these long-established stereotypes now look arbitrary and incomprehensible. This is exactly the point Žižek is trying to make in his use of the concept of ideology. These stereotypical descriptions do not become popular because they are true or accurate. Their power is not based on their making factual claims; something else is at work in supporting them. The Nazi descriptions of the so-called Jewish race were not based on scientific data. There is no such thing as a Jewish race (which is seen quite easily when one puts an Arabic Jew, a Russian Jew and an Ethiopian Jew together in one room). But these ideological stereotypes seem convincing for many people, not because they are true, but because they serve an important ideological function in the culture of the period.

How to Make an Ideological Quilt

Taking this discussion one step further brings the main point of the concept of ideology into view. The meaning of different terms in the Symbolic Order emerges out of the complex relationships they have to each other. For example, society does not construct the idea of 'woman' in isolation, but in comparison to other concepts – like 'man', 'children' and so forth. This is something that can be compared to the traditional practice of quilting, where scraps of cloth are stitched together to form a blanket. We use concepts to shape our understanding of society like a quilter uses pieces of fabric to shape a quilt. The different pieces of fabric look quite different depending on what they are attached to.

Continuing with this metaphorical description, because concepts cannot fully describe reality (i.e. words are not the objects they refer to) something is always left out in this process. Our 'quilt' will always have a few holes in it. This situation is described by Žižek (following Lacan) as 'the Real'. The 'Real' includes all of the things left out of the Symbolic Order; it is what remains unsaid, undescribed or beyond our capacity to know or express.

Human beings find this imperfect and unresolved dimension of culture uncomfortable. Without some sense of completeness, there is often disorder and confusion, and so societies frequently seek to achieve closure. Returning to our metaphor, human beings continue to try to 'patch' the quilt. Žižek argues that this is frequently achieved by establishing one primary concept or symbol as the organizing principle, which serves to give other ideas and concepts their meaning. Following Lacan, he calls this one overarching concept the 'Master-signifier' or the 'big Other'. This is the 'patch' that is supposed to complete the incomplete quilt of the Symbolic Order. This dynamic is how Žižek understands the functioning of ideology.

The diagram represented in Figure 1 illustrates the nature of this ideological function. Human society is shaped by the ideological quilt of the Symbolic Order. The 'quilt' in the image has a hole in it. This might signify an unresolved social problem, a gap in knowledge or understanding that is proving problematic, or some other disruptive situation. The space that remains unresolved is frequently experienced as threatening and chaotic. One does not enjoy the disorientation that results by achieving a brief (and elusive) glimpse of the presence of the 'Real', just as one never enjoys feeling a draft through the holes of

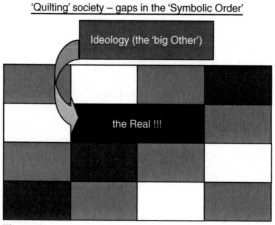

Figure 1

a warm blanket on a cold day. This discomfort leads people to try to patch the hole in their cultural 'quilt' with something that restores a sense of order. The key patch that will hold it all together is what Žižek means by ideology (particularly in the form of the 'big Other').[21]

Ideological concepts are not true and accurate descriptions of reality. When one sees them in hindsight, they often appear ridiculous, and one can hardly understand how people could possibly have been so foolish as to believe them. But the power of an ideology is not based on its truth; rather, an ideological concept becomes convincing simply because, for the time being, it serves to hold together the quilt in which a society wraps itself in to remain comfortable. So it is not so much that an ideology tricks people by convincing them that it is the truth. Instead, it is more accurate to conceive of ideology that it 'feels right'; it convinces by subtly holding a sense of reality in place and making one comfortable. Žižek often speaks of the 'master-signifier' as being 'empty'. It actually has no essential meaning, but can adapt its content to suit a particular context and situation.

For example, within Nazi Germany, different Christians believed all kinds of different and contradictory things about 'the Jew', but the ideological function of the concept of 'the Jew' could hold all of these wild ideas together, even when they contradicted each other, because the idea of 'the Jew' was serving as a 'Master signifier', that held their vision of reality together. In that time and place, the 'Jew' served to represent all the grievances and frustrations of a nation experiencing tremendous economic and political disruption. This scapegoat concept enabled many to continue to trust and celebrate their idea of 'the German people', because the cultural 'quilt' was held together by the idea that the 'Jews' were to blame for all their problems.

Ideology and 9/11

In *Welcome to the Desert of the Real*, Žižek interprets many of the reactions to the terrorist attacks of 11 September 2001 through the lens of his theory of ideology. Like Susan Buck-Morss, Žižek argues that in the wake of the catastrophe, most people did not seek or achieve an 'in-depth understanding' of the events surrounding the attacks. Instead, many clung desperately to whatever supports they could find that would bring comfort, and Žižek thinks many of these comforts were actually ideological. They were merely patches to cover over the holes in their cultural quilt. Žižek writes, 'today, all the main terms we use to designate the present conflict . . . are false terms, mystifying our perception of the situation instead of allowing us to think it.'[22] He continues, 'In the traumatic aftermath of September 11, when the old security seemed to be momentarily shattered, what could be more "natural" than taking refuge in the innocence of a firm ideological identification.'[23]

As people in the midst of this terrible cultural shock reached for the comfort of the nearest ideological patch to hold their worldview together, Žižek criticizes what he calls the twentieth century's aim 'at delivering the thing itself'.[24] He is concerned with the demand many people voiced after 9/11 for a quick and immediate solution to the situation, which assumes that human beings can build the perfect society, in which all problems and complications in the world would vanish. This is another version of the 'faith in progress' which characterized Western culture in the eighteenth and nineteenth centuries. Zizek criticizes this tendency with reference to the sinking of the Titanic: the presumption that human beings had finally built a ship that could never sink. Of course, in both these cases, the 'thing itself' was not delivered. The effort fell short of its ultimate goals.

Žižek's intention in these remarks is to criticize a propensity that he calls a 'passion for the Real'. He suggests that human beings repeatedly forget that 'the Real' is elusive by its very nature, so that one can never know something completely and absolutely (speaking theologically, one might refer to the tradition that only God has perfect knowledge, so that all human knowledge is to be understood as limited and incomplete). According to Žižek, forgetting that our knowledge is imperfect is one way to fall into an ideological position, and this tendency has practical consequences. Human beings cause great problems in the world, he suggests, when they think they can actually possess the 'Real'. When people forget that their words and assumptions are not complete, they begin to act as if they can construct a perfect society.

One might have the impression that, ideally, human beings would desire to overcome this barrier to 'the Real' and achieve perfect knowledge. Not according to Žižek. In his opinion, not only is this impossible, but, on those rare occasions when a person catches a brief glimpse of the incompleteness of our grasp of the world, or when he or she experiences a phenomena he calls 'the return of the Real, many individuals find this a very troubling event. When one actually does achieve a breakthrough in one's limited language or understanding, often one does not like what this new vision presents. As the old

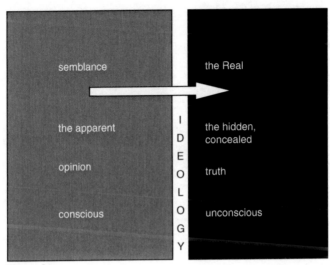

Figure 2

saying has it, 'ignorance is bliss.' This begins to communicate what is meant here. Consider the challenge of undertaking personal counselling or therapy: one often begins counselling rather naively – to help 'get over' some issue or to 'learn more about oneself'. But once one starts making some progress – working one's way deeper into one's emotional life and approaching a breakthrough of understanding – one may be suddenly tempted to shut down, or even stop going to counselling altogether. Why do people so frequently behave in this manner? According to Žižek and many in the counselling profession, it is because the process of self-discovery becomes uncomfortable and even painful. People often do not like what they learn about themselves. The truth hurts, as the saying goes.

The following two diagrams illustrate this idea as Žižek describes it. Figure 2 represents the desire to push beyond regular appearances ('semblance' in philosophical terms) and through ideology, to those things that elude conscious knowledge.

Normally one would imagine that human beings would like to cross from the incomplete side of this diagram – the limited sphere of the symbolic – and enter into the mysterious realm of the unknown: the 'Real'. We imagine that what we want to do is to escape from the clutches of ideology and achieve a clear and untainted understanding of reality. But what happens should one actually achieve a partial

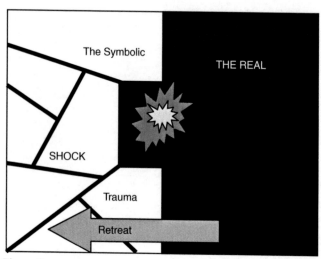

Figure 3

breech in this barrier? Often, what we discover upsets us. Rather than achieving a greater sense of peace and understanding, what we discover may actually disorient us and call into question those things we assumed we already knew and understood. Instead of being glad that the ideological or Symbolic line between us and the Real has been breached, we want to plug it up again – as soon as possible – with almost anything that may get the job done. Figure 3 illustrates this.

Rather than appreciate a successful glimpse of what eludes present experience, the breech in the ideological quilt is experienced as disruptive and threatening. The symbolic system starts to crack and rupture as 'the Real' breaks in, upsetting assumptions and resulting in confusion. Thus many may scramble to try to patch the hole as quickly as they can, with anything that will stop the traumatic interruption of our routines and assumptions.

Žižek argues that September 11 was this kind of experience. The events of 9/11 disrupted the cultures of North Atlantic societies in a traumatic manner, particularly in the United States. Beyond the physical attack of the airplanes, it was a trauma that brought a brief experience of the 'Real' into culture, and this shocked many that experienced it. This idea connects directly with the observations about the symbolic nature of the attack with which this chapter began. Recall Lincoln's description of 9/11 as being like Hiroshima: it was meant to have a 'sign value' that would suggest unprecedented power and shock. Žižek writes, 'the "terrorists" themselves did not do it primarily to provoke real material damage, but *for the spectacular effect of it.*'[25] In Žižek's view, the attack brought with it a brief experience of 'the Real', which is why it both shocked and fascinated so many people. He recalls how people watched the events on television over and over; 'our gaze was transfixed by the images of the planes hitting one of the WTC towers . . . We wanted to see it again and again.' Žižek compares this experience to the dynamic of being both attracted to and fascinated with the 'Real', but also being horrified and frightened by it. And it is these two experiences at the same time – attraction and repulsion – that make the event and understanding it so complicated.

Žižek often refers to the movie *The Matrix* in *Welcome to the Desert of the Real*, the title of which is taken from a statement in the film. This science-fiction story presents a narrative about someone who discovers that the world he lives in is not real. It is an illusion, a computer-generated program, or 'virtual reality'. Over the course of the film, the main character gradually realizes that something is wrong, and he is offered the opportunity to discover what the world is really like. The moment is presented to him as a decision over what sort of pharmaceutical he will ingest. He is offered the choice between a red pill and a blue pill. If he takes one, he will free his mind to see the world as it really is. If he selects the other, he is told that he will forget that there is any problem, and go on living as before.

Žižek suggests that the events of September 11 confronted Western societies with a similar choice. The tragedy signalled that something was not right in the world and set up an either/or decision to be made: to try to go deeper into the problem to find out what is going on, or turn away from the problem, out of fear or laziness, and go on as before. The question one is left with in the wake of 9/11, Žižek thinks, is this: do we really want to know how our world works? This is his challenge when he writes,

> Now, in the months following the attacks, it is as if we are living in the unique time between a traumatic event and its symbolic impact, as in those brief moments after we have been deeply cut, before the extent of the pain strikes us. We do not yet know how the events will be symbolized . . . what acts they will be evoked to justify.[26]

Do You Want to Know the Truth?
The 'Fake Passion for the Real'

Like Bruce Lincoln, Žižek refers to the post-9/11 speeches of George W. Bush and of Osama bin Laden, and observes how both paint the world in dualistic terms and demand that one choose whose side one is on. But Žižek goes further than Lincoln does in his analysis. He argues that 'the choice between Bush and bin Laden is not our choice; they are both "Them" against Us.'[27] He understands the 'Us' and 'Them' to be closely interrelated, like two sides of the same coin. Žižek reaches this point after wrestling with a great tension confronting the world after 9/11, which he calls 'the temptation of a double blackmail'.[28] He refers to the dilemma of choosing one of the typical responses on offer to citizens:

(a) poor innocent America was attacked and victimized by evil forces;

(b) America got what it deserved because it exploits the Third World.

In Žižek's view, *neither* of these choices is adequate. Both contain some truth, but both are also problematic. Both are, in fact, ideologies. For each option depends on a calculation of who suffers more (what Žižek calls the 'mathematics of guilt'). But neither side is purely good and innocent, and neither side is purely evil; but this is often how the rhetorical responses to 9/11 talk about the event. Either Bush and America are evil, or Arabs and the terrorists are evil. Either global capitalism is evil, or Islam is evil. According to Žižek, the so-called evils of capitalism and the "evils" of Islam mutually support one another. They are two sides of the same coin, because they operate according to similar logics. He adds,

> precisely in such moments of apparent clarity of choice, *mystification is total*. The choice proposed is not the true choice. Today, more than ever, we should summon up the strength to step back and reflect upon the background of the situation.[29]

Žižek encourages his reader to notice this, to observe that all of the simple and 'common sense' responses to September 11 are often highly ideological, and, in the end, structurally quite similar. There is no pure, innocent or uncomplicated answer to the event. The situation requires a response that steps beyond all of the simplistic demands to choose. Instead, he urges us to try something more paradoxical: 'to adopt both positions simultaneously'. Rather than calculate which side has been most victimized, 'the only appropriate stance is unconditional solidarity with *all* victims.'[30] Žižek urges his audience not to simply choose one of the two options that political society presented to them in the wake of a terrorist attack. He asks that one choose to focus on the victims on both sides and to shape any response to the terrible events accordingly.

That last sentence by Žižek has an attractive sentiment to it, but there is a risk that one could turn this profound vision into nice Hallmark-card sentimentality. Žižek himself warns of this possibility, arguing that 'it is precisely such moments of transparent innocence, of "back to basics," when the gesture of identification seems "natural," that are, from the standpoint of the critique of ideology, the most obscure.'[31] Elsewhere he also warns,

> The problem with the twentieth-century 'passion for the Real' was not that it was a passion for the real, but that it was a fake passion whose ruthless pursuit of the Real behind appearances was *the ultimate stratagem to avoid confronting the Real*.[32]

This cryptic remark requires some unpacking. Recall the explication above, in which it was noted how Žižek argues that, when one encounters a tiny piece of the 'Real', one actually does not like what is discovered. This relates to the warning in the above quotation. Because human beings do not *really* want to upset their comfortable grasp of reality, they often pretend to pursue the Real while secretly (even unconsciously) hoping that they do not achieve their goal.

An example from a recent form of ecumenical Christian social activism serves to illustrate the relevance of the point here. As the year 2000 approached, a cause developed in the ecumenical movement of the churches that called for a 'Year of Jubilee'. In the Hebrew Bible and Old Testament (Leviticus 25), there is mention of a regular cycle of the cancelling of debts and the freeing of indentured servants (occurring every fifty years). This tradition emerged from the recognition that after a period of time, great imbalances develop within a society, so that it is helpful to occasionally rebalance the situation and start again. The 'Jubilee 2000' movement was a call for a similar action in the contemporary world; particularly, it was a call for the G8 nations to forgive Africa's debt. Unfortunately, despite a small level of influence by the churches, most of the debt was not cancelled.[33]

Following from the logic of Žižek's concept of a 'fake passion for the Real', here is the point: did the churches *really* want their governments to cancel the debt? Was this pursuit of the Real actually a 'fake passion'? On what basis might one ask such a seemingly insensitive question? It relates to why so many governments refused to cancel Africa's debt. The politicians may well have thought that if they actually did do what it would take to wipe the African debts away, the citizens they represent, including those who are members of the Christian churches, would immediately vote them out of office for disrupting national economies and budgets. Might it be that the politicians realized at some level that, although Christians liked the sentiment of the idea of the year of Jubilee, they were not really prepared to pay the cost of *actually* doing it? Perhaps such a question is uncharitable, but there is some force to it. There is a distinct difference, for example, between churches asking governments to cancel Africa's debt without the churches themselves having to do anything to make this happen, and an act of solidarity in which churches approaching governments make an offer of how they will help pay for this debt cancellation (e.g. by offering to allow governments to tax church income). Whether or not this challenge is fair in this example, the illustration is clear. A 'fake passion for the Real' is an insincere or incomplete attempt to change a situation. The insincerity may actually be unrecognized, even unconscious, for swimming in a sea of ideologies, one may not even realize that one does not really want what one says one wants.

Žižek on Responses to 9/11

It is out of this perspective that a number of Žižek's remarks about common responses to September 11 emerge. Žižek is no supporter of the Bush administration, or of the war in Iraq, but many of his critical comments are also directed at the left-wing and liberal responses to these events. Žižek's basic caution is to suggest that even criticisms of a system can often remain within the same system of logic. Criticizing the status quo can actually serve to support the status quo. Žižek observes that, sometimes, in a hypocritical action, people address 'the Master with a demand which will be impossible for him to meet'.

Perhaps the simplest example of this dynamic is when Žižek speaks of 'calling the other's bluff'. Here one thinks of a tired and frustrated parent on a long road trip yelling into the backseat of a car: 'If you don't quiet down back there, I'll make you walk home!' Of course, the parent would be absolutely horrified if the child actually called this bluff, for the last thing the parent would do is actually leave their child in the middle of nowhere on a cold winter's night. In this situation a protest is uttered, but the critic in no way actually wants to deal with the consequences of what was said. And so, should this bluff be called (should the child say, 'Okay, I'll walk home') the status quo will only be strengthened, for the child will discover that the threatened consequences of their loud noise is empty, and so they will continue their annoying behaviour with all the more determination.

Being the one person to admit that the Emperor has no clothes is often not appreciated by the crowd of imperial admirers, not to mention the Emperor. This, of course, is not to discourage the quest for knowledge. Rather, it is to recognize an important dynamic to think about when analysing responses to events like September 11. When one asks 'Why did this happen?' it is significant to consider whether one really wants to know the answer. Žižek suggests that, often, people in contemporary Western societies are actually rather satisfied with the status quo and would prefer to keep going happily along as things are.

Belief and the Radical 'Act'

With this theoretical background in place, one can now begin to grasp how Žižek interprets religion after 11 September 2001. Though himself an atheist, his approach to religion is dialectical. He notes that the critics of religion, 'start by denouncing religion as a force of oppression which threatens human freedom; in fighting religion, however, they are compelled to forsake freedom itself, thus sacrificing precisely that which they wanted to defend.' He continues with a quotation from G. K. Chesterton; 'The secularists have not wrecked divine things; but the secularists have wrecked secular things, if that is any comfort to them.' [34] In order to defend the freedoms cherished by secular democracies from the perceived dangers caused by religion, Žižek observes that many governments have actually had to restrict the freedoms of their citizens in order to establish higher levels of security. In other words, what they are fighting to protect, governments actually have to sacrifice in order to pursue their goal. This suggests to Žižek that a rigid opposition between religion and the secular may not be as pure a dualism as it is taken to be.

In *Welcome to the Desert of the Real*, Žižek closely relates any comments regarding religion to a concern for truth. Despite his complex practice of holding together opposites, Žižek is very concerned with the concept and pursuit of truth. He longs for firm commitment and decision. He laments the lack of this in the contemporary situation; 'today we really need new courage, and it is a lack of this courage . . . which is most conspicuous in the reaction of American (and European) intellectuals to September 11 and its aftermath.'[35] But Žižek does not think that most contemporary people operate this way. He suggests that, in a cynical and sophisticated modern cultural environment, most people keep such firm commitments at a distance. He first suggests this with an illustration from the science-fiction movie *Unbreakable*, which is the story of a regular guy who becomes a superhero when he discovers that he is invincible to pain. When the main character tries to deny his power, and any corresponding responsibility for events around him, Žižek remarks, 'it is difficult, properly traumatic, for a human animal to accept that his or her life . . . is in the service of a Truth.'[36] This is what Žižek thinks the contemporary ideological environment has made of belief. We 'perform our symbolic mandates' without 'taking them seriously'.

At this point, Žižek has added another layer to the problem of an ideological 'quilt'. He is suggesting that, all too frequently, individuals do not necessarily believe that the ideologies they cling to are actually 'true', but that they act like they are simply because they serve as a convenient way to hold their Symbolic explanations of the world together. Thus, perhaps many Americans never really believed that Iraq had weapons of mass destruction, but it was easier to act like they believed that Iraq had them. But a domestic and less controversial illustration is probably more appropriate here: my father continues to be a devoted supporter of the ice hockey team the Toronto Maple Leafs, who have failed to win the league championship since 1967. He continues to confidently assert, however, that they will finally win the Stanley Cup once again before he dies. I wonder, though, whether he *really* believes this, or simply repeats it because it makes him feel better when confronted by the team's discouraging performance.

Žižek laments the rather cynical and relative attitude many people in contemporary Western societies have towards the values and ideals they claim to 'believe' in. In a post-9/11 world, many scholars and politicians employ concepts like 'human rights', but Žižek wonders how committed many are to actually standing up to defend them. It is due to his concern with questions like this that Žižek's recent work has turned to a detailed analysis of belief and religion. When he refers to religion positively, he looks to those moments when religion encourages people to act decisively for the truth. He appreciates 'Christ's famous words about how he has come to bring the sword and division, not unity and peace'. In the apostle Paul, he sees a call to 'commit ourselves to an excessive intensity which puts us beyond "mere life"'.[37]

This is how Žižek understands the challenge confronting people after September 11. He thinks most of the protests and responses against this tragedy – including religious ones – amounted to a 'fake Passion for the Real'. Thus Žižek challenges his audience to become aware of the ideological dynamic that they are often caught up in. Žižek challenges his reader to find ways to respond to the cultural shocks of our world which break out of this cycle. He wants us to act so that the ideological positions that make up the present situation are interrupted. Žižek calls this kind of response to events like September 11 a 'radical Act'. Such an action refuses to choose one of the either/or options thrust at us: either the United States or Islam; either the Bush administration or bin Laden. Instead, a 'radical Act' looks for a creative third option. Not either/or, but something completely different and new.

Žižek suggests an interesting concrete example of what he means by a 'radical Act', pointing to the Refusenik movement in contemporary Israel. This group of soldiers were (and are) members of the Israeli military. When ordered to serve in the Occupied territories, however, they refused, on the grounds that the occupation (of Gaza and the West Bank) was morally wrong. Why does Žižek think this is a radical 'Act'? Because he recognizes that this situation in Israel is usually portrayed in either/or terms: *either* you are with Israel and against the Palestinians; *or* you are with the Palestinians and against Israel. The Refuseniks made a third choice. They did not allow themselves to be defined by these two options. They did something new. They said, 'No', we will not oppress the Palestinians in the Occupied territories. However, they also said, 'But', we will also continue to serve as soldiers and defend Israel from attack. So they did not resign from the army, become pacifists, or join the Palestinian resistance. They chose none of the obvious options pushed at them. They did something unique, arguing that 'Yes', Israel must be defended from attacks; but also 'No', there are things we will not do to defend Israel. Zizek claims that 'such a gesture of drawing a line, of refusing to participate, is an authentic *ethical act*.'[37]

The Act and Belief as Pascal's Wager

In his famous book *Pensées*, Blaise Pascal (1623–1662) developed what is referred to as 'Pascal's wager'. Pascal thought that, although one cannot prove the existence of God, one can demonstrate the importance and usefulness of belief. Pascal wrote,

> God is, or He is not. But to which side shall we incline? Reason can decide nothing here. Which will you choose then? Let us see. Since you must choose, let us see which interests you least. Let us weigh the gain and the loss in wagering that God is . . . If you gain, you gain all; if you lose, you lose nothing. Wager, then, without hesitation that He is.[39]

Pascal's point is that, faced with uncertainty, it is better to 'wager' on the existence of God than to be an atheist, because the gain one attains if one is correct is very high; and non-belief promises nothing at all. Believing, he argues, is so much more potentially advantageous than not believing.

This reference to Pascal and his 'wager' on God is relevant because Žižek calls his idea of the 'radical Act' a 'Pascalean wager'.[40] One cannot prove that an Act will be successful or that it will make the situation better. Žižek suggests, however, that in an antagonistic world of dualistic ideological options, it is more advantageous to risk an Act than it is to merely 'go with the flow'. For him, this is the main lesson to be gleaned from 9/11, while the primary temptation is to become mute and passive in the face of a complex world. In an ideological context which nurtures cynicism, uncommitted critical distance or self-satisfied irony, Žižek argues that one must have the courage to act and to engage in counterfactual wagers. To achieve this, he hopes to harness the energy and commitment that he perceives in religious belief and redirect it towards progressive political action. For, in his view, 'All emancipatory politics is lost without this kind of belief.'

Such a concern to co-opt what he understands to be religion's capacity to motivate and foster commitment on the part of its adherents is what encourages Žižek's post-9/11 'turn to religion'. He is not, of course, interested in religion *as such*, nor does he advocate that one become an adherent of any religious community; rather, Žižek is interested in theology and religion only insofar as they illustrate the dynamics of 'belief' and moral commitment. In his view, such belief has a similar logic and emotional structure to what is required in order to perform an 'Act'. Just as an Act 'restructures the very symbolic coordinates of an agent's situation' (by choosing a third option beyond the conventional choices presented to it), he argues that belief involves the same process: 'religious belief, far from being the pacifying consolation, is the most traumatic thing to accept.' Why 'traumatic'? Because belief involves 'an intrusion which momentarily suspends the causal network of our daily lives'.[41]

This adoption of the dynamics of religious belief as a strategy with which to confront the ideological situation that emerges in the aftermath of September 11 2001 is an intriguing proposal. Žižek's work offers a compelling theory of ideology for analysing responses to a historical catastrophe like 9/11, and his secular and atheist appreciation of elements of Christianity is a stimulating conversation partner. Žižek suggests that theology's unique contribution to Western thought is to describe as divine the sort of engagement with the world that he describes as a 'radical Act': 'Perhaps the true achievement of Christianity is to elevate a loving (imperfect) Being to the place of God, that is of ultimate perfection.'[42] This is based on his reading of Christianity's description of Jesus Christ as both divine and human, and how it portrays the loving self-sacrifice of Jesus on the cross as a model for how to live a godly life.[43] Despite these provocative proposals, there are two problematic issues concerning Žižek's co-option of 'belief', which should be raised here. The first has to do with the formal and abstract way in which he employs the concept 'belief' as being the core component of religion. The second issue undermining Žižek's position is that his concepts of belief and the 'racial Act' take on a somewhat Gnostic undertone (in the sense of unmediated and without roots in material history) when he emphasizes their novelty. There is a sense in which both of these resources for progressive political action are creations *ex nihilo*. As the analysis below shows, this becomes of particular concern when this formulation reveals that Žižek employs 'belief' for largely instrumental purposes. But can the motivational power of 'belief' be harnessed when severed from any link to particular content?

Privileging Belief over Practice?

To question whether Žižek's interpretation of belief operates at only a 'formal' level is to note that he seldom analyses, or even takes into account, the practices or rituals of specific religious traditions or communities (Christian or otherwise). Below it will be acknowledged that, at the theoretical level, Žižek does not reduce belief to cognition, but when he discusses religion as a form of belief, it is noteworthy that he seldom explores in detail the practices of religious communities.

Žižek's interpretation of Christianity is largely based on G. K. Chesterton's book *Orthodoxy*, written in the early part of the twentieth century.[44] He takes little account of the wider theological tradition, nor of the significance of embodied '*practice*' in Christian churches, which many contemporary scholars of religion consider at least as important as religious '*belief*'.[45] The anthropologist Talal Asad, for example, has criticized Clifford Geertz's definition of religion as a 'symbolic system', in which symbols shape the moods and motivations of its adherents. Asad argues that such a theory overemphasizes the cognitive element in religious experience. It privileges cognition by focusing on ideas rather than the practices that shape an adherent's life. Asad's point is that the practices religious communities engage in shape how they understand the beliefs they articulate; 'embodied practices . . . form a precondition for varieties of religious experience.'[46] One need not privilege 'practices' to the extent that Asad does in order to acknowledge that a religion is a thicker cultural phenomenon that the narrow concept of 'belief' implies.[47] 'Beliefs' are not so easily abstracted out of the communities and practices from which they emerge.

This approach to belief is problematic in the case of Christianity, but perhaps even more so when considering other world religions more generally. The religion most frequently criticized by Žižek' is Buddhism, at least in its 'Western' form and as articulated by the Dalai Lama. He argues that Buddhism teaches its adherents to 'uncouple' from passionate concerns of this world so as to retain 'inner peace', which, in his view, actually functions as the 'perfect ideological supplement' to capitalism.[48] But this interpretation of Buddhist ritual as simply seeking to 'let oneself go' is a rather shallow description of a highly complex tradition.[49] At the very least, his analysis does not explore the ways in which Buddhist communities live their lives and engage with the world.

There is a degree to which Žižek's account recognizes the significance of practice for belief. He refers to ritual as 'materialized beliefs', and goes so far as to describe 'culture' as 'the name for all those things we practice without really believing in them'.[50] This is related to his theory of ideology, which, as we have seen, describes how ideology functions by encouraging and supporting the desire of the subject for a solid and non-contradictory sense of the world. In what Žižek calls a 'fake passion for the Real', he uncovers how people often assert beliefs without taking them seriously. Thus far we are following Žižek's line of argumentation, but here is the critical point: does not the problem that he diagnoses (the predominance of 'suspended belief') undermine the emphasis that he places on 'belief' as a cognitive phenomenon? His critique of the 'fake passion for the Real' would actually suggest that people are as shaped by their habits, fears and environments as they are by their consciously affirmed 'beliefs'.

Such nuance is evident in *Sublime Object of Ideology*, when Žižek discusses Tibetan prayer wheels (one instance in which his discussion of Buddhism goes beyond criticizing the rhetoric of the Dalai Lama). He describes how prayers are written down and placed on these rotating drums, after which the wheel is spun. In Žižek's rendering of this phenomenon, 'the wheel prays for you'.[51] Such an understanding suggests that belief has an 'exterior' element, a form of materialist practice, which reaffirms in a concrete way what the belief suggests. Žižek compares this dynamic to the way a 'laugh track' (or 'canned laughter') during a 'sitcom' programme on television 'laughs for us'.[52] One feels comforted by watching the comedy and does not even have to laugh (or necessarily find the humour amusing) because the television is amused on behalf of the person watching. In this sense, Žižek does not reduce belief to mere cognition or ideas about the world, but recognizes a subtle but powerful dynamic between the idea and its material embodiment. He writes, 'Religious belief . . . is not . . . primarily an inner conviction; but the Church as an institution and its rituals . . . stands for the very mechanism that generates it.'[53]

That he conceives of belief as being rooted in materiality raises a very different question about Žižek's concept, however, for if it remains very much a part of its cultural context, why does he not think that is any less problematically 'ideological' than other forms of thought? Previous chapters have demonstrated the extent to which religious beliefs can be tainted by ideology; how does Žižek think his conception escapes this?

Belief as an Ungrounded Leap

Žižek's appropriation of Christianity focuses generally on the description of the person of Christ by the apostle Paul, which he associates with his own concept of a 'radical Act'. We have already observed that Žižek describes an 'Act' as involving a capacity to 'unplug' one-self from the available ideological options, in order to adopt a new innovation. This is how he interprets the apostle Paul's idea that 'In Christ' there is neither Jew nor Greek, slave nor free, male or female (Gal. 3.28). Žižek applauds this vision as representing a leap from Law to Life, suggesting that it is a totally free 'Event' that may ground 'a Politics of Truth', a 'new collectivity', and a 'new universalism'.[54] Although one of Žižek's targets in this discussion is what he considers to be contemporary versions of Gnostic spirituality (which emphasize inner purity against the external events of the world), there is a sense in which this rendering of a pure 'Act' based on 'unplugged' belief is itself Gnostic. The 'Act', and the belief which motivates it, are celebrated because they emerge *ex nihilo* ('out of nothing') from beyond the messy ideological polarities in society. Such a 'politics of Truth' emerges without historical mediation; but without such mediation, what resources could possibly shape, develop or support it? In order to be an 'Act', it must be completely 'new' so as not to be contaminated by the dominant ideological positions of the age.

It is in this sense, then, that Žižek's position has a Gnostic flavouring. The believing subject who achieves this new form of politics achieves this on the basis on a subjective leap that knows no mediation. This amounts to a Pascalian wager based on a desire for a possible new world (a changed society), without equal attention to the possible costs or contradictions this might involve for the acting subject or others around him or her.

Numerous critics of Žižek have raised related concerns about this aspect of his thought. Geoff Boucher warns that it suggests a form of 'irrational fundamentalism'.[55] Yannis Stavrakakis thinks that Žižek's adoption of the dynamics of religious belief implies 'political absolutisation'.[56] Of the concept of the 'Act', Walter A. Davis writes, 'Sworn foe to mystification, in proposing this solution Žižek indulges in a striking mystification of his own.'[57] Matthew Sharpe describes what he calls Žižek's 'heterodox Christianity' as an updated version of Thomas Hobbes's description of the social order. Because the world is invariably full of violence and conflict, Hobbes argued that a society needs a dominant sovereign to impose order. When Žižek's work describes society in a similar manner, Sharpe argues (along with Geoff Boucher) that the result is a political theology which flirts with 'wholesale irrationalist reactions against modernity', and shares more in common with a medieval worldview than the democratic ideals of the Enlightenment.[58]

Marcus Pound argues that such criticisms exaggerate the implications of Žižek's position, although he acknowledges that his 'religious absolutism' does risk sliding into 'political absolutism'.[59] Nevertheless, according to Pound, one should not associate Žižek's concepts of belief or 'radical Act' with connotations of 'fundamentalism'. To explain why, it is necessary to return briefly to his theory of ideology.

In Žižek's interpretation of Jacques Lacan, he borrows the concept of the 'big Other' to refer to the mistaken idea that it is possible to achieve a foundational and solid form of knowledge of the world which is clear and accessible. Recall how he argues that all forms of thought are incomplete and embedded in ideological structures. What Lacan's work emphasizes, and Žižek follows him on this point, is that the task for psychoanalysis is to recognize the non-existence of the 'big Other' – that no solid ground of knowledge exists to stabilize and perfect the world. Acceptance of this fact allows people to accept the world as it is and thus to avoid violent or aggressive attempts to patch the hole in the ideological quilt because it disturbs the stability of a (false) notion of the 'big Other'.

This is how Žižek interprets the cry that Jesus of Nazareth utters from the cross during his crucifixion ('My God, my god, why have you forsaken me'). Pound describes how this reading resonates with Žižek's concept of ideology: 'Any critique of ideology involves the suspension of the big Other as the locus of support, repeating Christ's cry of dereliction, and thereby constituting a kind of *imitatio Christi*.'[60] For Žižek, this 'suspension' involves opening up a gap between the subject and its own speech. The example Pound employs is the fact that as soon as one begins to talk about oneself, the self is suddenly referred to as an object outside the self (e.g. who is the 'Christopher' who describes 'Christopher'?). There is a mysterious gap here between the speaker and his referent. The same is true, according to Žižek, of the dynamics of belief. There is no 'belief' without the 'believer', and so the two elements cannot be easily separated from each other. Pound argues, with Žižek, that this suggests that belief always evades rational argumentation, and so it is always unconditional and the product of a 'leap'. For this reason, critics who accuse Žižek of 'irrationalism' or 'fundamentalism' miss the point, for 'there is no faith or belief . . . that is not in the final analysis unconditional, i.e. simply accepted through the imposition of a signified.'[61]

Despite the helpful clarifications Pound provides, the problem with this defence of Žižek's emphasis on an ungrounded leap is that it makes a virtue out of a problem. So doing, it becomes too enthusiastic and comfortable with this description of a paradox, to the extent that it becomes license to 'Act' without needing to provide (at least provisional) justification.

As significant as these issues are, the discussion has become rather abstract and distant from our focus on responses to historical disasters; therefore, it is useful at this point to focus on an illustration, which is provided by returning to Camus's novel *The Plague*.

'Believe Everything, or Deny Everything'

One could imagine Father Paneloux finding some comfort in Žižek's discussion. In the face of terrible suffering, rational arguments justifying belief in God are put under heavy strain, and traditional theodicies break down. Paneloux experienced this after preaching his first sermon. One could interpret the contribution that Žižek offers to this situation to be something like the following: 'fear not, for beliefs are always ungrounded and are not based on evidence, so the terrible plague cannot, therefore, undermine it. Rational theodicies are misguided, so the Christian need not despair when they fail in the face of suffering.'

Pound cautions that Žižek's ontology begins to fall apart at such a point, as the individual subject gets caught in a nihilistic position located between being and meaning, from which there is no escape beyond negativity. Returning to the illustration: why should Paneloux find comfort from the message that his faith is always unconditional, so that it is immune from the tragedies of history? If his reasons for believing in God have been undermined, how can his faith be sustained by nothingness? Pound argues that, unlike the position of nihilism (which is the experience of a void of meaninglessness), Christian theology asserts that being is to be understood through the primacy of gift. The void viewed by nihilism as a 'lack' or as a threatening and ungrounded nothingness, can thus be experienced as divine plenitude, so that the troubled world can be affirmed.[62]

This is not, however, what appears to motivate Paneloux in Camus's novel. The priest's response to the growing devastation of the plague is desperate in tone. His faith is defended for its own sake – not because it is heartfelt, or in response to a sense of divine 'gift' – but because the only other choice is despair; 'We must believe everything, or deny everything.' Structurally, the argument presents an either/or dualism: either traditional teachings about God are absolutely correct, or one must deny that there is any ground for joy or hope in the world. To a significant degree, Paneloux's sermon is an act of self-defence. In Žižekian jargon, he seeks to re-establish the 'big Other', or in the metaphor employed above to describe the function of ideology, Paneloux is desperately trying to patch the hole in his quilt. Because it is so difficult for him to believe in God when confronted by the plague, he decides to try all the harder to believe. He refuses not to believe, rather than tolerate the painful paradox and contradictions that confront him.

From Camus's published notebooks, one learns of a theoretical concern lying behind his composition of *The Plague*: the distaste he felt for Marxist political leaders in France at the time. Out of their conviction that 'nothing is pure' in a corrupt world, Camus argues that many radicals believe that they have the warrant to proclaim all things to be corrupt, except for what contributes to their political cause. Against such an attitude (which he ascribes to Marxists, and to John Paul Sartre in particular), Camus writes, 'There are some who take up falsehood like they take up religious life.'[63] He distrusts those who employ their own distrust of the status quo as an excuse for absolutism and an unwillingness to compromise.

Paneloux's attitude can be compared with the militant zeal Camus criticizes in his notebooks, which is why the priest is not presented as a hero in *The Plague*. In marked contrast to the emphasis on 'heroes' that emerged in post-9/11 American culture,[64] what Camus praises in his novel are 'anti-heroic' attitudes. The 'anti-hero' of the narrative is Dr. Rieux, who gradually comes to accept his role of helping combat the disease. Through his eyes, a key concept in the text is developed – 'modesty':[65]

> our townsfolk were like everybody else, wrapped up in themselves; in other words, they were humanists: they disbelieved in pestilences. A pestilence isn't a thing made to man's measure . . . Our townsfolk were not more to blame than others; they forgot to be modest, that was all, and thought that everything still was possible for them; which presupposed that pestilences were impossible.[66]

Without 'modesty', Rieux suggests, human beings develop an unproductive self-importance and self-centredness. In a crisis, this leaves people unprepared to deal with the situation and prone to disregard those around them. Rieux, like Camus, is distrustful of concepts like 'heroism', which imply that individuals are 'special' or supernaturally 'courageous' when they perform helpful acts. The hero thinks of himself as worthy of praise, which only encourages un-modest self-importance. What motivates people to act on behalf of others, Rieux argues, emerges only when such self-centredness is set aside and a more 'modest' attitude to the world is maintained:

> Those who enrolled in the 'sanitary squads' as they were called had, indeed, no such great merit in doing as they did, since they knew it was the only thing to do, and the unthinkable thing would have been not to bring themselves to do it. These groups enabled our townsfolk to come to grips with the disease and convinced them that now that the plague was among us, it was up to them to do whatever could be done to fight it. Since plague became in this way some men's duty, it revealed itself to be what it was: that is, the concern of all.[67]

Rieux's perspective considers 'comprehension', not 'courage', to be the most significant way to respond to this crisis, and the core virtue required to achieve this is 'modesty'. For it is such an attitude that helps people move out of ignorance (caused by the assumption that one knows everything) to a view which is motivated by concern for one's fellow human beings. The force of the concept of 'modesty' in Camus's novel is that the characters he admires do not act so as to 'prove' something. They do not respond to the plague in order to make themselves feel better or to be praised by others for being 'courageous' or 'noble'. Nor do they act to advance some political agenda, to reassure themselves that the world works in a certain way or to prove the existence of God. Camus describes his anti-heroes as 'saints without God' because their self-enclosed mentalities have been interrupted by the crisis, and they are now able to respond sincerely and directly to the needs of the people around them. They seek to diminish the suffering of their neighbours motivated by no other agenda than to help them.[68] Rieux and his colleague Tarrou have no interest in 'God', because they think that Christian belief is the sort of desperate reaching out for the sort of legitimation and support that Paneloux anxiously pursues. In their view, the priest's response demands that one sacrifice one's own dignity and agency in order to be protected by a divine 'big Other', which, for them, is merely the product of one's own subjective desire. In other words, in their view, Paneloux's leap of faith is not sufficiently 'modest'.

This response of Rieux and Tarrou towards the priest brings to mind the way a friend of mine always winces when she hears Christians use the word 'pastoral' as an adverb, as in the sentence, 'It was very "pastoral" of you to listen to that annoying person with such patience.' In her hearing, such an expression suggests that the Christian is being kind to someone in order to feel that he or she is being 'pastoral' (e.g. out of sense of duty); in other words, the Christian is acting on the basis of his or her own self-serving agenda. What would otherwise be an act of kindness is revealed to be insincere and self-centred. As my friend would proclaim in exasperation, 'Don't be "pastoral"! Be kind!'

This example summarizes the moral vision which shapes the narrative of *The Plague*, but it also helps to bring into clearer view the primary weakness in Žižek's otherwise insightful and stimulating engagement with Christianity and the concept of belief.[69] The basic limitation in his approach is that he employs 'belief' for instrumental purpose. He emphasizes the concept so that people will act like they believe in something, so as to achieve a progressive political agenda. There is a very subtle, but nevertheless significant, manipulation here which undermines the very reason that Žižek is interested in, religious belief in the first place. He wants to harness the motivational power of belief, without tarrying with the content of any particular tradition of belief.

The same issue arises with his discussion of a 'radical Act'. The Refuseniks did not sit down and think to themselves, 'Let's engage in a radical Act.' Rather, they wrestled with how to respond in an appropriate manner to very difficult circumstances. Žižek's description of their decision is insightful and provocative; however, his attempt to systematize this dynamic (or 'operationalize' it) by urging his audience to go forth and do likewise, turns his description into a proscription; the practical decision of the Refuseniks becomes a system for progressive political action. The basic problem with such slippage is summarized by paraphrasing my friend: 'don't engage in "radical Acts"! Help people!'[70]

Is this a minor point? Does it exaggerate the extent of the problem contained in Žižek's approach to 9/11? I do not believe so. For all the cleverness and insight of Žižek's writing, there is something absolute and almost desperate in his rhetoric when he emphasizes the 'madness of a decision' related to an 'Act'.[71] To fall short of this is to merely perpetuate the cycle of existing ideological patterns; it is to remain part of the problem rather than part of the solution.

A final illustration clarifies this concern: it is not uncommon for those working in food banks and shelters for the homeless to be criticized for merely putting 'bandages' on the problem of poverty. Feeding the hungry and sheltering the homeless – the argument goes – covers over the cracks of injustice in a corrupt social order, which only perpetuates the system. The implication is that one should not try to diminish the immediate level of human suffering, so that it can build in intensity until the whole society erupts in revolution, and a more just order can be introduced. This sort of challenge often leaves the front-line outreach worker feeling deeply ambiguous and troubled about her or his work, for this criticism exposes significant limitations inherent in such forms of social outreach. Most workers, however, will nevertheless carry on with their task, not because they imagine that they can 'make poverty history', but because they are not prepared to ignore the pain and suffering of the human beings who arrive on their doorsteps. The imperfect and 'modest' outreach worker is unwilling to chase after a 'grand narrative' of social revolution, or a courageous and miraculous 'radical Act', at the expense of their immediate neighbours. To employ a Žižekian turn of phrase, a choice between 'making poverty history' and applying 'bandages' to soothe the suffering of particular human beings is not a true choice. One should opt for both simultaneously. But in the absence of the arrival of a perfect society, one ought not to diminish one's commitment to the more modest project of simply doing what one can to help one's neighbour.

The logic behind the criticism that social outbreak work is less than revolutionary is a similar logic to what lies behind Paneloux's 'believe everything or deny everything', and it is ultimately the attitude behind Žižek's appropriation of the concept of 'belief' to resource his concept of a 'radical Act' and his version of political theology. For this reason, scholars and activists should approach his more positive theoretical proposals with a degree of caution. Though no authoritarian 'fundamentialist', Žižek's rhetorical and philosophical style lends itself to conceiving of political action in absolute and unmediated terms. Despite his emphasis on acknowledging the 'other', his ethical vision on the 'Otherness' of the 'Real' is frequently achieved only by blurring attention away from the immediate presence of concrete human beings.

The limitations of these elements of Žižek's thought do not diminish, however, the contribution that his insights on the nature of ideology make to any analysis of the ways in which human beings respond to crises and the challenges of life. His work alerts his reader to the many ways that thought and emotions can distract themselves from attending to the issues that require their attention, and he deepens understanding of the ways in which theology can become shaped and distorted by the dynamics of ideology.

Following from this examination of an atheistic adoption of religious 'belief', the next chapter approaches similar themes from another direction and perspective as it analyses a theological critique of the concept 'religion'. In his early work, the Protestant theologian Karl Barth writes with rhetorical flair, and his approach has some similarities to that of Žižek. Barth argues that 'Religion must die. In God we are rid of it.' What he means by this challenging remark complements Žižek's warning about the pervasiveness of ideology, and an analysis of his position will help to deepen theology's appreciation of the complexities of religion at the 'Ground Zero' moments of human history.

Notes

[1] Albert Camus, *The Plague*, trans. Stuart Gilbert (New York: Knopf, 1957), 86–7.
[2] Ibid., 200.
[3] Ibid., 202.
[4] See, for example, Richard Dien Winfield, *Modernity, Religion, and the War on Terror* (Aldershot: Ashgate, 2007); Jürgen Habermas, *Between Naturalism and Religion: Philosophical Essays*, trans. Ciaran Cronin (Cambridge: Polity Press, 2008); Jeffrey Stout, *Democracy and Tradition* (Princeton, NJ: Princeton University Press, 2005); Sloterdik, Peter, *God's Zeal: The Battle of the Three Monotheisms*, trans. Wieland Hoban (Cambridge: Polity Press, 2009).
[5] Tom Rockmore et al. (eds), *The Philosophical Challenge of September 11* (Oxford: Blackwell, 2005), 3.
[6] For an influential argument along these lines, see Michael Ignatieff, *The Lesser Evil: Political Ethics in an Age of Terror* (Princeton, NJ: Princeton University Press, 2004).
[7] Richard Rorty, Religion as a Conversation Stopper; *Philosophy* and *Social Hope* (Lonon: Penguin Books, 1999) 168–74.
[8] Gene Ray, *Terror and the Sublime in Art and Critical Theory* (Gordonsville, PA: Palgrave Macmillan, 2005), 1.
[9] Nieman, *Evil*, 285.
[10] Quoted in Giovanna Borradori, *Philosophy in a Time of Terror* (Chicago: University of Chicago Press, 2003), 32.
[11] Ibid., 65.
[12] Paul Berman, *Terror and Liberalism* (London and New York: W. W. Norton & Co, 2003), 208.
[13] Peter Alexander Meyers, 'Terrorism and the Assault on Politics', in *Understanding September 11*, ed. Craig Calhoun, Paul Price and Ashley Timmer (New York: W. W. Norton & Co., 2002), 255.
[14] Thomas Brudholm and Thomas Cushman, 'Introduction,' in *Religious Responses to Mass Atrocity: Interdisciplinary Perspectives*, ed. Thomas Brudholm and Thomas Cushman (Cambridge: Cambridge University Press, 2009), 2.

[15] Lincoln, *Holy Terrors*, 17–18. Jürgen Habermas similarly criticizes comparisons between 9/11 and Pearl Harbor, but rather than Hiroshima, suggests that the appropriate parallel is August 1914. As such, his comparison suggests a rather grim sense of foreboding, for the outbreak of World War One 'signalled the end of a peaceful and, in retrospect, somewhat unsuspecting era, unleashing an age of warfare.' In Borradori, *Philosophy in a Time of Terror*, 26.

[16] A common figure in such an approach is Karl Mannheim, *Ideology and Utopia* (London: Routledge, 1936).

[17] Slavoj Žižek, *Welcome to the Desert of the Real* (London and New York: Verso, 2002), 2.

[18] For a concise presentation of Žižek's understanding of the concept 'ideology', see 'The Spectre of Ideology', *Mapping Ideology*, ed. Slavoj Žižek (London and New York: Verso, 1994), 1–33.

[19] Eberhard Busch, *Karl Barth: His Life from Letters and Autobiographical Texts* (Minneapolis, MN: Fortress Press, 1976), 81.

[20] Žižek, *Iraq: The Borrowed Kettle* (London and New York: Verso, 2004), 1.

[21] For useful discussion Žižek, see Marcus Pound, *Žižek: A (Very) Critical Introduction* (Grand Rapids, MI: Eerdmans, 2008); Adrian Johnston, *Žižek's Ontology* (Evanston, IL: Northwestern University Press, 2008).

[22] Žižek, *Welcome to the Desert of the Real*, 2.

[23] Ibid., 45.

[24] Ibid., 5.

[25] Ibid., 11.

[26] Ibid., 44.

[27] Ibid., 51.

[28] Ibid., 50,

[29] Ibid., 54.

[30] Ibid., 51.

[31] Ibid., 45.

[32] Ibid., 24.

[33] See Martin Dent and Bill Peters, *The Crisis of Poverty and Debt in the Third World* (Aldershot: Ashgate Publishing, 1999).

[34] Ibid., 83–4.

[35] Ibid., 75.

[36] Ibid., 69–70.

[37] Ibid., 68, 88.

[38] Ibid., 116.

[39] Blaise Pascal, *Pascal's Pensées* (New York: E. P. Dutton & Co., 1958), 66.

[40] Ibid., 153.

[41] Žižek, *On Belief* (London and New York: Routledge, 2001), 85–6.

[42] Žižek, *The Puppet and the Dwarf: The Perverse Core of Christianity* (London: MIT Press, 2003), 115.

[43] For examinations of Žižek's discussion of Christianity, see Adam Kotsko, *Žižek and Theology* (London: T&T Clark, 2008) and Marcus Pound, *Žižek: A (Very) Critical introduction* (Grand Rapids, MI: Eerdmans, 2008).

[44] G. K. Chesterton, *Orthodoxy* (New York: Bantam Doubleday, 1996).

[45] See, for example, Miroslav Volf (ed.), *Practicing Christianity: Beliefs and Practices in Christian Life* (Grand Rapids, MI: Eerdmans, 2001).

[46] Talal Asad, *Genealogies of Religion* (Baltimore: John Hopkins University Press, 1993), 35–44.

[47] For a critical analysis of Asad, see Christopher Craig Brittain, 'The "Secular" as a Tragic Category: On Talal Asad, Religion and Representation', *Method and Theory in the Study of Religion* 17.2 (2005), 149–65.

[48] Žižek, *On Belief*, 12.

[49] Robert E. Buswell. *Encyclopaedia of Buddhism* (New York: MacMillan Reference Books, 2003).

[50] Žižek, *The Puppet and the Dwarf*, 5, 7.

[51] Žižek, *The Sublime Object of Ideology* (London and New York: Verso, 2002), 34.

[52] Žižek, *The Žižek Reader* (Oxford: Blackwell, 1999), 104.

[53] Ibid., 65–6.

[54] Žižek, *The Puppet and the Dwarf*, 108.

[55] Geoff Boucher, *Traversing the Fantasy*, ed. Geoff Boucher, Jason Glynos and Matthew Sharpe (Aldershot: Ashgate, 2005), 23.

[56] Ibid., 44.

[57] Walter A. Davis, *Death's Dream Kingdom: The American Psyche Since 9/11* (London: Pluto Press, 2006), 84.

[58] Matthew Sharpe and Geoff Boucher, *Žižek and Politics: A Critical Introduction* (Edinburgh: Edinburgh University Press, 2010), 213–18.

[59] Marcus Pound, *Žižek: A (Very) Critical Introduction* (Grand Rapids, MI: Eerdmans, 2008), 3.

[60] Ibid., 59.

[61] Ibid., 62.

[62] Pound, *Žižek*, 66.

[63] Albert Camus, *Notebooks: 1935–1951*, trans. Philip Thody (New York: Marlowe & Company, 1998), 158.

[64] See Susan Faludi, *The Terror Dream: What 9/11 Revealed about America* (London: Atlantic Books, 2007).

[65] I owe this observation to Thomas Merton, *Albert Camus' 'The Plague'* (New York: The Salisbury Press, 1968), 15.

[66] Camus, *The Plague*, 34–5.

[67] Ibid., 110.

[68] Ibid., 208.

[69] There are some further and intriguing similarities between Žižek's interpretation of Christianity and this discussion of *The Plague*, which cannot be explored in the context of this chapter. For a helpful analysis of this aspect of Žižek's thought, see Pound, *Žižek* and Kotsko, *Žižek and Theology*.

[70] If it were possible address Žižek's ethics in a more sustained manner here, this point could be expanded substantially. In his approach, ethics is not primarily a matter of relations between subjects; it emerges in and as the gap that appears within reality and experience. Ethical action is more a withdrawal from the everyday than an engagement with it. The 'Other' he discusses is not the other person who may happen to cross one's path. The concept of the 'Other' is analysed through Lacan's register of the Imaginary, Symbolic and Real, so that the 'neighbour' is described as a 'Thing', as an 'unfathomable abyss of radical Otherness' which cannot be gentrified. Such a theoretical stance, according to Žižek, is necessary to prevent reducing the neighbour to a mirror image of the self. He argues for a theoretic shift away from Levinas's

emphasis on the 'Face' of the other and towards the 'faceless Third'. This might serve to 'cleanse' our approach towards the neighbour 'of all imaginary lure', but as he focuses almost exclusively on the limits of subjectivity, it becomes increasingly difficult to imagine that the 'neighbour' being discussed in this text has anything to do with the stranger sitting next to me on the bus. See Žižek, 'Neighbors and Other Monsters: A Plea for Ethical Violence', *The Neighbor: Three Inquiries in Political Theology*, ed. Slavoj Žižek, Eric L. Santner and Kenneth Reinhard (Chicago: University of Chicago Press, 2005), 134–90.

[71] Žižek, *Welcome to the Desert of the Real*, 152.

Chapter 6

Religion as Ground Zero?

The previous chapter focused on the problem of ideology as a factor influencing responses to the terrorist attacks of 11 September 2001, but also impacting on other disasters and catastrophes in human history. The analysis of how ideology may influence religion in this discussion was explored from a non-theological perspective, although it was demonstrated that Žižek's own position resembles the sort of zealous leap which theologians are frequently accused of making. In this chapter, the criticism of religion will be developed from a theological perspective. The primary focus will be on Karl Barth's critical engagement with the concept of religion in his early work *The Epistle to the Romans*. The discussion demonstrates that Barth is keenly alert to the ways in which religion can be shaped and driven by human interests and concerns, rather than by a deep quest for knowledge of God. At the same time, however, just as Žižek showed that human beings cannot escape from the problem of ideology, Barth acknowledges that there can be no question of easily evading the problem of religion that he diagnoses. Building on his analysis of religion as a site of interruption and confusion, as well as of contestation and tension, this Christian concept of 'religion' can be metaphorically described as a 'ground zero' of sorts; for the way in which members of Christian communities respond to the challenges they encounter as they practice their religion will have a profound impact on their lives and their environment.

Following from the analysis of Barth's treatment of religion, the discussion will proceed to confront a practical application he makes of his position to one of the crises of his time: the rise of Nazism in Germany and the general acquiescence of the Protestant Church to its authority. The rhetorical slogan that Barth employs to challenge this – to 'do theology as if nothing has happened' – will be critically discussed in detail. This analysis demonstrates that, despite its theological insight, this slogan cannot serve as a general response to catastrophe, or in particular as a reaction to 9/11 or 7/7. This argument is developed in dialogue with contemporary explorations of the relationship between theology and trauma theory, as well as with the theologies of Emil Fackenheim and Johann Baptist Metz. The general point that will be defended is that in the face of trauma and catastrophe, theology should proceed as if something has happened.

The chapter closes with a critical discussion of the centrality of memory in Metz's political theology. The remembrance of past suffering is an important element of healing from trauma, but also as an antidote to theology's tendency to fall into ideology and self-serving agendas. In dialogue with Susan Sontag and Dominic LaCapra, however, the limits of memory will also be explored, which highlights the critical importance, even in the midst of the turmoil of the aftermath of a catastrophe, of nurturing self-critical thought.

God as Interruption

In 1914, Karl Barth wrote a sentence that would challenge comfortable attitudes towards the Christian religion.[1] He wrote, 'The little clause "God is" signifies a revolution.'[2] He argues that this clause represents an interruption of human assumptions and of the tendency to reduce the idea of 'God' to one's own views and purposes. As he witnesses the military build-up in Europe in anticipation of war, Barth laments to a friend over the failure of his contemporaries to distinguish their own political agendas from the Christian religion:

> The unconditional truths of the gospel are simply suspended for the time being and in the meantime a German war-theology is put to work, its Christian trimming consisting of a lot of talk about sacrifice and the like . . . it is truly sad![3]

Barth's remarks represent a theological protest over the outbreak of the First World War. The direction that this perspective took in his subsequent thinking was intensified by the rise of Hitler and the Nazi party in the 1930s, when he would become a major critic of the regime and would be forced to leave his teaching position in Germany. In this early period of his writing, Barth develops a theological critique of the concept of religion, particularly in a theological commentary on Paul's letter to the Romans. Without going into the rich complexity and depth of Barth's later thought, this section explores his criticism of religion at it appears in the seventh chapter of his Romans commentary[4]. In this discussion, Barth is trying to articulate how he thinks Christian theology challenges the culture of his day, which he presents as both profound and overwhelming.

In *The Epistle to the Romans*, Barth develops what will later be called a 'Theology of Crisis'. This label is sometimes misunderstood as referring simply to the fact that it was written during a time of crisis – the outbreak of war – but this misses its principal meaning. Barth's notion of a 'theology of Crisis' is rather that the Christian gospel is something that confronts human society with a crisis, by calling it into question. The gospel, he says, interrupts the assumptions of our world. The God of the Christian bible brings human culture under judgement.

In Paul's letter to the Romans, the author suggests that he was 'set apart for the gospel of God' (1.1), and that human beings are 'called to belong to Jesus Christ' (1.6). Barth understands this as suggesting that Christians are placed in an 'either-or' situation. The Christian's status under grace is not a warm and fuzzy feeling. To receive the gift of God's grace does not mean, for Barth, that all things about human life and culture are accepted by God. Instead, he suggests that 'Grace is the relation of God to [human beings] which admits of no compromise.'[5] He is not calling his audience to an unthinking obedience to an external authority. Despite the tone, this is not his point. What he is concerned about is how easily Christians fall into self-deception and become vulnerable to the seduction of what he calls 'ideology'. Thus he is suggesting that Christians must always remember that there is a gap between human culture and God. When this is forgotten, human beings are vulnerable to defining God according to their own limited understandings and preferences.

Barth's intention during this discussion is to highlight 'the dangerous ambiguity of religion'.[6] He wants his readers to be very wary of the needs and desires that lead them to turn to religion. This might at first seem like a rather strange thing for a Christina theologian to say, and also an unusual way to interpret chapter seven of Paul's epistle; but for Barth this warning about the problem of 'religion' gets to the heart of the nature of Christian theology.

The seventh chapter of Paul's letter to the Romans is an extended discussion of the status of the Jewish law after the death and resurrection of Jesus Christ. Paul suggests that the Jewish law had a very important role to play in God's salvation history, but that, in Christ, Christians have 'died to the law' (Rom. 7.4). Barth translates this Pauline discussion to his own context. Rather than emphasize 'the law', his concern is with 'religion'. Barth thinks that his culture uses the idea of 'religion' in the same way that Paul thinks of the 'law'. Barth's basic point is this: 'religion' is a creation of human beings. It is rooted in the finite world and limited by culture, human ambition and human failings. Religion, then, is not itself holy or sacred. It is, to use the Pauline language, 'of the flesh'. It is finite and created by human beings. Barth writes, 'above all the occurrences of human life there hangs a smoke-screen of religion, sometimes heavy, sometimes light.'[7]

This description of religion brings to mind the way in which Žižek presents the function of the Symbolic order in its relation to ideology. Barth suggests that religion is a 'smoke-screen' that one tries to peer through in order to see the truth of existence. It is a cultural device that human beings use to try to articulate something about their experience, but because it is a human creation, religion never fully captures or contains what it seeks to hold – God. Religion thus can be manipulated, and might be used to manipulate, and so it must be dealt with carefully and critically. Barth continues, 'The [religious person] changes colour like a film of oil on the top of the water. Every moment inevitably [s/he] changes . . . colour.'[8] For this reason, Barth is very critical of religion. He warns,

> Religion . . . acts . . . like a drug which has been extremely skilfully administered. Instead of counteracting human illusions, it does no more than introduce an alternative condition of pleasurable emotion . . . What human passion is more obviously temporary than the passion of religion?[9]

This perspective could serve as a description of many ways that religion has been used in reaction to 11 September 2001, and in many other reactions to the catastrophes of human history. As previous chapters in this book have demonstrated, religion is frequently used to further an ideological agenda, to manipulate, to seek after selfish purposes; it is blamed for the violence of the world and used as a weapon against others. For Barth, this sad state of affairs cannot be denied by the theologian. The memorial shrines that are constructed after a disaster, the affirmations that 'the world will never be the same', the pious-sounding speeches may all have a function, perhaps even a value, in helping human beings respond to the tragedy and trauma. However, Barth warns that such religious activity should not be understood as necessarily involving God, or expressing God's attitude towards the situation. Frequently these activities are simply the creations of human beings, products of ideology, things that are produced by human need and desire. Thus, one must be cautious to avoid speaking naively about this strange and controversial word – 'religion'.

Barth's criticism of religion is by no means an outright assault. Although he says that religion is 'dangerous', he also calls it 'ambiguous'.[10] His treatment of religion is much the same as Paul's treatment of the 'law'. He views religion as deeply problematic, finite and vulnerable to manipulation, and ultimately, unable to 'save' human beings; however, he also wants to be clear that all this does not imply that we should adopt 'a war against religion'. Barth wants to clarify that 'We do not escape from sin by removing ourselves from religion and taking up with some other and superior thing – if indeed that were possible.'[11] In fact, he suggests that this is simply not possible. Just as Žižek argues that human beings cannot escape from ideology, Barth thinks that all human striving involves elements that he calls religious. He writes, 'The veritable KRISIS under which religion stands consists first in the impossibility of escape from it *as long as* a man *liveth*.'[12]

On this point Barth's manner of argumentation is dialectical, as he is concerned to avoid simplistic and one-sided positions in the face of a complex dynamic. Barth thinks that simply deciding to abandon religion because it is so problematic is simplistic. First, he asks, after you abandon religion, what pure realm of thought and experience will you adopt? What other areas of human culture escape the problems of ideology, bias and human error which can be found in religion? Barth argues that there are no pure areas of culture, so abandoning religion in itself solves nothing. It will not prevent conflict, prejudice, hatred or disagreement. And it will not automatically encourage compassion or understanding.

Second, just as Paul values the contributions of the 'law', Barth values the contributions of religion. He argues that we need to recognize and understand 'the double position which the law [and religion] occupies as the loftiest peak of human possibility'.[13] Religion, like the law, represents an attempt to live the good life and to encounter God. It seeks the truth. Only, because it is part of limited and finite creation, it cannot achieve what it reaches for. As a product of culture, religion will always be fallible and imperfect. At its best, it represents humanity's pursuit of the divine and of truth. This is important and necessary. The problem arises when human beings think that their religion is itself divine and the truth.

The meaning or function of religion is thus, for Barth, the same as the law is for Paul: it instructs human beings of their need for God:

> Religion compels us to the perception that God is not to be found in religion . . . Religion, as the final human possibility, commands us to halt. Religion brings us to the place where we must wait, in order that God may confront us – on the other side of the frontier of religion.[14]

Barth suggests that, if human beings are truly attentive in their religious striving, they will discover that they themselves cannot actually live according to their deepest desires. People cannot live their religion as they intend. This is similar to Paul's observation that, no matter how hard he tried, he could not obey the law. The meaning of the law, then, is that 'it sharpens our intelligence that we may perceive the sheer impossibility of attaining that freedom from the law.'[15] By helping human beings recognize this, religion becomes the path to the knowledge of God; but, crucially, this is not to say that religion is itself knowledge of God. Such knowledge can only be granted by God godself, through what Barth calls God's self-revelation. Human claims about God must be interrupted and humbled, according to Barth, as people wait for God to reveal godself to them.

Religion as Ground Zero

Due to the complicated and hazardous nature of all supposedly 'religious' motivations and expressions, Barth argues that 'religion is an abyss: it is terror.'[16] This is an intriguing warning for a Christian theologian to make. Barth continues: in the face of religion's problematic nature, Christians 'must submit to the full paradox of our situation.' One ought not to panic over this problem or start grasping for easy answers. He admits, however, that few people actually want to do this. Human beings do not like inhabiting this ambiguous situation. They want clear answers and direction from their religion – especially in the midst of a cultural shock. Barth likens the situation of people inhabiting a religion to the complaining of the Israelites wandering in the wilderness, longing for the 'flesh-pots of Egypt'. In the context of such wilderness wanderings, we are tempted to 'content ourselves with some lesser, more feeble possibility of religion.'[17] Previous chapters have illustrated some examples of these more 'feeble' religious expressions, in which individuals employ religious terminology and symbolism in order to forward quite limited individual personal agendas or political positions.

If the term 'ground zero' refers to the exact ground where an explosion has occurred, it is in such a sense, following on from the perspective articulated by Barth, that 'religion' can be described as being itself a form of 'ground zero'. It is the site where an explosive interruption of human assumptions and conventions frequently occurs. Religion is a site where the worst of our human prejudices and frustrations are vented, while at the same time also being a source of great beauty and acts of kindness, which have in their own way had enormous and far-reaching influence on human society. Religion is a site of tension and a source of potential disruption, leaving in its wake both terrible violence and also considerable inspiration and consolation.

Many people, including (even especially?) those who are religious, try to avoid this interruptive force of religion. This is especially true in the midst of terrible human tragedies, when such vivid and disturbing interruptions of human life make individuals and communities long for comfort and security. At such times, many do not want a form of faith that calls them into question, but a faith that provides firm ground upon which to stand.

In his commentary on Romans, however, Barth suggests that there is no firm ground to stand on in this world. The only solid thing we have, he says, is God – but not a God packaged and delivered according to our wants and desires; and not a God who controls the events of our world as we would have them run. Rather, Barth's view of the 'Wholly Other' God is one that can only be reached out to, prayed to and awaited.[18] God's power is not something human beings can try to harness for their own purposes. Decorating the explosive power of religion with nice piety can only contain religion's troubling power for so long; 'the bomb, which [the human being] has so carefully decked out with flowers, will soon or later explode. Religion breaks [human beings] into two halves.'[19] Given this disturbing element in religion, Barth asks, 'Can we resist the temptation of easing religion of its heavy burden and uncharging it of its dangerous dynamite?' His answer is simple and direct: 'God forbid.'

Barth offers a vision of religion as having both the potential to interrupt human self-absorption and ideology, and also the capacity to become reduced to both such problems. It is thus a field of contestation. His intention is to humble the human understanding of 'religion' without dismissing the search for the divine. By guarding against the limitations of the all-too-human dimensions of religion, he trusts that individuals and communities will be enabled to experience the God who will reveal godself to them. Barth's emphasis is to ensure that it is God who is viewed as having the agency and initiative in the life of faith, not human needs or agendas.

There is much to appreciate about this honest admission of the dangers of religion on the part of this Christian theologian; however, what remains unclear is how Barth moves from this self-reflexive caution to a capacity to receive the positive reality of God. His emphasis on the idea that it is God who is interrupting human beings does not eliminate the problem that it is only imperfect human beings who interpret and express this reality, even as Barth emphasizes that God's revelation breaks through these schemas. There is a tendency in Barth to treat God's interruption of human beings as a foundational event, which, once experienced, cleanses the Christian religion of its ideological and fallible content, so that it can subsequently witness to the truth of God's revelation. Stated so bluntly, this is not Barth's intention, and his attention to the reality of sin certainly acknowledges that human beings remain fallible and will continue to misconstrue the object of faith. Barth's entire project is conceived as a dialectical movement of sinful human beings continuously being interrupted by the in-breaking of God's revelation. Nevertheless, his emphasis on a decision for God in the midst of the abyss of religion suggests the achievement of a positive access to the objective reality of God; 'we stretch out our failing arms towards the "Yes" which confronts us invisibly in the "No" by which we are imprisoned.'[20] The grace of God's 'Yes' rescues human beings from their sinful state. These are the two poles of Barth's theology: fallen humanity and the God of grace. Religion is the middle ground between these two poles. While remaining sensitive to the deeply problematic nature of religion, Barth's subsequent work in dogmatic theology does not linger sufficiently on the complexity of this middle position. After writing, 'religion must die. In God we are rid of it', he proceeds as if theology can articulate knowledge of God despite the messiness of 'religion'.[21] This is due to his confidence in the reliability of God's ongoing revelation through the reading of Holy Scripture, as well as the witness of the community of saints, in the form of the dogmatic tradition of the church.[22] Nevertheless, if God does indeed 'rid' human beings of religion, this achievement is only temporary, as people continually return to the more limited desires and needs they seek to satisfy through their religion.

Although Barth's work illuminates this difficulty, he does not continue to wrestle with it directly. If religion is 'ground zero', the site of interruption, in the sense of being a field of contestation, in which human identity is called into question and reshaped, and where a struggle between ideological agendas and the search for truth is played out, how does the religious theologian avoid redeploying a new ideological or self-serving agenda? Barth employs the language of disruption and catastrophe to describe the interruption of God's revelation into the world, without attending to the effect that such disruptions have on the human beings who experience them.

Theology and Trauma

On this point, contemporary conversations between theology and trauma theory have an important contribution to make. Shelly Rambo, for example, argues that the effects of a traumatic event do not simply fade into the past or go away once a crisis situation has returned to normal, but that the impacts of the trauma linger and remain. The wounds left behind by traumatic interruption can result in disconnection from one's former life and may change one's relationship to the past and future. She writes, 'Persons who experience trauma live in the suspended middle territory, between death and life.'[23] For the wounds left behind by a catastrophic event are not simply 'gotten over' once the immediate danger passes. In the aftermath of a disaster, people's sense of life is often mixed with death. The memory of those who have died, but also one's own sense of vulnerability and fear, continue to haunt any supposed 'return to normalcy'.

Rambo articulates the significance of this dynamic for a theology of trauma as follows: 'Trauma is the suffering that does not go away. The study of trauma is the study of what remains.'[24] Barth's critique of religion in *The Epistle to the Romans* certainly acknowledges that the difficulties and challenges human beings confront and articulate in 'religion' do not ever go away. What his theology does not linger on, however, is this second element of Rambo's interest: the study of what remains, in the ways in which death pervades life in the life of the individual, and, more generally, in the ways in which theology is pervaded by the limitations of religion. Stated more theoretically, in his work Barth moves from the negativity of suffering and sinful reality, to the positivity of God and the experience of grace, leaving the experience of dwelling in the space in between these realities undeveloped.

The concept of 'trauma' in psychoanalysis and psychiatry refers to a break or wound in an individual's psychological well-being. The psychologist John Erichsen describes trauma's effect as resembling what happens when a magnet is dropped on the floor: although no obvious damage is visible, it may have lost its magnetic properties.[25] Theologians who study the disorienting effects of trauma are interested in how it impacts on an individual's healing process, as well as on their faith and spirituality. But their reflections often go beyond this to explore how the insights of trauma theory can teach the theologian something about the limits of theological reflection itself. In the face of catastrophic events such as those with which this book is concerned, and, as Barth acknowledges, the extent to which religion itself can be its own form of terror and an experience of the abyss, the ways in which theological reflection may itself be disrupted by the disorienting nature of traumatic experience requires further examination.

When Serene Jones explores the impact of the terrorist attacks of September 11, she argue that the trauma of the events left many people stuck in a 'playback loop', in which their structures of meaning collapsed and their minds continued to remain preoccupied with the violence and destruction they had witnessed. The result was a significant collective sense of powerlessness and loss of trust, along with many other traditional symptoms of Post Traumatic Stress Disorder (PTSD) among many American citizens. The task for theology in such a situation, Jones continues, is to 'take the repetitive violence of 9/11 and reframe it in the context of the story of our faith'.[26] This involves demonstrating the ways in which the many 'story lines' or accounts of the meaning of the event (e.g. heroism, family values, patriotism) part ways with the Christian story. Theology's task in such an environment, Jones argues, is 'to renarrate to us what we have yet to imagine'.[27] This involves creating the space for people to tell the story of their suffering and grief, to provide witnesses to listen to this testimony, and, finally, to begin to tell a new story that breaks the cycle of violence and looks to an alternative future.

Rambo's approach to theology and trauma develops a similar emphasis, but she lingers longer than does Jones on the middle space between a traumatic event and the experience of grace. For her, theology ought to attend to 'the mixed terrain of remaining', which is to account for 'the excess, or remainder, of death in life that is central to trauma'.[28] In order to faithfully offer witness to the trauma of others, Christian theologians need to linger on the incompleteness and brokenness of this middle space. In the liturgical language of the primary event of the Christian year, it is neither to focus on the suffering of Good Friday when Jesus was crucified, nor on the miraculous resurrection from the dead on Easter Sunday; rather, Rambo argues that theological attention should focus more generally on Holy Saturday. Drawing from Hans von Balthasar's interpretation of Adreinne von Speyr's mystical meditations on Christ's descent into Hell, Rambo emphasizes that in the Christian story, on Holy Saturday, active suffering ceases, but a different kind of anguish begins. It is a suffering based on absence, rather than a present event; on loneliness, feeling forsaken, disconnected or abandoned. She writes, 'One does not take on sufferings in hell; one endures what it is to be abandoned.'[29]

If this is the hellish location that many people find themselves in, and, more generally, when a world of frequent catastrophes and horror stories has become the context in which Christian theology is articulated, how does the theologian understand the task of articulating positive visions of hope and promise, which are the reasons many turn to churches and their theological traditions in time of need? Given the criticisms of the traditions of theodicy developed earlier in this book, as well as the dangers of ideology for theological reflection, how might theology avoid becoming reduced to sentimentality, wish-fulfilment or mere repetition of the slogans of the status quo?

Rambo's book offers some useful direction in relation to these concerns. She highlights how two models of witnessing – proclamation and imitation – have frequently been deployed in Christian thought, both of which are interpreted primarily in relation to the figure of Jesus of Nazareth, in the sense of imitating his paradigmatic example. Rambo challenges this approach, arguing that from the perspective of a traumatic event, and for those who inhabit the middle position left in the wake of catastrophe, 'the centrality and stability of both the figure of Jesus and the clear identification of the message that the disciples are receiving' can no longer be assumed.[30] The shift of focus she alludes to here is a calling into question of the location of redemption in either death (theology of the cross, salvation through suffering) or resurrection (salvation by the erasure of death), in order to emphasize the persistence of love in the midst of suffering.

This is a witnessing to the suffering and death that remain in the aftermath of a trauma, or, theologically speaking, in the crucifixions and Golgothas which persist in human history. For this task, theology cannot simply focus on God's promised future, but must linger on the truth of suffering's ongoing devastation, on the cracks within the peaceful running of the world, which highlight the 'not yet' status of the Kingdom of God. It is to make visible what human culture, the ideologies of the world and, as Barth has astutely shown, even religion, would prefer to render invisible: the pain that lingers and haunts human history.

Doing Theology as If Nothing Had Happened

This emphasis on theological attention to incompleteness and the persistence of suffering and death even in the midst of life may meet with some obvious resistance: 'Ought theology not focus on the preaching of the Good News?' 'Does not this presentation of Christianity diminish the promise of resurrection and new life for all people?' One can imagine Paul's celebrated statement being quoted in resistance to the argument in the previous discussion of theology and trauma: 'If there is no resurrection of the dead, then Christ has not been raised; and if Christ has not been raised, then our proclamation has been in vain and your faith has been in vain.' (1 Cor. 15.13–14) There are also some obvious non-theological objections that can be made to the 'theology of the middle' being advanced here. Some rational choice theorists, for example, might warn that any church that does not have a clear message of consolation as its central focus will fail to attract a wide membership, since the function of religion, in their view, is largely to offer the promise of a heavenly reward to those who suffer lack in the present world.[31] In similar fashion, recall from Chapter One how Koenig emphasized the possible value of religion serviing as a 'positive worldview' in the wake of a disaster.

These objections, however, only represent avoidance strategies which dodge the problem that has emerged over the course of this book: the interwoven relationship between religion and violence, as well as theology and ideology. The intention of Christian theologians who study trauma theory is to explore forms of spirituality and faith that are mindful of the limits of human knowledge and human striving. They caution against the ease with which theology falls into sentimentality and simplistic dualisms, which allow it to be manipulated and exploited for all-too-human ends. It is in order to resist such threats to the integrity of theology as an academic discipline, but also as a faithful witness to God, which leads to the conclusion that theology cannot simply continue to articulate a positive and hopeful message in the context of a hellish and broken world. Before developing this position further, however, it is instructive to turn once again to Barth's early writing, since he offers a powerful and compelling alternative proposal.

In 1933, four months after Adolf Hitler became chancellor of Germany, Barth wrote an essay that was controversial at the time, and remains so today. In the wake of the rise of Nazism, which horrified him, he stated, 'I intend to do theology, and nothing but theology, as if nothing had happened.'[32] These puzzling words have sometimes been understood as a call to quietism and withdrawal from the world, but Barth's motivations are otherwise.[33] Rather than asking people to ignore historical events, Barth calls upon them to root any response to troubling experiences in the Christian faith. He warns that if one 'does theology' simply when and because something bad has happened, then this urgent need will be what religion is driven by, which will only domesticate or manipulate it. For it is only by refusing to react in panic that one might find the room for the miraculous encounter with God's grace, or as Žižek might say, a creative 'Act'. Barth's description of grace suggests that it 'can be found and sought, conceived and apprehended, only as Miracle, Beginning, and Creation'.[34] In this important sense, then, God is not something to be summoned or referenced simply when the occasion would seem to demand it.

Clearly any theological reflection worthy of its name would seek to avoid being reduced to constantly trying to respond to the fashions of its age. In his own thoughtful and moving response to 9/11, Charles Mathewes applauds a friend who decided to proceed to teach his class on Barth's 'Theological Existence Today' on 11 September 2001, despite the fact that it was only a few hours after news of the terrorist attacks had spread among his students. Mathewes views this decision as 'profoundly wise', for it helps to clarify that Christian theology is a 'particular way of thinking', distinct from other ways of conceiving of politics, as well as moral and religious struggle. To have cancelled the class, or to have changed its focus in order to talk about the events of the morning and what they might mean, would have been to allow the terrorists attacks to dictate the agenda of their lives and to become the thing that was most important to focus on.[35]

There is indeed wisdom here, in that it encourages caution against reducing theology to an instrumental task, focused on getting results to the questions and concerns people might have at any given moment.

One can find an example of what Barth imagines such theological attention involves in a lecture he delivered to a group of Christian pastors in 1922 on the topic 'The Need and Promise of Christian Preaching'. In these remarks, he admits that when faced with the two 'great magnitudes' – the Bible and daily life – the preacher feels caught between a rock and a hard place. It is not an easy task to help Christians move from the hopes and promises of the biblical text to the complexities and disappointments of daily life.

Faced with this challenge, Barth councils that the most basic and faithful message that is to be delivered is: 'God is present!' How does this help clarify the problem? He continues by acknowledging that this is a difficult issue for all people, and for Christians an answer can only begin to form when the Bible is opened and engaged with. Barth writes,

> If the congregation brings to church the great *question* of human life and *seeks* an *answer* for it, the Bible contrariwise brings an *answer*, and *seeks* the *question* corresponding to this answer: it seeks questioning *people* who are eager to find and able to understand that its seeking of them is the very answer to their question.[36]

For Barth, then, when people come to their place of worship looking for an answer to *their question*, the important work of the preacher, the Bible and the Church, is to help people find the space they need to move from *their question* and a need for *their answer*, in order to be able to meet the challenge of a new and different question: 'Are we asking after God?' In this process, according to Barth, the question moves from our question to God's question to us. The focus is thus changed from the preoccupations of human beings, to a focus on discerning the will of God. As for an answer to these questions: this becomes clearer once one begins to ask the right question: 'The question is the answer.' Barth concludes, 'In the Bible it is not *we* who seek answers to questions about *our* life, *our* affairs, *our* wants and wishes, but it is the *Lord* who seeks labourers in *his* vineyard.' This is to say that the preacher, faced with the needs and desires of the people, is indeed called to give an answer. But as to what this answer is, Barth writes: 'as the minister of the Bible, he must be the first to be prepared to submit to God's *question* by asking the question about God . . . If he answer's the *people's question* but answers it as a man who has been *questioned by God*, then he speaks – the word of God.'[37]

In the tone and emphasis of these statements, one encounters once again Barth's concern to describe human agendas as being interrupted by divine agency. What remains unclear (or at least undeveloped) in this lecture is how the preacher who submits to being 'questioned by God' arrives at such a capacity to speak 'the word of God'. The Christian leader has indeed been interrupted, but it appears that Barth is confident that this is but a temporary state; she or he will subsequently be empowered to proceed in a positive fashion, preaching the Word 'as if nothing has happened'. The time for being questioned comes to an end, so that the moment of delivering an answer might arrive. The pastor has moved from interruption to witnessing to a received truth. Barth's confidence in God's capacity to move the pastor to faithful proclamation is impressive and inspiring; yet, might the way he describes the departure from the very human questions and concerns of the Christian be underdeveloped? There is a wide hermeneutical divide between the interruption Barth invokes and the answer of the 'Word of God' he privileges.

Barth was, of course, aware of this reality, and there is a sense in which the problem with his framing of this issue, as well as his slogan 'doing theology as if nothing had happened', is more a product of emphasizing his rhetoric in a simplistic manner. For there is, in fact, something disingenuous in his cry for theological purity; he publishes his slogan precisely *because something had happened*: the capitulation of the Protestant churches in Germany to the authority of the Nazi agenda. Martin Rumscheidt argues that, in this essay, 'Barth meant his work to be an assessment of what being a Christian in the Third Reich meant . . . It was, in fact, a Christian clarion call against what was happening.'[38] A contextual reading of Barth's slogan, therefore, suggests that his rhetoric had a strategic purpose in response to his reading of the particularities of the situation he was confronting. For many postwar theologians in Germany, however, the new situation called for a very different form of theological response.

Theology in the Aftermath: As If Something Has Happened

In his theological reflection on the impact of the Holocaust on Jewish theology, Emil Fackenheim refers to a statement by Leo Strauss which could be taken as support for Barth's emphasis on doing theology as if nothing has happened:

> It is safer to understand the low in the light of the high than the high in light of the low. In doing the latter one necessarily distorts the high, whereas in doing the former one does not deprive the low of the freedom to reveal itself fully for what it is.[39]

Fackenheim responds to this advice by noting that the events he is concerned with – the rise of Nazism and the Holocaust – do not reveal themselves fully from the perspective of the 'high'. Any form of thought that is able to begin to understand such catastrophes, he argues, is one that has first confronted them, been challenged and 'shattered' by them. Furthermore, thought can only oppose such horrors with its own sense of horror. After the rupture caused by the Holocaust, Fackenheim suggests that 'the high is accessible only through an act of recovery, and this must bridge what is no mere gap but rather an abyss.'[40]

In the face of historical catastrophes, Fackenheim argues that philosophy and theology can only be conceived of as exercises in 'mending' (*Tikkun*) and 'bridge building'. In the same way that it destroyed human beings, Auschwitz annihilated philosophical concepts like human dignity; likewise, theologically, it disrupted the concept of God. To simply go on as before was impossible. Fackenheim thus argues that those who turn to the philosophical or theological traditions must begin again and learn to engage with it anew, for both had failed to prevent the worst from happening. Chapter Three explored this emphasis in some detail, but it is worth recalling how he develops this view as a challenge to Christian theology in particular. Focusing his criticism on the thought of Kierkegaard, he writes,

> Are we wrong if we weep, protest, accuse on their [the victims of the Holocaust] behalf? Can any conceivable relation to God *edify* us as we hear those screams and gasps, and that no less terrible silence? Surely the Christian Good News that God saves in the Christ is itself broken by *this* news.[41]

For Fackenheim, something as devastating as the Holocaust demands more from religious adherents than, for example, an admission of sin on the part of Christians who had fallen short of their calling, or had allowed their faith to be used for ideological purposes. The rupture of the theological tradition goes deeper than this; the failure of Christians to stand up to Nazis to defend the Jewish people remains, he argues, an unresolved and frequently unacknowledged 'trauma'.

The Catholic theologian Johann Baptist Metz takes up the challenge articulated by Fackenheim and argues a similar point when he suggests, 'We Christians can never again go back behind Auschwitz; to go beyond Auschwitz, if we see clearly, is impossible for us of ourselves. It is possible only together with the victims of Auschwitz.'[42] It is at this point that the problem with a contemporary interpretation of Barth's statement of continuing to do theology 'as if nothing happened' comes more clearly into view. Despite the noble and heroic-sounding clarity of this position, and even though it can be understood as startegically appropriate to the situation Barth was confronting, as a rhetorical device, it can easily slide into a denial or forgetting of historical suffering.

As a young German man in postwar Germany, Metz became increasingly disconcerted with the relative lack of discussion within German society of the traumas of the war, and particularly about the Holocaust. W. G. Sebald has noted a similar absence within postwar German literature:

> People's ability to forget what they do not want to know, to overlook what is before their eyes, was seldom put to the test better than in Germany at that time. The population decided – out of sheer panic at first – to carry on as if nothing had happened.[43]

It is such a failure to confront the terrible suffering of the past which Metz's 'political theology' intends to challenge. From within post-Holocaust Germany, he asks 'why one sees and hears so little in our theology of such a catastrophe, or of the whole history of human suffering?'[44] Metz argues that theology cannot proceed as if nothing has happened because, left to its own recourses (i.e. those of individual theologians), the memory of the devastation wrought by the catastrophe will often be forgotten or ignored. He recalls how 'Auschwitz worked like an ultimatum for me', and it leads him to ask, 'Does theology really ever heal every wound?'

Theology in the aftermath of disaster, Metz continues, is only possible when it is conducted in solidarity with the victims of the tragedy. Without listening to the voices of those who suffered, and who continue to suffer, theology is blind and deaf about the world that it claims is redeemed. Moreover, it may be unable to recognize what redemption even involves. For Metz, theology must make an 'about-face', a turn towards the suffering of others. After Auschwitz, theology can no longer be conceived as a 'system', but only in terms of human beings.[45]

Metz's emphasis recalls Rambo's concern to describe theology in the wake of deep suffering as 'fractured language, always broken, and never complete'.[46] Theology is fractured because the world has fractured. It is broken because of its incapacity to fully describe, console or heal those who have been victimized. Perhaps a Barth-inspired voice might protest at this point that such a position makes the object of theology – God – the subject of human projection, confusing the world's brokenness with the reality of the divine. While the basic theological objection is an important one – that God is not dependent or defined by the state of the world – such a rebuttal also eludes the problem. For the claim is not that it is God who is fractured and broken, but the discipline of theology, as well as the theologians who articulate it and the community to which it speaks, the church. The claim being made here is not that God is traumatized by catastrophe, but that theology, theologians and the church are. They are not the same in the aftermath of a disaster, and so they cannot proceed with integrity 'as if nothing has happened'. Barth's position really only defends the idea that the object of theology – God – may not have changed; but it is not God who is writing theology.

Theology as Memory of the Catastrophe

Metz's work emphasizes a view of history as catastrophe. The progress of world history is a story of savagery and suffering, but contemporary society, particularly its dominant mode of subjectivity and rationality, represses and ignores this reality. In an aphorism, he writes, 'As Brecht has said, "When crime is committed, just as the rain falls, no one cries: Halt!"'[47] For Metz, a primary role of theology is to cry 'halt' in a world of catastrophe and suffering.

Metz develops his theology around an anamnestic understanding of reason, which is informed by his reading of Walter Benjamin and Theodor Adorno. In similar fashion to Adorno's concept of negative dialectics, which intends to think with the aid of concepts beyond the objectifying nature of rational thought, Metz's concept of 'dangerous memory' seeks to uncover the suffering that religion would often prefer to bury and forget. In this sense, both Adorno and Metz follow the same impulse: to save intuitions that have not been exhausted by modern philosophy. In other words, to uncover 'what is missing' from the story that modernity tells about itself.

For both Metz and Adorno, modern society encourages the repression of suffering, both among individuals and collectively. It prefers to ignore the suffering of the 'other', who contemporary society oppresses politically and modern rationality dominates theoretically, as thought forces all things to conform to its procedures and norms. Such a perspective resonates with concerns Metz developed out of his own experience as a young solider at the close of the Second World War, as well as his horror over the realities of the Holocaust. He writes, 'after Auschwitz I consider as blasphemy every Christian theodicy and all language about "meaning" when they are initiated outside this catastrophe.'[48]

Approaching Christian theology from such concerns, he draws from Walter Benjamin's concept of history as catastrophe to develop a concept of *memoria passionis* – the memory of suffering, or 'memory of the passion'. Benjamin argued that, rather than conceiving of history as progress, which focuses attention on movement towards the future at the expense of ignoring suffering in the past, critical thought must allow itself to be interrupted by catastrophes. Only with such acknowledgement of human suffering can thought resist the ways in which ideology distorts its understanding of the realities of historical existence.[49] In Metz's view, this perspective resonates with the Christian tradition's practice of remembering the passion of Jesus Christ on the cross, but also its ongoing recollection of the suffering of the people of Israel in the Old Testament and of the Christian martyrs and witnesses throughout the history of the church.

From Adorno and Max Horkheimer, Metz appropriates the concepts of 'instrument reason' – or rationality reduced to the function of calculation and control – and the critical category of the 'culture industry', which manipulates and shapes all aspects of human culture according to the demands of identity thinking and the capitalist market.[50] Driven by such concerns, a primary focus of Metz's writing is to develop a critique of 'bourgeois religion', by which he means an expression of Christianity focused on privatized interior life. When religion gets reduced to serving the needs of a heavily ideological cultural environment (the 'culture industry'), it degenerates into a spirituality intent on soothing and consoling the identity of the subject, at the price of covering over contradictions and injustices in the world, and in the silencing of the voice of the neighbour.

What interrupts this routine of thinking is, for Metz, attention to the suffering of another person. He writes: 'The Christian *memoria passionis* articulates itself as a memory that makes one free to suffer from the sufferings of others.'[51] Here his emphasis once again resonates with Adorno's writing, who suggests that tensions in social life testify to unresolved contradictions; 'suffering is objectivity that weighs upon the subject', and so 'the need to lend a voice to suffering is the condition of all truth.'[52]

In Metz's view, two things in particular distract Christian theology from such attentiveness to suffering in history: first, the predominance of evolutionary logic, which is driven by technical rationality and an understanding of time as the cult of the makeable and of progress; second, the drive to systematization and to consoling doctrinal answers that reconcile the problems of society and individual experience. Because of the power of these dynamics to tempt theology and lead it astray, Metz argues that, 'The Church needs something like an apocalyptic shock . . . The shock effect must be produced inside the Church by those who are open to what is outside the Church and what lies on its fringe.'[53] For Metz, theology is apocalyptic in this sense, which is no 'gentle eschatology' of timeless time. For the vision of the world opened up by an apocalyptic interruption is not the continuum of an idea of developing progress, but the trail of suffering.[54]

Metz recognizes that, up to this point, his eschatological concern has much in common with the work of theologians like Barth, Eberhard Jüngel, Jürgen Moltmann and Dietrich Bonhoeffer, but he then makes a distinction. He suggests that each of these theologians, in their own way, sublate attention to human suffering into the very being of God, so that suffering becomes a theme for understanding the triune nature of God. To make this step, however, represents for him 'too much of a response, soothing the eschatological questioning of God'. Metz considers this an example of the sort of systems-building he resists. It makes theology 'speculative' and an 'almost Gnostic reconciliation with God behind the back of the human history of suffering'.[55] Avoiding this failure requires maintaining a 'respect for the nontransferable negative mystery of human suffering'.[56] Thus, Metz writes, 'Not even Christian theology can allow Job's question to God, "How long yet?" to fall silent in a soothing answer.'[57]

For Metz, theology is properly understood as theodicy – but theodicy in a political rather than existential or metaphysical mode. He writes, 'discourse about God [is] the cry for the salvation of others.'[58] The interruption that the recollection of the catastrophes of history imposes is the inability to ignore 'abysmal histories of suffering in this world'. In the face of this recognition, according to Metz, theology ought not to try to eliminate this question or over-respond to it. Theology 'does not develop its answers reconciling everything, but rather directs its questioning incessantly back toward God.'[59] It follows, therefore, that Metz presents theology in largely a negative mode. It witnesses to the catastrophes of history by refusing to forget the suffering they cause and by protesting against this suffering. Theology as memory resists the desire of individual human beings, but also whole cultures, to try to conceal or repress the traumas they experience. By nurturing the *memoria passionis* within its thought and practice, Metz suggests that the church can help people acknowledge their own traumatic brokenness, while not being destroyed by it. He urges the Christian community to seek to embody the sort of 'bridge' that allows human beings to dwell in the 'middle space' of unreconciled history. Metz expresses this approach as follows, 'Christian theology must be able to perceive history in its negativity, in its catastrophic essence, so to speak.' He then adds, however, 'If this perception is not to turn tragic . . . then these catastrophes must be remembered with practical and political intent.'[60]

The concern raised here is similar to that developed by Rambo and Jones when they emphasize the need for victims of trauma to re-narrate their story. For Metz, a perception of catastrophe which turns tragic is one which seeks to escape from history: to flee from all care and connection to some empty but safe utopian void. *Memoria passionis* resists such a tendency, for it is a form of memory undertaken for the sake of those who have suffered unjustly. It is recollection grounded on a sense of connection and solidarity with all peoples. Such memories interrupt the drive to escapism, because one now recalls those who would have to be left behind to suffer their fate. Remembering for the sake of the neighbour thus becomes something practical and political, not in the sense of leading to a blueprint for a specific new social order, but because it motivates human resistance and protest against injustice. As such, it becomes the ground upon which people find the resources to carry on in the aftermath of catastrophic history, and some direction in which to re-narrate their lives. Metz writes, '*memoria passionis* is the only universal category of humanity open to us.'[61]

Metz's emphasis on memory and the negativity of suffering results in a theology with little room for positive foundations. There is a sense in which the *memoria passionis* remains focused on Good Friday rather than Rambo's Holy Saturday, let alone Easter Sunday. This leads one to ask whether what he himself calls a '*theologia negativa* of the future' implies a negative theology, offering little by way of positivity, but only an agenda defined as resistance to suffering. Such is the judgement of Joseph Columbo, who argues that Metz's theology amounts to a 'negative dialectics'.[62] Both R. R. Reno and Jan-Heiner Tück suggest that Metz's relentless focus on suffering and theodicy results in insufficient attention to the 'once and for all' victory of Christ's resurrection.[63] Although Metz himself resists such an implication, there is something to these observations. The question is whether this a flaw in his thinking or the natural consequence of his understanding of theology.

The issues this raises about the extent to which theology can offer 'positive' direction and reassurance will be addressed in the next chapter. In order to bring to a close this discussion of the ways in which religion metaphorically shares something of the impact of a 'ground zero' phenomena, one issue remains to be explored: the problem of whether witnessing the suffering of others does in fact result in a sense of connection and solidarity.

Witnessing the Pain of Others

In a reflection on the impact of wartime photographs and video footage, Susan Sontag confronts a theology like that of Metz, with its emphasis on solidarity with the suffering neighbour, with a dilemma. Sontag challenges the assumption that the viewing of images of suffering and catastrophe will cause a moral and ethical change in the viewer. Virginia Woolf, for example, argued that if people would only be exposed to pictures of the mangled bodies of children and adults from a battlefield, they would become pacifists. Such a position, Sontag suggests, presumes the following:

Not to be pained by these pictures, not to recoil from them, not to strive to abolish what causes this havoc, this carnage – these, for Woolf, would be the reactions of a moral monster. And, she is saying, we are not monsters, we are members of the educated class.

Our failure is one of imagination, of empathy: we have failed to hold this reality in mind.[64]

The rebuttal to Woolf's assumption that Sontag offers points to the sad reality that simply being exposed to images of damaged bodies has not been sufficient to stop wars from breaking out, or to inspire humanitarian outreach. Photographs *as such*, she argues, are not sufficient in themselves to change the empathic imaginations of many human beings. In an increasingly media-saturated culture, citizens of many countries are confronted daily with a steady stream of images of suffering. Relief agencies and social service organizations rely on such images in their fundraising campaigns. This is evidence that such pictures occasionally 'work', at least in the sense of inspiring some individuals to donate money to a 'worthy cause'. Yet, is not a more frequent response simply to turn off the television or to look down at the ground as one walks by the poster on the wall?

This issue is the flip-side of the problem of ideology demonstrated in Chapter Two, and explored theoretically through the thought of Žižek in Chapter Five. Images are also used to try to motivate people to fight in wars, as Sontag recognizes: 'If governments had their way, war photography, like most war poetry, would drum up support for soldier's sacrifice.'[65] Does the fact that people in North Atlantic societies live in a 'spectator culture', so that catastrophes, even when they occur in close proximity to them (such as 9/11 or 7/7), can seem 'unreal' or 'like something on TV', undermine the centrality that Metz places on the moral and theological role of memory? The mere observation that other people are suffering does not appear to be a sufficient interruption of the self-centredness of many human beings. Moreover, most psychologists and psychoanalytic theorists suggest that this failure does not imply that such people are 'moral monsters'. Christian theologians might add that there is a distinction to be made here between the sinfulness of human beings and their being considered 'evil monsters'.

The fact that observing human suffering does not necessarily lead to empathy does not undermine the significance of memory emphasized by Metz. In fact, it only highlights the importance of working to recover such acts of recollection, while at the same time demonstrating that more is required. Sontag's own reflections in *Regarding the Pain of Others* end with a consideration of the role of memory. The imperative 'Don't forget', she says, is an ethical act, as it suggests a commitment to remain connected to other human beings, even the

dead. Nevertheless, she offers a caution on making this the sole prior-
ity: 'There is simply too much injustice in the world. And too much
remembering (of ancient grievances: Serbs, Irish) embitters . . . To reconcile, it is necessary that memory be faulty and limited.'[66]

One way to respond to this challenge is to emphasize the concept
of imagination, which Metz argues is nurtured and grounded in the
roots of his *memoria passionis*: the biblical narratives about Jesus of
Nazareth and the people of Israel. Memory, for him, is shaped and
motivated by these biblical stories, enabling Christian memory to
'escape the system of the history of progress and triumph' and turning
mere recollection into solidarity, in the form of 'anamnesis'.[67]

There is a long legacy of Christian examples that demonstrate that
such a witness has been nurtured by the biblical narratives. The direction Metz offers to theology is a helpful and powerful contribution.
But the persistence of counter-examples – counter witnesses who have
failed to be moved by the suffering of their neighbours or to be motivated by the biblical narratives to lead lives of solidarity – suggest that
Christian 'memory' cannot in itself be instrumentalized and treated as
a cure for human apathy or cultural ideology. As Dominick LaCapra
warns, imagination and recollection following a traumatic event are
not inherently positive dynamics, but can be conflicted: comforting
and healing, or re-traumatizing and painful:

> The imagination may at times provide momentary release or an
> avenue of escape, but after the event the imagination may be over-
> whelmed by hallucinations, flashbacks, and other traumatic resi-
> dues that resist the potentially healing role of memory-work.[68]

For this reason, LaCapra argues that while memory is a necessary
starting point for healing (and for all symbolic activity for that matter), it is not a sufficient resource in and of itself:

> What is required may be both to remember and to check mem-
> ory with all the resources of critical inquiry in order to approach
> as closely as possible events that necessarily involve gaps, distor-
> tions, and limited evidence at least with respect to the experience
> of trauma itself.[69]

In her own response to the complexities of the motivating power
of symbolic images, memory and human empathy, Sontag does not

identify any one particular resource or safeguard against the capacity to remain unconcerned or unmoved by the suffering of others. Rather, the only resource she places her hope in is in the potential for human beings to step back from the intensities of suffering and trauma and to respond with reflection rather than the immediacies of rage or despair. For her, it is mature and engaged human thought that is called for at the 'ground zero' spaces of human history: 'Nobody can think and hit someone at the same time.'[70]

Shelly Rambo and other theologians might well raise some questions about the capacity of human 'thought' to be the solution to the suffering of history. Brilliant minds have proven to be capable of committing terrible crimes, and Chapter Three of this book demonstrated the terrible rationality and planning behind the implementation of the Nazi 'Final Solution'. Faced with the polarities of life and death, how does one bridge the gap between the two? Rambo argues that 'no human logic can postulate or even construct such a bridge.'[71] Rather than the potentials of human thought, she argues that it is only the divine Spirit who enables the embracing of life even in the midst of death. She clarifies that the Spirit is not itself the bridge, but it enables human beings to maintain the bridge between life and death at its most fragile point. It provides 'the capacity to imagine life where it cannot be envisioned as such'.[72]

Stated in this way, Rambo's position recalls the way Žižek describes the achievement of a radical 'Act' as 'something of a miracle'. Is this where theology is ultimately left in the face of a catastrophe: to throw up its hands and counsel people to hope for divine intervention? Does this result only in a reintroduction of traditional theodicy, which previous chapters have challenged and criticized? Are we left, once again, only presenting a divide between human reason, as Sontag describes it, and religious hope, as formulated differently by either Barth or Rambo? These are questions the next chapter will explore, as it turns to an examination of what it means to speak theologically in a time of terror.

Notes

[1] Barth's discussion uses the general term 'religion', which contemporary scholarship considers a problematic general term, if it intends to refer to a universal concept encompassing all world religions, in all their diversity. Rather than fault Barth for his terminology, it is more fruitful to treat his generic term 'religion' with the specificity with which he conceives of it – as referring to only to the Christian faith.

[2] Quoted in Eberhard Busch, *The Great Passion: An Introduction to Karl Barth's Theology*, trans. Geoffrey W. Bromiley (Grand Rapids, MI: William B. Eerdmans, 2004), 8.

[3] Karl Barth, *Revolutionary Theology in the Making*, trans. James D. Smart (Richmond, Virginia: John Knox Press, 1964), 26.

[4] The scope of the discussion in this chapter will not, therefore, cover the entirety of Barth's dogmatic theology, nor does it claim to be a complete summary of Barth's thought. Although I am sympathetic with the common distinction between an 'early' and a 'late' period in Barth's work, I am aware of the significant challenges to such a formulation. On this debate, see John Webster, *Barth* (London and New York: Continuum, 2000). 22ff.

[5] Karl Barth, *Epistle to the Romans*, trans. Edwyn C. Hoskyns (Oxford: Oxford University Press, 1968), 229.

[6] Ibid., 254.

[7] Ibid., 230.

[8] Ibid., 231.

[9] Ibid., 236.

[10] Ibid., 254.

[11] Ibid., 241.

[12] Ibid., 242.

[13] Ibid., 241.

[14] Ibid., 242.

[15] Ibid., 257.

[16] Ibid., 253.

[17] Ibid., 252.

[18] In later periods of his writing, Barth distances himself from the concept of God as 'Wholly Other'. See Webster, *Barth*, 49ff.

[19] Ibid., 268.

[20] Ibid., 257.

[21] Ibid., 238.

[22] For a brief summary of Barth's dogmatic project, see Karl Barth, *Dogmatics in Outline*, trans. G. T. Thompson (London: SCM Press, 1949).

[23] Shelly Rambo, *Spirit and Trauma: A Theology of Remaining* (Louisville, KY: Westminster John Knox Press, 2010), 25.

[24] Ibid., 15.

[25] Marcus Pound, *Theology, Psychoanalysis and Trauma* (London: SCM, 2007), 21.

[26] Serene Jones, *Trauma and Grace: Theology: Theology in a Ruptured World* (Louisville, KY: Westminster John Knox Press, 2009), 31.

[27] Ibid., 21.

[28] Rambo, *Spirit and Trauma*, 6.

[29] Ibid., 50.

[30] Ibid., 39.

[31] Lawrence A. Young, (ed.), *Rational Choice Theory and Religion* (New York and London: Routledge, 1997).

[32] Karl Barth, *Theological Existence Today*, trans. R. Birch Hoyle (London: Hodder & Stoughton, 1933), 9.

[33] For some useful discussion of this essay, see H. Martin Rumscheidt, 'Doing Theology as if Nothing Had Happened: Developments in the Theology of Karl Barth from 1919 to 1933', *Saint Luke's Journal of Theology* 30.1 (1986), 7–19; Timothy J. Goringe, *Karl Barth Against Hegemony* (Oxford: Oxford University Press, 1999).

34 Barth, *Epistle to the Romans*, 229.
35 Charles Mathewes, *The Republic of Grace: Augustinian Thoughts for Dark Times* (Grand Rapids, MI: Eerdmans, 2010), 1–3.
36 Barth, *The Word of God and the Word of Man*, trans. Douglas Horton (New York: Harper & Brothers Publishers, 1957), 116.
37 Ibid., 118–22.
38 Rumscheidt, 'Doing Theology as if Nothing Had Happened', 16.
39 Cited in Fackenheim, *To Mend the World* (Bloomington and Indianapolis: Indiana University Press, 1982), 262.
40 Ibid., 263.
41 Ibid., 279. For Fackenheim's criticism of Barth for his response to the Holocaust, see 133, 192–3, 284.
42 Johann Baptist Metz, *Love's Strategy*, ed. John K. Downey (Harrisburg, PA: Trinity Press International, 1999), 40.
43 W. G. Sebald, *On the Natural History of Destruction*, trans. Anthea Bell (Toronto: Vintage, 2004), 41.
44 Johann Baptist Metz, *A Passion for God: The Mystical-Political Dimension of Christianity*, trans. Matthew Ashley (New York: Paulist Press, 1998), 3.
45 Metz, *Love's Strategy*, 129.
46 Rambo, *Spirit and Trauma*,164.
47 Johann Baptist Metz, *Faith in History and Society: Towards a Practical Fundamental Theology* (New York: Seabury Press, 1980), 171.
48 Ibid., 41.
49 See Walter Benjamin, 'Theses on the Philosophy of History', *Illuminations*, ed. Hannah Arendt, trans. Harry Zohn (New York: Schocken Books, 1969), 245–55.
50 See Theodor W. Adorno and Max Horkheimer, *Dialectic of Enlightenment: Philosophical Fragments*, ed. Gunzelin Schmid Noerr, trans. Edmund Jephcott (Stanford, CA: Stanford University Press, 2002).
51 Johann Baptist Metz and Jürgen Moltmann, *Faith and the Future: Essays on Theology, Solidarity, and Modernity* (Markknoll, NY: Orbis, 1995), 11.
52 Theodor W. Adorno, *Negative Dialectics*, trans. E. B. Ashton (New York: Continuum, 1995), 17–18.
53 Metz, *Love's Strategy*, 152.
54 Metz, *A Passion for God*, 52–3.
55 Ibid., 69.
56 Ibid.,119.
57 Ibid., 71.
58 Metz, *A Passion for God*, 55.
59 Ibid., 56.
60 Ibid., 40.
61 Johann Baptist Metz and Elie Wiesel, *Hope against Hope*, ed. Ekkehard Schuster and Reinhold Baschert-Kimmig (New York: Paulist Press, 2000).
62 Joseph Columbo, *An Essay on Theology and History: Studies in Pannenberg, Metz, and the Frankfurt School*, (Atlanta: Scholars Press, 1990) 214.
63 R. R. Reno, 'Christology in Political and Liberation Theology,' *The Thomist* 56.2 (1992), 291–322; Jan-Heiner Tück, *Christologie und Theodizie bei Johann Metz* (Paderborn: Shoeningh, 1999).
64 Susan Sontag, *Regarding the Pain of Others* (London and New York: Penguin Books, 2003), 7.

[65] Ibid., 42.

[66] Ibid., 103.

[67] Metz, *Faith in History and Society*, 58.

[68] Dominick LaCapra, *History and Memory after Auschwitz* (Ithaca, NY and London: Cornell University Press, 1998), 181.

[69] Ibid., 183.

[70] Sontag, *Regarding the Pain of Others*, 106.

[71] Rambo, *Trauma and Spirit*, 74.

[72] Ibid., 123.

Chapter 7

Speaking of God in a Time of Terror

Rowan Williams was speaking a few blocks away from the World Trade Center on the morning of 11 September 2001, when the two passenger airlines slammed into the Twin Towers. He thus witnessed first hand the devastation and subsequent chaos of the terrorist attack on New York City. In the reflection he writes in response to this experience, Williams shares how he was stopped on the streets of New York City shortly after the attacks by a man who asked him angrily, 'What the hell was God doing when the planes hit the towers!?' Williams recalls that his 'fumbling' attempts to answer that God does not intervene in the world in that way seemed 'like a lame apology for some kind of "policy" on God's part', and that his words sounded 'heartless in the face of such suffering'. Williams admits that, in the midst of such a disaster, almost any answer he could give does little to relieve the pain or fear of the immediate moment. Given this recognition, Williams makes an important, if challenging, admission. He suggests that Christians must come to realize that they 'might be committed to a God who could seem useless in a crisis'. He then adds, 'Perhaps it's when we try to make God useful is crises, though, that we take the first steps towards the great lie of religion: the god who fits our agenda.'[1]

Such a position discourages the panicked scramble towards theodicy that Christians, along with members of other religious traditions, often gravitate towards. Williams argues that it is this demand for a firm answer to cling to that sometimes leads religious people to grab on to an ideological comfort that supports their assumptions about the world. This tendency does not help people respond maturely and faithfully to the situations confronting them, nor should it be understood as being motivated primarily by distinct 'religious' impulses or beliefs. Rather, demands for simple answers and scrambling to explain the meaning of suffering are more generally the result of very human emotions following from fear, confusion and anger. As Job might ask of such efforts, 'What provokes you to keep on talking?'

This concluding chapter explores the position of Williams in detail, as well as its implications for Christian theology. To some degree, Williams's caution shares similarities with the concerns of Barth's essay 'Theological Existence Today'. He warns that theology can turn to speaking about God 'too quickly' in the aftermath of a trauma, which risks reducing its language of the divine to an instrumental and self-serving ideology. This chapter begins with a discussion of the contrast between the murderous religious language of the terrorists and the simple, compassionate words of mourning left behind by the victims of the September 11 attacks. It then challenges Peter Sloterdijk's accusation that monotheisms are inherently violent, given their internal 'logic of the One', by making reference to Vincent Cornell's interpretation of 'Qur'anic universalism'. Although these reflections lead to a defence of speaking theologically in times of terror, the thought of Williams suggests that religion should be understood as 'planned frustration', and theology as 'wounded speech'. Such an approach to theological discourse recognizes the limited and incomplete nature of theology, which interrupts the demand that it must speak 'positively' in times of crisis. This perspective returns the analysis to the thought of Metz and Adorno, who together point to ways in which theology can inhabit the 'middle space' between life and death, which is continuously interrupted by an awareness of the suffering of others.

On the Dangers of Speaking Theologically

In his reflections on 9/11 in the book *Writing in the Dust*, Williams describes the terrorist attacks as having 'interrupted' those who observed its terrible devastation. It was an event that could not be ignored. It demanded recognition and called for a response of some kind. In this sense, the impact of the attack has some structural similarity to the interruption Barth describes as being inherent to what he calls 'religion'. It at least momentarily stopped people in their tracks and brought the status quo into question. For some, new priorities and concerns would result, while others would simply return to their prior ways of living as quickly as possible. Like Barth's concern to challenge religion's tendency to become reduced to satisfying immediate human needs and to an ideology, Williams similarity warns of the importance for theology to be cautious when responding to an event like 9/11. In this regard, he shares the basic concern that motivated Barth in 1933 to write of his intention 'to do theology as if nothing had happened'.

The circumstances of September 11, however, suggest to Williams that theologians cannot simply carry on with business as usual. For the terrible problem confronting theology at such a time is that the destruction has been inflicted by religious adherents, on behalf of their understanding of religion. The fact that the hijackers acted 'in the name of God' should give pause to any theologian who dares to speak of God at such a time. Thus Williams begins his reflections by admitting the challenge with which such a religiously motivated act of destruction confronts religious adherents. He states that one had 'better acknowledge the sheer danger of religiousness' before beginning to speak theologically.[2] This includes admitting that 'religion' is by no means a pure and wonderful thing. Like all human cultural phenomena, it can just as easily become something harmful as it can be a force for good. Like all other realms of human thought and experience, religion 'can be a tool to reinforce diseased perceptions of reality'. Thus, when one speaks of God in a time of terror, great care is required: 'Our religious talking, seeing, knowing, needs a kind of cleansing.'[3] Christians and all people of faith ought to guard against simplistic, sentimental and violent uses of their religious traditions for purposes that contradict what their religion claims to stand for. For this reason, although Williams wants his reader to think and speak of God, he also warms, 'Careful. You can do this too quickly.'[4]

Williams notes that a great contrast exists between the last 'religious' words left behind by the hijackers who flew the planes into the Twin Towers (discussed in Chapter Four) and the last words left behind by victims of the attacks in voice messages and emails to their loved ones. He observes that 'The nonreligious words are testimony to what religious language is supposed to be about.'[5] Williams has in mind, of course, the individuals trapped in the burning World Trade Center, the Pentagon or on United Airlines 93 over Pennsylvania, who, knowing what was happening to them, had the presence of mind to try to contact their loved ones in order to leave a final farewell message. For Williams, these very human words and emotions are far more powerful a witness to what should be valued and celebrated about life than what more directly 'religious' words and concepts might capture at such a time; for religious speech have largely been contaminated, or have at least lost credibility, in the face of having been employed in the name of terror and murder.

In an interview on an American television documentary, a Jewish leader makes a similar point. Rabbi Irwin Kula, president of the National Jewish Center for Leadership and Learning in New York, laments the extent to which 9/11 discredited traditional religious language. Describing his own shock over the attacks, he recalls,

> All of a sudden, I said, 'Wow. I know how dark religion is. I've been teaching for a long time that religions can do a lot of damage.' In the early parts of my rabbinate, the 55-year-olds (and I was 25 at the time) would say, 'Rabbi. You know religion killed more people than anything else . . . When 9/11 happened, it's the first thing I thought of within those first few days: 'Wow. Religion still is pretty murderous when it comes down to it. It's really pretty murderous.'[6]

Kula was deeply shaken by the attack on New York. He admits to having struggled to find a way to continue to teach and speak as a Jewish leader afterwards. One year after the attacks, he shares that he has found something to hold on to: the messages left behind by victims to their families. Kula describes his reaction to them:

> These are final conversations that were recorded on cell phones, recorded on voice mail. They seem to me to be incredible texts, because they were at the moment of confronting life or death. They're so pure about the expression of love between husband and wife, between mother and child . . . When I read them, I just felt they were texts as sacred as the text that we end up having recorded, that we transmit from generation to generation.

Kula treats these messages left behind as if they are modern Psalms. Just as a cantor in Jewish tradition chants the Psalms of the day, Kula has adapted this into a daily practice of chanting some of the voice messages and emails left behind. He sings these messages, because, for him, they are psalm-like examples of what religious language is meant to convey. This practice revolves around chanting messages like the following:

Hey, Jules. It's Brian. I'm on the plane and it's hijacked and it doesn't look good. I just wanted to let you know that I love you, and I hope to see you again. If I don't, please have fun in life, and live life the best you can. Know that I love you, and no matter what, I'll see you again.

It is clear why Kula and Williams consider such 'compassionately secular' words to be more powerful and resonant than the 'murderously spiritual' religious words of the hijackers.[7] The contrast does indeed put the religious discourse of the terrorists to shame. Does this imply, however, that the only appropriate way to speak of God in a time of terror is to shun overtly 'religious' language completely?

Kula himself appears to suggest such a position. Because religious language and traditions have become contaminated by the murderous religiosity of the terrorists (even though they themselves were Muslims, not Jewish like himself), this rabbi feels compelled to set the language of his own tradition aside and to pray using what seems to him a more 'authentic' expression of compassion and love. It is easy to be sympathetic to a degree with this response to the tragedy. Kula's practice could be understood as an act that preserves a memory of the victims, which resonates to some extent with the emphasis that Johann Baptist Metz places on remembrance. There is a sincere attempt in Kula's example to value the human lives that were lost in the attacks and to offer a degree of solidarity with them. Nevertheless, there is also something rather disquieting about Kula's adoption of these messages for his own spiritual devotion. After watching the documentary *Faith and Doubt at Ground Zero* and listening to Kula chanting what were the last words exchanged between a victim and her or his loved ones, many of my students have expressed considerable discomfort over his practice. Some thought the rabbi was being disrespectful for the way he uses the private emails or voice messages of others. Others have been scandalized by what they considered to be sacrilegious. Many students simply express discomfort, without being able to articulate what about Kula's chanting they found troubling beyond; 'It seems so morbid.'

I think my students are sensitive to something important when they covey a subtle critique of Kula's use of these messages. There is a sense in which his 'spiritual solidarity' with the victims of the attacks remains at an abstract and highly subjective level. This is to say that his religious use of these messages becomes his own way to cope with the impact and shock that 9/11 has had on *him*; this spirituality is an internal, rather than external, reaction. As such, to an extent, the practice ontologizes and sacralizes the terrorist attacks. To a significant degree, one might suggest that 9/11 has effectively become Kula's religion. It provides the symbols and the language of his worship, and the focus of his attention. In his interview for the PBS documentary, Kula himself acknowledges the centrality of the terrorist attacks in his life: 'there is not a day that goes by that I don't think about Sept. 11 and how fragile life is – not someone else's life, my life.' He adds, 'I felt that I could not go into the Sabbath without going to Ground Zero.' Recalling the discussion of Žižek's concept of ideology from Chapter Five, there is a real sense in which Kula's spirituality, which intends to protest against the suffering caused by 9/11, 'turns into its opposite': a veneration of an act of catastrophe. The testimonies of the victims have become a form of divine revelation: 'It's incredibly life-affirming, because it's knowledge from the Ground Zero.' What Kula has done is to replace words about God with the words of the victims of the attack, but this is not to speak theologically, but to sacralize messages intended for a very different purpose – to say farewell to loved ones. The words of the victims are not merely remembered, but are made use of in an instrumental manner.

Rowan Williams does not urge his reader to replace theological language with the language of the victims of 9/11; rather, he considers such testimony to serve only as an interruption of the ways in which religion has been corrupted by problematic ideologies. These testimonies prohibit speech about God from becoming sentimental or self-centred. For Williams, the contrast between religious terrorism and secular testimonies of love is something that ought to humble theology and encourage it to 'cleanse' itself. It calls for better, not less, theology.

The Logic of Theology as Inherently Violent?

Prior to exploring the direction that Williams's own position follows, it is instructive to first linger over the discomfort both he and Kula express due to their recognition of the dangers of religious rhetoric. It is such rhetoric that has fuelled the vehemence of the 'New Atheists' against religion. The attacks of September 11 led Richard Dawkins, for example, to argue that, 'To fill a world with religion, or religions of the Abrahamic kind, is like littering the streets with loaded guns.'[8] When, unlike Kula, Williams resists distancing himself from his own religious tradition, is he failing to recognize its inherent logic towards violence?

Such would be the position of Peter Sloterdijk, who argues that all monotheistic religions are driven to violence by their own internal logic. Given its emphasis on *one* God and thus *one* source of truth, Sloterdijk suggests that monotheism is structured by a 'logic of the one', which imposes a blueprint for 'zealous universalism'.[9] The different theologies of Christianity, Judaism and Islam, he continues, are all in their own ways shaped by an 'internally conditioned grammar' that is hostile to difference and to external worldviews. There is thus an 'inherent supremacism' in all monotheisms. This pushes their adherents towards zealous aggression and competition against all rival claims to the truth. The God of monotheism is a jealous God, who cannot tolerate rival idolatries. Sloterdijk writes,

> The logical origin of zealotry lies in bringing everything down to the number one, which tolerates no one and nothing beside itself. This number one is the mother of intolerance. It demands the radical *either* in which the *or* is ruled out. Whoever says 'two' is saying one too many.[10]

In such a rendering, a monotheistic religion is incapable of tolerance and is inherently anti-democratic. The logic of monotheism encourages impatience with the limitations of the external world, an attitude that Sloterdijk calls 'hastiness'.[11] When an adherent of a religion is willing to compromise with other belief systems, it can only be the result of inconsistency or a lack of faithfulness to the theological teachings of the tradition. Must any post-9/11 attempt to 'cleanse' a theological tradition acknowledge Sloterdijk's accusation that monotheisms are inherently violent?

It is important to recognize that the seemingly obvious empirical evidence which Sloterdijk draws on to support his position – although it is, admittedly, alarming and rhetorically powerful – does not represent how the majority of the members of monotheistic religions generally behave. For example, it is striking to recall the widespread denunciation of the 9/11 terrorist attacks that were issued by Muslim spokespeople from across the globe in the immediate aftermath of the event. Leaders in countries as diverse as Qatar, Pakistan, Malaysia, the Palestinian Authority, Egypt and the United Kingdom issued press releases criticizing the hijackers for misusing Islamic concepts and sacred texts, and for committing murder. Despite these acts of protest, it is the version of Islam found in the letter left behind by the hijackers that is commonly taken in the popular media to be the 'true' articulation of what Muslims 'really believe'. Sloterdijk's position implies that this witness of the majority of Islamic leaders in the world fails to conform to the inherently violent 'logic' of their own monotheism. But this argument requires adopting one of two assumptions in order to make sense of this phenomenon. Either one must develop a conspiracy theory, which suggests that the declarations of these Muslim leaders were insincere; or (and this is the view Sloterdijk opts for) one can argue that those leaders who advocate for peaceful coexistence do so only because they resist the logic of violence inherent to the Islamic tradition – i.e. they do not take their own tradition seriously. Neither of these assumptions is compelling.

Universalism with a Tolerant Face

The American Muslim Vincent Cornell presents a view that is the opposite to that of Sloterdijk. It is a position which offers an alternative way to interpret the public denunciations of Islamic terrorism by Islamic leaders. Cornell argues that it is a mistake to consider zealous fundamentalism (or Lincoln's 'maximalism') to be the necessary logical extension of a monotheistic religious tradition. Although he admits that some elements of Islam can be identified which seemingly support Sloterdijk's interpretation, Cornell emphasizes that the content of Islam also contains considerable resources which resist aggressive zeal against outsiders. This is to say that Sloterdijk's position simplifies the complexity and diversity found within the Islamic tradition. Cornell suggests that 'the nature of one's religion depends on the scriptures one reads.'[12] If one only reads texts in the Qur'an which emphasize conflict with non-believers, then these will shape one's religious orientation. In Cornell's view, however, such an approach to the sacred text is a limited and incomplete reading, which neglects counter-traditions that nuance and reinterpret the more aggressive passages.

To be clear, it is not Cornell's position that there are no problematic statements and passages in the Qur'an; nor does he suggest that there are purely 'bad' versions of Islam, and alternatively 'good' versions, which are located in completely different parts of the sacred text. Cornell's point is that the way that Muslims interpret the Qur'an is often driven by their own concerns and agendas. He writes, 'the interpretation of religion depends on human perceptions.'[13] Thus, when he observes how some of his fellow Muslims employ Islamic language to legitimate terrorism, he suggests that 'The fundamental problem with Islamic extremism is not that it is otherworldly, but that it is so worldly.' Such extremism seeks to force the external world to conform to the desires and agendas of the adherent, in the manner that Sloterdijk suggests, but Cornell disagrees that such behaviour is due to the logic of Islam itself. Instead, he argues, 'The logic of Islamic extremism is the logic of power.'[14] The problem with militant Islam, according to Cornell, is not that it is 'too religious' or 'too zealous', but that it is not religious or zealous enough. He suggests that such extremist movements worship *power*, not *Allah*. He laments the extent to which Islamic ways of speaking have become consumed in the present context by an emphasis on achieving access to power: 'In contemporary Muslim political discourse, God is mentioned but not engaged.'[15]

Cornell's antidote for Muslim extremism is not for Islam to become less monotheistic or less Islamic. His position could not be more opposed to that of Sloterdijk, for he argues that the way to counter extremism's 'logic of power' is to emphasize the monotheistic logic of Islam. It is precisely because Muslims believe that there is no other God but Allah, Cornell insists, that there can be no essential conflict between Islam and the West. Because Islam upholds a universal perspective, in which Allah is the God of all peoples and all cultures, he argues that 'there is nothing intrinsically "un-Islamic" about Western culture.' The logic of Islamic monotheism, or what he calls 'Qur'anic universalism', is such that, according to Cornell, Muslims are called to recognize that, under Allah, all peoples belong to God, so that no specific peoples or cultures can be considered inherently ungodly. Thus, Qur'anic universalism does not encourage a 'clash of civilizations', but calls upon all civilizations and peoples to struggle internally to find the right path for living.[16] Without denying the painfully destructive ways in which religious rhetoric can be used to motivate and legitimate acts of terror, Cornell's argument suggests that it would be simplistic to argue that ceasing to use religious language in public will result in the end of extremist terrorism.

Religion as 'Planned Frustration'

The response of Rowan Williams to the 9/11 terrorist attacks shares something with that of Vincent Cornell, in that he also suggests that it is precisely a more attentive appreciation of the particular content of Christianity which will help Christians to respond more adequately to the problems of the external world. But Williams is less confident that an alternative and universal Christian response presents itself in a clear and unproblematic manner. Even more than Cornell, Williams points to the significance of the attitudes and agendas which individual believers, as well as entire religious communities, bring with them when they turn to their sacred texts looking for comfort and reassurance during times of crisis.

In the midst of a cultural shock, Williams warns against allowing the 'dreadful innocence' of one's 'first surge of anger' to be the motivation for one's actions. In times of turmoil and confusion, he observes that human beings often feel a need to 'discharge' the tensions they feel, and so often lash out violently while under stress. Rather than communicate with the strangers who they fear might threaten them, people often turn them into 'symbols' – something their collective imagination can 'project its fears and tensions' onto.

In *Lost Icons*, Williams refers to the phenomena of 'road rage' as an example of how Western culture is often 'reactive' as opposed to being 'active'. He is concerned with the possibility that 'our cultural environment increasingly expects, imagines, provides for and nourishes panic.'[17] Williams observes that people are becoming less able to deal with tension and uncertainty, and therefore many panic at such times and lash out. They are unable to step back from a difficult situation, assess what is going on and choose a course of action based on mature consideration rather than emotional outburst. Many individuals, he continues, are often unable to accept or to deal with complexity – and so they 'snap' under stress – as in the strange phenomenon of 'road rage'.

The connection Williams makes between Western culture and 'road rage' informs the remarks he makes in *Writing in the Dust*. Although he is interested in the reasons people panic in reaction to events like 9/11, his message is more concerned with how he thinks people ought to respond to such events. This is why Williams councils against speaking about God 'too quickly'. He calls upon people to interrupt the momentum of the cycle of fear and anger that they find themselves caught up in, before beginning to speak about God. He uses metaphors about finding 'breathing space' or 'making room' in oneself, it order to interrupt oneself. This helps people to respond with 'comprehension' and 'modesty' (recalling Camus's Dr. Rieux), so that they might bring 'into the world something other than self-defensiveness.'[18] With such imagery, Williams outlines a very basic form of spiritual practice, one that encourages his readers in times of crisis to interrupt their reflex to respond out of immediate emotion and customary habit, and to step back for a moment in order to allow themselves to reflect prior to choosing what action to undertake in response to a situation.

Williams makes this plea 'not to run too fast' – so that people may 'explore feelings and recover the words' for speaking about God – because he does not think that the general cultural atmosphere in Western societies encourages the kind of response he advocates. Commenting on how the news media handled 9/11, he writes,

> The point at which we need to show more footage of collapsing towers or people jumping to their death, when we raise the temperature by injunctions never to forget – that is when something rather ambiguous enters in. We are trying to manipulate and direct the chaotic emotions of victims.[19]

For his model of an alternative way to respond, Williams refers to a story that appears in the eighth chapter of the Gospel of John. It is the familiar story of a woman who has been found guilty of committing adultery. She is dragged before Jesus of Nazareth by an angry crowd, who ask Jesus how she should be punished, reminding him that the usual custom would be to stone her to death. Recall how Jesus replies: 'Let the one who is without sin cast the first stone' (John 8.8). Williams focuses on another part of the story. He writes, 'When the accusation is made, Jesus at first makes no reply but writes with his finger on the ground. What on earth is he doing?'[20] This emphasis on a small detail in the text is often overlooked by biblical scholars, but Williams suggests it shows that Jesus hesitates. He does not get caught up in the intensity of the moment:

> Jesus does not draw a line, fix an interpretation, tell the woman who she is and what her fate should be. He allows a moment, a longish moment, in which people are given time to see themselves differently precisely because he refuses to make the sense they want. When he lifts his head, there is both judgement and release . . . So this is writing in the dust because it tries to hold that moment for a little longer, long enough for some of our demons to walk away.

Williams thinks that this act of Jesus – of writing in the dust as a way to defuse a tense situation and allow people to arrive at a place where they can think more clearly – was a 'radical Act' in the sense that Žižek might use the term. It did not grasp at the immediate options that presented themselves, but interrupted the momentum and panic of the moment by focusing on ways to be constructive. Jesus neither zealously followed what seemed the obvious thing to do based on the crowd's interpretation of the Jewish law, nor did he simply tell them that law was irrelevant (which would have only incensed them further). Instead, Jesus found a creative and new third option. Williams suggests that it is this kind of act that is a helpful response to the attacks of September 11. This, for him, is what it means to fall back on the faith in God which Christians are called to embody. Such hesitation and calm prior to acting, Williams suggests, is the promise and life-giving contribution that faith can contribute during times of crisis.

Williams hopes that, in the aftermath of a catastrophe, the Christian religion will help human beings to avoid allowing the stress and fear they feel to overwhelm or control them. He acknowledges that this is difficult to avoid, for 'drama is another addictive drug in all sorts of contexts.'[21] In a world where death is the inevitable end point of life, and in which terrible tragedies unfortunately occur, he suggests that people must learn to respond to these difficult realities in a way that does not control them – either through fear and anxiety, or due to a determined effort to ignore reality. He praises those who, despite the suffering in the world, are able 'to practice living in the presence of death'.[22] Such a capacity does not ignore suffering, but does what it can to combat it, only in a manner that does not demand 'dramatic immortality' for itself or become a prideful mission on behalf of a great 'cause'. This is to say that such a response does not instrumentalize the suffering in the name of some self-serving agenda (including one's own sense of self-worth), nor does it allow the present difficult moment to define the entirety of the world.

Williams hopes that Christian theology and the church might assist people to develop such a capacity to respond to tragedies in the world. He thinks an important role for theology is to help 'train ourselves in becoming familiar with risk and death, so that we recognize what needs to be done in a crisis'.[23] This is his version of 'doing theology as if nothing has happened'. It is not to ignore the tragedy that presents itself, nor is it to minimize it; rather, such an approach shifts the focus of theology – but also of human emotional response – away from a preoccupation with explaining suffering, and towards a determination to help do what is possible to ameliorate it. Theology is to be primarily concerned with helping Christians become the sort of people who do not panic when confronted with death, but who have the capacity to respond to it with maturity and wisdom, so as not to be consumed by it.

Williams is not ignorant of the fact that such a way of responding to a crisis is extraordinarily difficult to manage. Often it is only conceivable that bystanders will have the capacity to respond in this way, rather than those most impacted by the trauma. This is why he speaks metaphorically about the need to be 'trained' to achieve such a way of life. For him, this goes to the core of what religion is about, for in his view, one's faith involves not only belief in God, but also includes the desire to become the sort of person God calls one to be. The 'religious' problem presented by panic in the face of a disaster, therefore, is that it results in a 'loss of self'. When one is consumed by fear, anger or hatred, it is such negative emotions that are in control of one's self, not the vision of life one desires and longs for. Williams writes,

> Authentic religious (in this case, Christian) practice begins in the attempt to attend to the moment of self-questioning – to refuse to cover over, evade, or explain the pain and shock of whatever brings the self into question, to hold on to the difficulty before the almost inevitable descent into pathos and personal drama begins.[24]

Being able to engage with one's life in a way that attends to more than the dramas, fears or frustrations of the given moment is what, for Williams, marks the sign of a healthy spiritual life. What Christianity can help people do, he hopes, is to learn to live in a way that makes this possible. Williams suggests that a successful experience of psychological counselling might be described as undertaking 'planned frustration' for the sake of healing.[25] Drawing from this image, the proper function of theology can be described as serving to assist Christians to engage in a reflective 'planned frustration', which interrupts the ideologies they must confront in times of crisis.

Theology as Wounded Speech

Williams warns that, when speaking about God in a crisis or a time of terror, 'it becomes very important to know how to use the language of belief'.[26] The primary error to avoid, in his view, is the temptation to 'bind God to our own purposes'. This is no easy task, and he has already admitted that people want God to be 'useful' to them in a crisis. 'Why else have faith?' someone might ask. Not being able to control, or at least be able to anticipate, the way the world works understandably challenges what many think religion is supposed to offer: reassurance that things will work out as they should, because God is in control. This is why learning that Christian faith is not founded on, nor does it guarantee, a stable and peaceful world usually requires a willingness to engage in some 'planned frustration'.

In a critical analysis of the theodicy of Mary McCord Adams, Williams demonstrates how difficult it is to embody this sort of attitude, even at the theoretical level. For even a theologian as sensitive and thoughtful as Adams is unable to avoid the temptation to cover over the wounds that suffering causes. This tendency develops when she succumbs to the enticement to speak as if knowledge of God makes all things acceptable, or at least bearable. Adams intends to construct a Christology that is mindful of the horrors that occur in the world. In her view, the only thing that can make life worth living in the face of horrendous evil is to know that even these horrors are 'incommensurate' with the goodness of God. This is to say that, although nothing 'of this world' is capable of compensating for the terrible evils people must suffer, people can be comforted by the knowledge of two things: that divine Goodness beyond the present situation outweighs the evil within it, and that God identifies with the suffering of human beings, which enables God to 'endow the worst that creatures can suffer, be, or do with great positive meaning.'[27] Williams presents three reasons to reject the position presented by Adams, with its 'promised post-mortem beatitude'. First, he argues that Adams privileges the perspective of the observer, rather than that of the person who suffers; second, the emphasis on God's presence in suffering devalues the particular suffering of the individual human being; third, it reduces God's role to a 'balancing act', so that divine providence becomes a task of reacting to historical tragedies. It is instructive to linger over each issue in turn.

Adams privileges the observer's point of view, Williams argues, when she proceeds as if the theologian is able to weigh what proportion of divine Goodness is required in order to balance a given amount of human suffering. Williams acknowledges that Adams herself observes that different people respond to suffering in different ways, so that no two people can be assumed to 'experience' suffering in precisely the same way. Yet this recognition does not prevent her from comparing

differing levels of suffering, or of emphasizing God's capacity to provide a level of relief that is incommensurate with any suffering one
may experience. Williams argues, against Adams, that the recognition
that people respond in diverse ways 'ought to suggest that we abandon the pseudo-aesthetic mode in talking about such matters.'[28] Any
'calculus' that weighs the balance between the level of 'good' and 'bad'
experiences turns theology to a 'language of proportion', which only
the objective standpoint of the distant theologian can measure. As
such, the theologian is put in the position of evaluating and measuring
the level of suffering experienced by another human being, and then
uses that measurement for the purpose of positive theological speech
about the divine.

The discussion of trauma in Chapter Six has, hopefully, helped to
clarify why this is a problem. Rambo observes that trauma causes
suffering that is 'not fully masterable by cognition'. It can cause dis-
tortions in memory or in one's sense of identity, and may linger in a
person's psyche long after the event causing the trauma has passed.[29]
Some events may be traumatic for certain individuals, while the same
situation does not impact on another person in the same manner. The
complexities of such forms of suffering make the sort of emphasis
on 'proportional' levels of suffering that the Christology of Adams
depends on highly questionable.

The discussion in Chapter Three of the philosophy of Emil Fackenheim
illustrated some significant problems with any theodicy that deals with
suffering by arguing that human beings are comforted by the knowledge that God suffers with them. Williams is sensitive to this concern
in his criticism of Adams. He argues that her theology essentially suggests that suffering cannot be thought of as separating human beings
from the divine, because, through the incarnation, God in Christ par-
ticipates fully in the fragility and vulnerability of suffering creation.
Essentially, this point is followed with the affirmation that God 'feels
our pain' and knows exactly what it is that any individual human
being is experiencing. Finally, it is inferred that this somehow brings
one closer to the 'inner life' of God. The problem with such a theodicy,
according to Williams, is that it once again acts as if the observing
theologian is able evaluate and measure another person's suffering,
without taking that individual's own description of their situation
sufficiently seriously.[30] This devalues the particular history of the individual and suggests that different levels of suffering are proportional
to each other. The caution Williams is offering is essentially this: that

theology cannot tell those who are suffering, irrespective of their own account of their situation, how God heals them or makes their suffering meaningful.

The BBC journalist Johnston McKay tells a story about the biblical scholar William Barclay, whose daughter drowned while sailing in Northern Ireland. Of the story about Jesus calming a storm to comfort the frightened disciples, Barclay once remarked, 'If Jesus stilled a storm once upon a time, that doesn't do much for me.'[31] Recall from Chapter Two how Studdert Kennedy answered a wounded man's question, 'What is God like', by pointing to a crucifix, and how unhelpful that man found his answer. Being told that 'God is with you' or 'feels your pain' may be meaningful to some, but others may find it brings little comfort to a person in agony. For Williams, to insist that it should is both insensitive and theologically suspect.

A third objection to the theodicy of Adams that Williams mentions is that her image of God and of providential divine action 'is essentially reactive'.[32] This concern is raised following statements by Adams like the following:

> Given our record to date, for God to continue a radical non-interference policy would be to turn the alleged divine aim at loving and creative relationships from an intention to a pious hope or idle wish.[33]

There are numerous problems with this position, some of which Williams addresses. The first issue he raises is that this statement implies an image of the divine in which God is an agent in the same way as human beings, so that God acts in time and space just as people do. This implies, Williams says, that God inhabits a context or an environment, just like human beings, and is compelled to respond to that environment as events within it unfold. In opposition to such an image of the divine, Williams argues that God's action is identical with God's being, which means that 'what God does is nothing other than God's being actively real.'[34]

Beyond this theological objection to the way Adams conceives of divine action, there is also a moral problem with it. In the same PBS documentary that features Irwin Kula, another Jewish Rabbi, Brad Hirschfield, describes how he hears many people in New York City ascribe 'miraculous acts' of divine intervention during the events of 9/11:

people come and say, 'I feel I was saved by God because my wife called me and sent me to the market' – this is a real story. Someone calls me and explains to me, 'I was saved by God on Sept. 11. My wife called me, and reached me between Metro North. When I got on the subway to go downtown to stop and do an errand, that was the hand of God.'[35]

Hirschfield admits to feeling the compelling emotional power of such stories, but he also acknowledges a real problem with this understanding of divine action:

what do you say to the person who's the wife who didn't call the husband, or the husband who didn't call the wife, and who now just has a photograph and not even a body to bury? That God didn't love them? They were being punished for some sin?

This is a problem with many theodicies, as well as with the way in which Adams conceives of divine activity and providence. Hirschfield's subsequent remarks highlight the depth of the moral problem:

If you're going to tell me about how the plan saved you, you'd better also be able to explain how the plan killed them. And the test of that has nothing to do with saying it in your synagogue or your church. The test of that has to do with going and saying it to the person who just buried someone and look in their eyes and tell them, 'God's plan was to blow your loved one apart.' Look at them and tell them that God's plan was that their children should go to bed every night for the rest of their lives without a parent. If you can say that, well, at least you're honest. I don't worship the same God. But that at least has integrity.

This is one reason that Williams resists the way in which Adams describes divine action. God's actions simply cannot be employed as a 'balancing factor' to restore confidence that God is actively doing things to make sure the world has more Good in it than Evil, or that God will act at some point in historical time to compensate all the suffering than people have endured.[36] To make this argument, one had better be prepared to look into the eyes of someone in agony and try to tell them that, somehow, God has a plan for their suffering.

If this is not what ought to be said, then what would Williams suggest? It should be clear by now that he does not recommend one respond to tragedy by constructing a theodicy. He notes that 'the problem of theodicy is not experienced as such by those for whom, according to all the discussions, it ought to be an agonising primary question.'[37] This is to say that a theodicy is generally written and demanded by observers of human tragedy, not those who are presently suffering from it directly. In the biblical story, Job's friends are the ones who compose possible theodicies, not Job himself. On this point, Williams makes an astute observation about Adams's work. He suggests that she 'seems to presuppose that the purpose of theodicy is to make the world of human experience capable of being contemplated without despair.'[38] Such an assumption or goal, however, acts as if a good theodicy is capable of making everything seem acceptable, as if to say, 'if only you understood the situation properly, you would agree that the situation isn't as bad as it seems.'

Williams argues, alternatively, that rather than constructing a theodicy, theology should instead focus on the question of 'how we remain faithful to *human* ways of seeing suffering'. The task of 'a good theology', he continues, is to 'reacquaint us with our own materiality and mortality'.[39] Such as task involves learning how to 'grieve properly', by which he means, 'to grieve without the consolation of drama, martyrdom, resentment and projection'.[40] This form of grieving makes one more human, because it is not just for oneself – i.e. it is not merely self-directed and self-absorbed (what Freud called melancholy[41]) – but the grief is focused on those other people one is connected to and whose experiences one is concerned with.

To a significant degree, theology, as Williams employs it, is wounded speech, rather than a language of consolation. It seeks after a 'knowledge of suffering as without explanation or compensation', and ensures that it sees 'suffering always in its historical particularity'.[42] The language of theology cannot become, therefore, a form of speech that explains why suffering exists in the world, or why an earthquake killed *these* people, but not *those* people. Instead, Williams argues that theology must remain open to the perspective of the sufferer and be worried more about suffering and evil, so as to be compelled to try to ameliorate or challenge them, rather than constructing theoretical accounts of their meaning. In this regard, his emphasis on attending to the particularities of historical suffering shares much in common with the *memoria passionis* as understood by Metz. The language of theology cannot eliminate the pain of seemingly senseless suffering in the world. As such, it is always incomplete. Theology as a way of speaking is itself challenged and broken by the wounds it witnesses to.

What does such a manner of speaking about God look like? Unfortunately, Williams has had occasion to be called upon to provide us with an example.

Speaking of God after 7/7: 'The Language of Wounds'

On 7 July 2005, fifty-two people were killed by four suicide bomb explosions in London, and seven hundred and seventy others were injured. Three bombs were denoted on the London Underground at 8:50 am, during the busy morning rush hour. Just under one hour later, another bomb exploded on a double-decker bus. The bombers were all Muslim residents of the United Kingdom, none of whom were previously suspected of criminal activity by the authorities. Two of the men left behind pre-recorded video messages, which were aired on the television network *Al Jazeera*. In these testimonies, the men explain that they were motivated by a desire to protest British atrocities against Muslims throughout the world and to condemn the support of the UK government for the rulers of Saudi Arabia, as well as by the teachings of Osama bin Laden.

In his capacity as Archbishop of Canterbury, Rowan Williams is a significant public figure in the United Kingdom, and it was thus incumbent upon him to offer some public reaction to the attacks. One prominent occasion occurred on 1 November, during a memorial service on All Soul's Day in St. Paul's Cathedral. In his sermon, Williams does not try to explain why the victims of the attacks were made to suffer, nor does he suggest that their deaths had any meaning. No theodicy is presented; rather, he admits quite directly that

> those who so pointlessly and terribly died were, each one of them, precious, non-replaceable . . . Time gives perspective and may bring healing; but the trauma of violence, and even more the death of someone we love makes a difference that nothing will ever completely unmake.[43]

Williams quotes from the poet W. H. Auden, adding that 'the language of wounds' will continue to haunt all those who mourn the terrible event. What is noteworthy is the way in which he describes how the 'language of wounds' not only expresses grief, but also 'resists terror'. In this his own version of *memoria passionis*, one observes how the emphasis that Williams makes on attending to the particularities of historical suffering becomes a resource for theology. In his view, attention to suffering and taking it seriously inherently involves a critique and protest against those actions which inflicted the suffering. At the same time, it also inversely points towards a different vision of the world.

Williams contrasts the attitude exhibited by the terrorists on 7/7 with that of those who have gathered to mourn at St. Paul's. He emphasizes how the suicide bombers treated their victims as anonymous and faceless; 'the shock of terrorist violence is just this sense of arbitrariness'. The fact that they killed Christians, Muslims, Hindus and atheists was irrelevant to them. Their victims were not particular human beings, but merely generic objects to kill in order to get the attention of the world. As such, he observes, the terrorists are not simply attacking a system or government, but 'the whole idea that we are each of us unique and responsible and non-replaceable'. When people gather to remember and mourn those who were killed, however, they are demonstrating and embodying the falsity of the terrorist attitude towards human life: 'We are here grieving, after all, because those who so pointlessly and terribly died were, each one of them, precious, non-replaceable.' By uttering 'the language of wounds', one articulates a protest against actions which ignore the value of human life. This implies commitment to the view that 'Every life is a special sort of gift.' This, for Williams, is the purpose and function of speaking religiously during a time of terror; 'When we behave as if that were true, we do what's most important for the defeat of terror and indiscriminate violence.'

Such acts of memory demonstrate 'that death, even violent and untimely death, cannot destroy our relationships at the most important level; that love is indeed, as the Bible says, strong as death.' This suggests that what is to be feared most during a time of terror is not death, for it cannot destroy the love one has for other human beings; rather, the more sinister danger about such a tragedy is that the pain, anger and fear it causes can transform and control the hearts and minds of those it engulfs and cause them to lose their vision and commitment to the idea that all human beings are unique and worthy of respect. In this caution, Williams is alerting his audience to the dangers of the way in which trauma and fear can unleash aggression and anger against other people. He is concerned to prevent the British people from succumbing to the dynamics of dualistic Us/Them thinking which was analysed in Chapter Four; he wants to encourage his audience to avoid responding to their pain in ways that resemble 'road rage'; he hopes that people will not turn to their religion 'too quickly' in order to construct a God that will be 'useful' to them, but will in reality be nothing but an ideological idol.

On the Demand to Speak Positively

In the previous chapter, in the examination of Metz's emphasis on the memory of past suffering, the question arose over the extent to which theology ought to provide 'positive' direction and consolation in the face of catastrophe. In order to begin to address this issue, the discussion will now depart away from the theology of Williams, although the way in which he responded to 7/7 already hints at how the question of positivity will be addressed in what follows.

The demand to 'say something positive' presumes that theology possesses an answer to suffering that should satisfy everyone or that can resolve any agony someone is experiencing. As demonstrated in the critique of the theodicy of Adams, however, the presumption that theology can provide an answer to how another person experiences their suffering requires that theologians privilege their own perspective over that of the person in distress. There is still another issue that emerges out of the analysis of the work of Adams: that certain 'answers' can only work for certain people (because they experience their own suffering in differing ways). This raises the question of the 'truthfulness' of any such answer. The theologian might, for example, say something that 'works' for a certain individual (in the sense of making them 'feel better' or 'accept' their situation more easily), but which does not help another person in the same way. But does the fact that this answer does or does not 'work' demonstrate whether or not it is 'true'? Recall the discussion of ideology in Chapter Five: how ideology often functions to 'repair' the holes in one's worldview, in order to cover over disturbing issues one would prefer not to have to deal with. Similarly, in Chapter Six, Barth warned against the tendency of 'religion' to function like an 'addictive drug' (or, as Marx would put it, an 'opiate'). These observations suggest that caution is required prior to assuming that ways of speaking which 'work' are necessarily signs of theology's truth or faithfulness.

In his reflections on the impact of Auschwitz on philosophy, Theodor Adorno raises a problem at the heart of the demand that theology be able to speak 'a positive message' in times of crisis. He argues that clichés, such as 'there are no atheists in foxholes' or 'danger teaches us to pray', are illogical

> because the situations in which people are forced to think 'positively' simply in order to survive are themselves situations of compulsion, which force people back on pure self-preservation . . . to a point where the *truth content* of what they think is hopelessly undermined and utterly destroyed.[44]

This is to say that the demand to say something positive, in the absence of any basis upon which to say it, is merely an act of desperation, not an act of resistance; nor is it an example of speaking theologically with integrity. For besides the moral and logical problem with speaking positively for positivity's sake, there is a theological issue here as well. For theological speech, if motivated by a felt need to say something consoling, cannot be said to be speech that is motivated by 'faith seeking understanding'. It is the precise opposite of Barth's concern to 'do theology as if nothing has happened'. Adorno and his colleague Max Horkheimer articulated this rather bluntly when they wrote, 'When language grows apologetic, it is already corrupted.' Because of this, in their view, 'There is only one expression for truth: the thought which repudiates injustice.'[45]

An obvious rebuttal to this argument would be to insist upon the need to offer people hope in a time of terror. Jürgen Moltmann, for example, suggests that a Christian interpretation of 9/11 must view the tragedy from an eschatological perspective. In direct opposition to Adorno's statement that 'There is no true life in the life that is false', Moltmann argues that Christian hope in Christ 'is the real beginning of true life in the very midst of this false life'. He continues, 'In the light of the resurrected Christ, we perceive the world under the cross.' This allows the Christian to recognize that the crucified God suffers with them, and that, through the resurrection, 'Christian hope recognises the deliverance from evil that is present in the beginning of the new life and the new creation of all things.'[46]

Moltmann's position is a powerful reading of the Christian tradition, but note that it implies a similar theodicy to that of Mary McCord Adams. The suffering of human beings is consoled by pointing to the fact that Christ also suffered. Furthermore, Moltmann implies that when we understand 'the resurrection of Christ as a divine process of transformation from mortality to immortality and from shame to glory', this perspective should allow the Christian to be immune from despair over the state of world. That Moltmann's 'balancing act' privileges the observer's perspective becomes clear when he assimilates the experience of Jewish children in the Holocaust with the resurrected Christ:

> The children in the concentration camp of Theresienstadt painted butterflies in the face of their death: when the poor caterpillar dies, the beautiful butterfly is born and will fly into freedom.[47]

At this point, the danger of falling into the trap of a 'language of proportion' becomes all too clear. Moltmann constructs a terribly unfortunate metaphorical formula: the suffering of Jesus on the cross is comparable to the suffering of children in Theresienstadt, which is comparable to the metamorphosis of a caterpillar (and is it necessary to point out that here the caterpillar does not 'die' but undergoes metamorphism?). Whose perspective is privileged in such a rendering, and for what purpose? As was the case with Adams, such an equation sublates human suffering into the being of God, which is the sort of theological move that Metz argues becomes an 'almost Gnostic reconciliation with God behind the back of the human history of suffering'.[48] By contrast, Metz insists that theology cannot engage in dispensing hope and consolation in such a fashion; 'Not even Christian theology can allow Job's question to God, "How long yet?" to fall silent in a soothing answer.'[49]

Does calling for reserve on the part of theology against dispensing messages of hope and consolation imply that life is hopeless in the face of catastrophe, or that hope for the future ought to be discouraged? Charles Mathewes warns against a tendency among Christian intellectuals to fall victim to a form of Gnosticism that recoils from the horrors of the world, and describes a vision of radical estrangement, 'a sense that the world is not properly one's home.'[50] This is an important caution, but this is not what is being encouraged here. A more nuanced approach to the question of hope demonstrates how this is so.

Hoping Against Hope

The apostle Paul describes the patriarch Abraham's reaction to his call by God as 'hoping against hope' (Rom. 4.8). When Abraham is promised that his descendents will be as numerous as the stars (Gen.15.5),

Paul writes, 'he did not weaken in faith when he considered his own body, which was already good as dead' (Rom. 4.19). Abraham sees the reality of his own situation clearly and acknowledges the barrenness of his wife, Sarah. He has no idea how the strange divine promise could possibly be fulfilled. He and his partner can only proceed 'as if' this promise can be achieved. He has no reason to hope, but will proceed as though he can trust that the unexpected is nevertheless possible.

Such a hoping against hope is the way to conceive of the impulse of longing for a better future in a manner that avoids the tendency to impose an 'observer's perspective' on suffering and which avoids the danger of presenting the world as if one is radically estranged from it. Hoping against hope is a stance which protests against what ought not to be. Rather than resting on an assured 'positive' message, it is rather a negative theology of the future, one which knows less about what is to come, not more, but which also interrupts despair and suspicion of one's environment. Hoping against hope emerges from a perspective that acknowledges the particularities of the sufferings of the world as they present themselves, so as to avoid the temptation to cover over the wounds of history, or to sublate them into a consoling narrative. Hope in the mode of negation results from a recognition of the catastrophic nature of time. Such a vision of the future is not based on continuity with what is known in the present, nor is it allowed to simply become a statement of wish-fulfilment. As Metz describes it, such a perspective establishes 'prohibitions against thinking of the future as an empty screen upon which images can be projected.'[51] This is to say that when theology speaks of such hope, it shuns the construction of any blueprints of what the future will look like or positive expectations of what will be. That this is a difficult attitude to sustain is witnessed to by recalling that neither Abraham nor Sarah modelled such a perspective flawlessly. Considerable suffering and pain resulted when, growing impatient with their ongoing childlessness, they conspired to use their slave Hagar as a surrogate mother, only to banish both she and Ishmael when Abraham's 'real' son Isaac was finally born (Gen. 15 and 21). At this point, Sarah and Abraham are no longer living in the mode of hoping against hope, but have shifted to projecting their own blueprint onto the blank screen of the future. The result is that they are no longer cognizant of the suffering dwelling among them in the present time, including that of Hagar and her young son Ishmael. That the text describes how God refuses to forget the suffering of these victims of Abraham and Sarah's actions demonstrates how the biblical story itself subtly criticizes an instrumental approach to hope in the

mode of 'positivity'. Is a positive ontology, therefore, really a require-
ment for moral judgement and for theology?

Moltmann presents an argument in his theology of hope that could
be taken as an interjection at this point. In his presentation of a more
positive theological vision, he writes, 'We first perceive the darkness of
the night in the light of the new day. We recognise evil only in the light
of the good, and we feel the deadliness of death only through our love
for life.'[52] This statement not only raises a challenge to Metz's position,
it also recalls an argument mentioned in Chapter One, when Nieman
suggests that a judgement that something should not have happened
can only be posited on the basis of a positive order of things. Does this
challenge demand that theology maintain a more 'positive' approach
to speaking about God, despite the issues raised here?

There is a sense in which Metz himself grants this point. He suggests
that his own emphasis on *memoria passionis* should be conceived in
relation to a *memoria resurrectionis* ('memory of the resurrection'),
because 'a resurrection faith is expressed inasmuch as it acts "counter-
factually" in making us bear in mind the sufferings and hopes of the
past.' In this position, there is a glimpse of a 'positive order of things',
which is offered as a contrast to the sufferings of the world; but note
that it is a rather weak version, presented in a tentative and fragmen-
tary manner. Metz argues that to speak of the resurrection means that
the dead 'have a meaning that is as yet unrealised'; it is to say that
history 'does not depend only on the survivors'.[53] In this rendering,
resurrection is more a hoping against hope than present fulfilment. In
his view, to say more risks reducing theology to ideology. His 'eschatological reserve' goes all the way down; he refuses to say more about
what resurrection means for the dead, or how it might account for,
or heal, past sufferings. Offering anything more 'positive' than this,
for him, is a political task, which can only be lived by acting to resist
suffering; it cannot be existentially or metaphysically articulated as a
blueprint prior to such action.

This position of Metz is illuminated still further by returning to the
thought of Theodor Adorno. For Adorno, 'negative dialectics', which
refuses to ground philosophy on any sort of positive foundation, helps
to clarify why failing to speak positively does not imply that philosophy
abandons itself to despair. In response to Moltmann's assertion that 'we
recognise evil only in light of the good', Adorno's thought implies that
the opposite is the case. In a world in which ideology abounds, and
where even the beautiful forms of human culture can become reduced
to supporting acts of terror (Islam employed to fly passenger planes

into buildings, Christianity used to legitimate slavery, Bach's music to entertain prison guards at Auschwitz), human thought and emotion get easily distracted from things they would prefer not to recognize. For this reason, Adorno argues that 'Thought as such, before all particular contents, is an act of negation, of resistance to that which is forced upon it.' In a phrase that could be taken as a summary of Metz's concept of *memoria passionis*, Adorno adds, 'The need to lend a voice to suffering is the condition of all truth.'[54] Such a perspective inverts that of Moltmann. Recognition of the good emerges out of opposition to the bad. Only in this way can religion be thought of as an 'interrupting' catastrophe, or theology as being 'surprised by grace'.

It might be tempting to dismiss this position as being 'mere negativity', but Adorno argues that his 'inverse theology' offers brief glimpses of a better possible world, which nurture and sustain the capacity to carry on living despite the terrible state of the world.[55] Criticizing what one knows to be false carries within it a subtle recognition of what ought-to-be, or more precisely as Adorno conceives of it, one catches a brief glimpse of the possibility of a better world through the act of criticizing present injustice. Thus, although Adorno's 'anti-theodicy' offers no 'positive' consolations for suffering, he does not think this leaves one abandoned to one's fate. In the face of a seemingly meaningless or absurd world, the cry, 'Is that all?' manifests itself as a negative illumination of the fact that the world could be otherwise. And when thought is not distracted by the desire to 'explain' the meaning of this suffering, it is motivated to get on with the task of seeking to actively diminish it.

If this view sounds overly abstract, or seems to be at some distance from the earlier discussion in this chapter, a brief return to Williams's 7/7 memorial sermon helps illustrate Adorno's point. Recall how Williams draws a negative contrast between the attitude of the terrorists towards their victims – so that the victims become anonymous and without value – and the reaction of horror articulated by many as a protest against the murders. He suggests that it is the negative critique against this horror implied by those gathered in the cathedral which illuminates a deep commitment to a view of human beings as non-interchangeable and unique. This is a way of speaking theologically that does not follow Moltmann's move from positivity to negative criticism, but proceeds in the opposite direction. As Adorno would present the matter: 'How could I love good if I did not hate evil?'[56] On this point, one also recalls a tragic phenomenon about human relationships: one frequently does not fully appreciate how important someone is to one-self, until one loses them or feels the danger of losing them.

When is Life Grievable?

Making this emphasis requires a return to the challenge encountered in Chapter Six, when Sontag pointed to the problem that witnessing suffering does not automatically cause people to feel empathy.[57] In her own reflections on Sontag's essay, Judith Butler highlights how this problem illuminates how the way in which suffering is presented affects one's responsiveness to it. Her concern in this discussion has less to do with the failure of some images to impact on the emotions of people, and more with how any such emotional response frequently involves assumptions about who is sufficiently 'human' to deserve empathy. The act of judging over which examples of suffering merit attention, or indeed, over what represents unacceptable 'suffering', involves subtle acts of anthropocentrism: 'Wherever there is the human, there is the inhuman.'[58] We only grieve those we think belong to 'us'; those to whom we feel connected; those who matter because they are like us. If one is not 'haunted' by the suffering of others, there can be no acknowledgement of loss. Thus 'grievability [is] the precondition of life.'[59]

If grief and mourning are shaped by how one 'frames' the human, then the failure of someone to be moved by the suffering of others is explained by the fact that the suffering individual is not recognized as being connected to them. Recall the terrible witness to this capacity in Chapter Three, when the discussion revisited how Jewish people were exterminated by the Nazis because they were not considered fully human. One need not feel empathy for 'Them', for they are not like 'Us'. Even witnessing 'Their' suffering may thus fail to move 'Us'.

Butler's discussion acknowledges that it is difficult to 'learn to see the frame that binds us' and prevents us from acknowledging the suffering of the other person.[60] The negative theology of the future discussed in this chapter is a perspective which helps to challenge and crack the frames which prevent theology from recognizing the suffering of the neighbour. There is no way of conceiving the world that is immune to the problem Sontag and Butler illuminate. All forms of human thought are inherently 'anthropocentric' and incomplete, just as Žižek's concept of the Symbolic always embodies a lack, and theology's speech of God is never adequate to its object. These limitations are no reason to abandon thought or cease to attempt to speak about God, for such a decision would simply leave one mute. But these limitations are the reason that the critical approach to theology articulated by Metz and Adorno, and to a limited degree modelled by Williams, is the appropriate way to conceive of speaking of God in a time of terror. For Butler's warning alerts one to the limitation found in Moltmann's insistence that one knows the darkness only by having seen the light; such a view already 'frames' what counts as the 'Light', and so can easily succumb to failing to perceive good things among what initially appears as 'darkness'.

Adorno offers a metaphor to describe the state of post-Holocaust philosophy, and it is one that can be usefully applied to theology. Speaking to an audience of German students, he warns against imagining that 'if only the debris of culture could be finally cleared away access could be gained to the original truth.' Adorno compares the philosopher who thinks one can simply 'clean up' the past and 'start over again' with the image of people in the immediate postwar years scrambling to gather up the rubble of the buildings in order to rebuid them with the same material.[61] He then adds, however, that this ought not to be misunderstood in order to rebuild them with the same material as implying that everything that German culture is destroyed and worthless, and should be thus left on the scrap heap. His position is not the view that, 'in negativity one encounters positivity'(i.e. that starting again demands jettisoning the past entirely); rather, he argues that it is in the capacity and willingness to confront the negativity and protest against it that human thought can continue on with integrity. He thus offers an image to complement that of living in the midsr of rubble and ruins:

> there is really no other possibility, no opportunity . . . [than] to work one's way through the darkness without a lamp, without possessing the positive through the higher concept of the negation of negation, and to immerse oneself in the darkness as deeply as one can.[62]

Call this 'planned frustration', *memoria passionis*, 'hoping against hope', or simply mature critical thought; it is, however, the way for theology to inhabit what Rambo calls the 'middle space' of trauma. In such a way of conceiving the work of theology, not as much can be said about a situation as one would want to be able to say, nor will it be as positive a contribution as many will want it to be or, indeed, as many understandably will demand it to be. In my view, however, it is the only way to speak of God at ground zero in a way we can realistically hope does not contribute further to the suffering of the world and which just might serve to illuminate, if only momentarily, a sense that the current catastrophe is not all that there is.

Notes

[1] Rowan Williams, *Writing in the Dust: after September 11* (Grand Rapids, MI: Eerdmans, 2002), 8–9.

[2] Ibid., 5.

[3] Ibid.

[4] Ibid., 6.

[5] Ibid., 3.

[6] The interview is available at: http://www.pbs.org/wgbh/pages/frontline/shows/faith/interviews/kula.html [last accessed 4 December 2010]. The documentary *Faith and Doubt at Ground Zero*, written by Helen Whitney and Ron Rosenbaum, first aired 3 September 2002 on PBS's 'Frontline' (USA).

[7] Williams, *Writing in the Dust*, 12.

[8] Richard Dawkins, 'Religion's Misguided Missiles', *The Guardian* 15 September 2001.

[9] Peter Sloterdijk, *God's Zeal: The Battle of the Three Monotheisms*, trans. Wieland Hoban (Cambridge: Polity, 2009), 82.

[10] Ibid., 96.

[11] Ibid., 144.

[12] Vincent Cornell, 'A Muslim to Muslims: Reflections after September 11', *Dissent from the Homeland*, Stanley Hauerwas and Frank Lenticchia (eds) (Durham, NC: Duke University Press, 2002), 328.

[13] Ibid., 329.

[14] Ibid., 330.

[15] Ibid., 335. When making this point, Cornell observes that many Islamic radicals are engineers and computer programmers – i.e. people whose skills often focus on controlling events in the world. For a discussion of this phenomenon, see Diego Gambetta and Steffan Hertog, 'Why are There so Many engineers among Islamic Radicals', *Archive for.european.sociology* L, 2 (2009), 201–30.

[16] Ibid., 332. For an intriguing discussion of a version of Christian supremacy from medieval Poland that was developed precisely to legitimize the toleration of non-Christian people, see Michael Ostling, 'Be Kind to the Antichrist: Millenarianism and Religious Tolerance in the Edict of Pskov', *Studies in Religion/Sciences Religieuses* 30.3–4 (2001), 261–76.

[17] Rowan Williams, *Lost Icons* (Harrisburg, MA: Morehouse Pub., 2000), 141–3.

[18] Williams, *Writing in the Dust*, 6.

[19] Ibid., 19.

[20] Ibid., 78.

[21] Ibid., 42.

[22] Ibid., 43.

[23] Ibid., 44.

[24] Williams, *Lost Icons*, 149.

25 Ibid., 150.
26 Williams, *Writing in the Dust*, 11.
27 Mary McCord Adams, 'Evil and the God-who-does-nothing-in-particular', in *Religion and Morality*, ed. D. Z. Philips (New York: St. Martin's Press, 1996), 114–15; quoted in Rowan Williams, *Wrestling with Angels: Conversations in Modern Theology*, ed. Mike Higton (London: SCM Press, 2007), 256. See also Mary McCord Adams, *Christ and Horrors: The Coherence of Christology* (Cambridge: Cambridge University Press, 2006).
28 Williams, *Wrestling with Angels*, 257.
29 Shelly Rambo, *Spirit and Trauma*, (Louisville, KY: Westminster John Knox Press, 2010) 29–32.
30 Ibid., 262.
31 Johnston McKay, *Glimpses of Hope: God Beyond Ground Zero* (Edinburgh: St. Andrew Press, 2002), 128.
32 Williams, *Wrestling with Angels*, 266.
33 Adams, 'Evil and the God-who-does-nothing-in-particular', 119; quoted in Williams, *Wrestling with Angels*, 264.
34 Williams, *Wrestling with Angels*, 268.
35 http://www.pbs.org/wgbh/pages/frontline/shows/faith/interviews/hirschfield.html [accessed 11 December 2010].
36 Williams, *Wrestling with Angels*, 270.
37 Ibid., 271.
38 Ibid.
39 Ibid.
40 Williams, *Writing in the Dust*, 72.
41 Sigmund Freud, 'Mourning and Melancholia', in *The Standard Edition of the Complete Psychological Works of Sigmund Freud*, ed. James Strachey, vol. XIV (London: Hogarth, 1966), 237–58.
42 Williams, *Wrestling with Angels*, 272.
43 Rowan Williams, 'Today Is Not an Occasion for Us to Focus on Fear', *The Guardian* 1 November 2005. http://www.guardian.co.uk/uk/2005/nov/01/july7.politics [accessed 10 December 2010].
44 Theodor W. Adorno, *Metaphysics: Concepts and Problems*, trans. Edmund Jephcott, ed. Rolf Tiedemann (Stanford, CA: Stanford University Press, 2000), 124.
45 Theodor W. Adorno and Max Horkheimer, *Dialectic of Enlightenment: Philosophical Fragments*, trans. Edmund Jephcott, ed. Gunselin Schmid Noerr (Stanford, CA: Stanford University Press, 2002), 181.
46 Jürgen Moltmann, 'Hope in a Time of Arrogance and Terror', in *Strike Terror no More: Theology, Ethics, and the New War*, ed. Jon L. Berquist (St. Louis, MO: Chalice Press, 2002), 178.
47 Ibid., 179.
48 Johannes Baptist Metz, *A Passion for God*, trans. Matthew Ashley (New York: Continuum, 1995), 69.
49 Ibid., 71.
50 Charles T. Mathewes, 'Christian Intellectuals and Escapism after 9/11', *Strike Terror no More*, ed. Jon L. Brequist (St. Louis, MO: Chalicw Press, 2002), 310.
51 Metz, *Faith in History and Society: Towards a practical Fundamental Theology* (New York: Seabury Press, 1980), 176.
52 Moltmann, 'Hope in a Time of Arrogance and Terror', 179.

53 Metz, *Faith in History and Society*, 11–12.
54 Adorno, *Negative Dialectics*, 18–19.
55 For a fuller discussion of Adorno's 'inverse theology', see Christopher Craig Brittain, *Adorno and Theology* (London: T&T Clark, 2010).
56 Adorno, *Metaphysics*, 126.
57 Another useful text on this issue is Carolyn J. Dean, *The Fragility of Empathy: After the Holocaust* (Ithaca and London: Cornell University Press, 2004).
58 Judith Butler, *Frames of War: When is Life Grievable?* (London and New York: Verso, 2009), 76.
59 Ibid., 98.
60 Ibid., 100.
61 Adorno, *Metaphysics*, 127.
62 Ibid., 144.

Afterword

Speaking Theologically in a Time of Terror

In lieu of a tidy or 'positive' conclusion, this book can only end where it began. Recall how the Introduction to this volume described my encounter with 'Roger' on 9/11, a Christian who, after the traumas of that day, began to call for the bombing of women and children in Muslim counties he could not even identify by name. His words and the look in his eyes haunted me for the rest of the day, and weighed on me when I was called upon to preach a sermon in a Christian church the very next day. The church was almost full that afternoon, and the congregation included many travellers whose planes had been grounded because of the attacks and who were staying in the hotels in the surrounding neighbourhood. 'Roger' was not in the congregation, but I was preaching to him. I conclude this book with an excerpt from that sermon, in recognition of both the inadequacy of speaking about God at such a time and also the importance of not being rendered mute in the face of people's ongoing suffering and fear.

This week it is all too evident that we have lost a great deal. We have lost our sense of security; our confidence. Our world is obviously lacking in justice and fairness. Some have lost their faith in the power of God's love and compassion; and, of course, many have lost those that they love.

At a time when so much has been lost, God needs people to continue to be *like* the shepherd who looks for the lost member of the flock; *like* the woman looking for a lost coin (Lk. 15.3–10). We all can understand the anger and despair around us, for we all to some extent share in it. But I encourage you to resist becoming like those authorities grumbling against Jesus in the story from the Gospel of Luke. They have given up the search for a better world. They will only hear what they already assume to be the case.

God is the one who continues seeking for what has been lost, and we are called upon to search along with God – to continue the search for love and compassion; for security and trust among all peoples; for justice and fairness in our world. The lesson of this week is not that we have been too narrowly 'religious'; that our societies are too welcoming to 'foreigners'; or that we have been too compassionate towards strangers. The real lesson for Christians is that our search for God's kingdom is very far from over. At such a time, the call to Christians is for them to recommit themselves to God's love; not to retreat in fear.

So today we gather together to pray, and to share in the breaking of bread at the Eucharist. And we do this, not because these acts will save us from sorrow, or make us immune to the pain and fear around us, but because our prayers and our sharing of the sacrament can save us from the power of this sorrow and fear. They can help prevent us from being controlled by the terror that confronts us. As people of faith, we are not to be transformed by the tragedies and sorrows of this world into hardened and pessimistic people. Instead, we are to be transformed by the grace of God's love into a sign of light to our troubled world. We do not know what challenges the days ahead will bring; but we are reminded today what sort of people we do not want to be, and we are reminded that the world as it looks today is not as God would have it be.

Bibliography

Adams, John Esslemont (1915), *The Chaplain and the War*. Edinburgh: T&T Clark.

Adams, Mary McCord (2006), *Christ and Horrors: The Coherence of Christology*. Cambridge: Cambridge University Press.

—(1996), 'Evil and the God-who-does-nothing-in-particular', in *Religion and Morality*, ed. D. Z. Philips. New York: St. Martin's Press, 107–131.

Addley, Esther (2010), '7/7 inquests: We know who did it and why. But this is more than just catharsis', *The Guardian* 27 October

Adorno, Theodor W. (2000), *Metaphysics: Concepts and Problems*, trans. Edmund Jephcott, ed. Rolf Tiedemann. Stanford, CA: Stanford University Press.

—(1995), *Negative Dialectics*, trans. E. B. Ashton. New York: Continuum.

—(1981), *Prisms*, trans. Samuel and Shierry Weber. Cambridge, MA: The MIT Press.

Adorno, Theodor W. and Max Horkheimer (2002), *Dialectic of Enlightenment: Philosophical Fragments*, trans. Edmund Jephcott, ed. Gunzelin Schmid Noerr. Stanford, CA: Stanford University Press.

Agamben, Giorgio (1999), *Remnants of Auschwitz: The Witness and the Archive*, trans. Daniel Heller-Roazen. New York: Zone Books.

Alexander, David (1990), 'Psychological Intervention for Victims and Helpers After Disasters', *British Journal of General Practice* 40 (August), 345–8.

Alexander, David A. and Susan Klein (2003), 'Biochemical Terrorism: Too Awful to Contemplate, Too Serious to Ignore', *British Journal of Psychiatry* 183, 491–7.

—(2005), 'The Psychological Aspects of Terrorism: from Denial to Hyperbole', *Journal of the Royal Society of Medicine* 98 (December), 557–62.

Amarasingam, Amarnath (ed.) (2010), *Religion and the New Atheism*. Leiden: Brill, 2010.

Amis, Martin (2008), *The Second Plane*. London: Vintage Books.

Anonymous (1755), *An Account of the Late Dreadful Earthquake and Fire, which Destroyed the City of Lisbon*. London: J. Payne.

—(1756), *A Letter from a Clergyman at London to the Remaining Disconsolate Inhabitants of Lisbon Occasioned by the Late Dreadfull Earthquake*. London: R. Griffiths.

—(1755), *A Letter from a Portuguese Officer to a Friend in Paris Giving an Account of the Late Dreadful Earthquake, by Which the City of Lisbon was Destroyed*. London: M. Cooper.

—(1756) *A Satirical Review of the Manifold Falshoods and Absurdities Hitherto Publish'd Concerning the Earthquake*. London: A. and C. Corbett.

Arnal, William E. (2000), 'Definition', in *Guide to the Study of Religion*. London: Cassell, 21–34.

Asad, Talal (1993), *Genealogies of Religion*. Baltimore: John Hopkins University Press.

Bailey, Charles E. (1984), 'The British Protestant Theologians in the First World War: Germanophobia Unleashed', *Harvard Theological Review* 77.2, 195–221.

—(1989), 'The Verdict of French Protestantism Against Germany in the First World War', *Church History* 58.1, 66–82.

Barth, Karl (1949), *Dogmatics in Outline*, trans. G. T. Thompson. London: SCM Press.

—(1968), *Epistle to the Romans*, trans. Edwyn C. Hoskyns. Oxford: Oxford University Press.

—(1964), *Revolutionary Theology in the Making*, trans. James D. Smart. Richmond, VA: John Knox Press.

—(1933), *Theological Existence Today*, trans. R. Birch Hoyle. London: Hodder & Stoughton.

—(1957), *The Word of God and the Word of Man*, trans. Douglas Horton. New York: Harper & Brothers Publishers.

BeDuhn, Jason David (2002), *The Manichaean Body: In Discipline and Ritual.* Baltimore: Johns Hopkins University Press.

Benjamin, Walter (1969), 'Theses on the Philosophy of History', in *Illuminations*, ed. Hannah Arendt, trans. Harry Zohn. New York: Schocken Books.

Bergen, Doris L. (ed.) (2004), *The Sword of the Lord: Military Chaplains from the First to the Twenty-First Century.* Notre Dame: IN University of Notre Dame Press.

Berhardi, Friedrich von (1914), *Germany and the Next War*, trans. Allen H. Powles. London: Edward Arnold.

Berkovits, Eliezer (1977), *Faith after the Holocaust.* Jersey City: Ktav Publishing.

Berman, Paul (2003), *Terror and Liberalism.* New York and London: W. W. Norton.

Biddulph, John(17550, *A Poem on the Earthquake at Lisbon.* London: W. Owen.]

Borradori, Giovanna (2003), *Philosophy in a Time of Terror: Dialogues with Jürgen Habermas and Jacques Derrida.* Chicago: University of Chicago Press.

Boucher, Geoff, Jason Glynos and Matthew Sharpe (eds) (2005), *Traversing the Fantasy: Critical Responses to Slavoj Žižek.* Aldershot: Ashgate.

Braiterman, Zachary (1998) *(God) After Auschwitz: Tradition and Change in Post-Holocaust Jewish Thought.* Princeton: Princeton University Press.

Brenda, Julien (1927), *La Trahison des Clercs.* Paris: Bernard Grasset.

Brittain, Christopher Craig (2010), *Adorno and Theology.* London: T&T Clark.

—(2005), 'The "Secular" as a Tragic Category: On Talal Asad, Religion and Representation', *Method and Theory in the Study of Religion* 17.2, 149–65.

Brown, J. and A. Martin (2005), 'New Orleans Residents: God's Mercy Evident in Katrina's Wake', *Agape Press.* http://headlines.agapepress.org/archive/9/22005b.asp [accessed 14 December 2005].

Brudholm, Thomas and Thomas Cushman (eds) (2009), *Religious Responses to Mass Atrocity: Interdisciplinary Perspectives.* Cambridge: Cambridge University Press.

Buber, Martin (1952), *Eclipse of God: Studies in the Relation between Religion and Philosophy.* New York and Evanston: Harper & Row.

Buck-Morss, Susan (2003), *Thinking Past Terror.* London and New York: Verso.

Busch, Eberhard (2004), *The Great Passion: An Introduction to Karl Barth's Theology*, trans. Geoffrey W. Bromiley. Grand Rapids, MI: William B. Eerdmans.

—(1976), *Karl Barth: His Life from Letters and Autobiographical Texts.* Minneapolis, MN: Fortress Press.

Bush George, (2001), 'Remarks of the President Upon Arrival http://georgewbush-whitehouse.archives.gov/news/releases/2001/09/200/0916-2.ht [last accessed 19 April 2011].

—(2001), Text of Bush's Speech,' CNN.com. http://edition.cnn.com/2001/US/09/11bush. speech.text/ [last accessed April 2011].

Buswell, Robert E. (ed.) (2003), *Encyclopedia of Buddhism*. New York: MacMillan Reference Books.

Butler, Judith (2009), *Frames of War: When is Life Grievable?* London and New York: Verso.

Calhoun, Craig, Paul Price and Ashley Timmer (eds) (2002), *Understanding September 11*, New York: W. W. Norton & Co.

Camus, Albert (1998), *Notebooks: 1935–1951*, trans. Philip Theody. New York: Marlowe & Company.

—(1957), *The Plague*, trans. Stuart Gilbert. New York: Knopf.

Carless, Martyn S., 'Tsunami: God's Anger Revealed' http://www.moriel.org/articles/discernment/church-issues/tsunami_gods_anger_revealed.ht# [last accessed 10 April 2011].

Cavanaugh, William T. (2010), *The Myth of Religious Violence*. Oxford: Oxford University Press.

Chapman, Mark D. (1995), 'Theology, Nationalism and the First World War: Christian Ethics and the Constraints of Politics', *Studies in Christian Ethics* 8, 13–35.

Chesterton, G. K. (1996), *Orthodoxy*. New York: Bantam Doubleday.

Chomsky, Noam (2001), *9/11*. New York: Open MediaSeven Stories Press, 2001.

Cohen, Arthur A. (1998), *The Cohen Reader*, ed. David Stern and Paul Mendes-Flohr. Detroit: Wayne State University Press.

—(1981), *The Tremendum*. New York: Crossroad.

Cole, Tim (1999), *Selling the Holocaust*. London: Routledge.

Columbo, Joseph (1990), *An Essay on Theology and History: Studies in Pannenberg, Metz, and the Frankfurt School*. Atlanta: Scholars Press.

Connolly, William E. (1991), *Identity/Difference: Democratic Negotiations of Political Paradox*. Minneapolis, MN: University of Minnesota Press.

Cornell, Vincent (2002), 'A Muslim to Muslims: Reflections after September 11', in *Dissent from the Homeland*, ed. Stanley Hauerwas and Frank Lenticchia. Durham, NC: Duke University Press, 325–36.

Cornwell, John (2000), *Hitler's Pope: The Secret History of Pius XII*. London: Penguin.

Crowe, David (2005), 'Why Katrina?' www.restoreamerica.org/content/why_katrina.pdf [last accessed 12 December 2010].

Davis, Walter A. (2006), *Death's Dream Kingdom: The American Psyche Since 9/11*. London: Pluto Press.

Dawidowicz, Lucy S. (1976), *The War Against the Jews*. Toronto, New York, London: Bantam Books.

Dawkins, Richard (2008), *The God Delusion*. New York: First Mariner Books.

—(2001), 'Religion's Misguided Missiles', *The Guardian*. London, 15 September.

Dean, Carolyn J. (2004), *The Fragility of Empathy: After the Holocaust*. Ithaca and London: Cornell University Press.

Delillo, Don (2007), *Falling Man*. London: Picador.

Dent, Martin and Bill Peters (1999), *The Crisis of Poverty and Debt in the Third World*. Aldershot: Ashgate Publishing.

Dews, Peter (2009), 'The Intolerability of Meaning', in *The Religious in Responses to Mass Atrocity*, ed. Thomas Brudholm and Thomas Cushman. Cambridge: Cambridge University Press, 60–78.

Eksteins, Modris (1989), *The Rites of Spring: The Great War and the Birth of the Modern Age*. Toronto: Lester & Orpen Dennys.

Eliott, T. S. (1980), *The Complete Plays and Poetry: 1909–1950*. London and New York: Harcourt Brace & Company.

Elliot, Michael (2001), 'America Will Never Be the Same' *Time Magazine Online* 11 September 2001. http://www.time.com/time/nation/article/0,8599,174540,00.html [last accessed 19 April 2011].

Esposito, John L. (2002), *Unholy War: Terror in the Name of Islam*. Oxford: Oxford University Press.

Fackenheim, Emil L. (1972), *God's Presence in History*. New York, Evanston, London: Harper & Row.

—(1982), *To Mend the World: Foundations of Post-Holocaust Jewish Thought*. Bloomington and Indianapolis: Indiana University Press.

Faith and Doubt at Ground Zero, (2002), Helen Whitney and Ron Rosenbaum, first aired 3 September 2002 on PBS's 'Frontline' (USA). http://www.pbs.org/wgbh/pages/frontline/shows/faith/interviews/kula.html [last accessed 4 December 2010]

Faludi, Susan (2007), *The Terror Dream: What 9/11 Revealed about America*. London: Atlantic Books.

Faramarzi, Scheherezade (2010), 'Iranian Cleric: Promiscuous Women Cause Quakes', *Washington Post* 20 April.

Fiddes, Paul S. (1988), *The Creative Suffering of God*. Oxford: Oxford University Press.

Findley, Timothy (1978), *The Wars*. London: Macmillan.

Finkelstein, Norman G. (2003), *The Holocaust Industry: Reflections on the Exploitation of Jewish Suffering*. London: Verso.

Fischer, Fritz (1967), *Germany's Aims in the First World War*, trans. James Joll. London: Chatto & Windus.

Freud, Sigmund (1966), *The Standard Edition of the Complete Psychological Works of Sigmund Freud*, ed. James Strachey, vol. XIV. London: Hogarth.

Fromkin, David (2004), *Europe's Last Summer: Who Started the Great War in 1914?* New York: Knopf.

Gambetta, Diego and Steffan Hertog (2009), 'Why are there so many engineers among Islamic Radicals', *Archive for.european.sociology* L, 2, 201–30.

'To God, an age-old question', *The Telegraph* (Calcutta, India) 31 December 2004.

Goldhagen, Daniel J. (1995), *Hitler's Willing Executioners: Ordinary Germans and the Holocaust*. New York: A. Knopf.

Goringe, Timothy J. (1999), *Karl Barth Against Hegemony*. Oxford: Oxford University Press.

Graham, Ron (2001), 'Death's Gift to Life', *Macleans* (17 December), 15–16.

Granberg-Michaelson, Wes (2005), 'Acts of God or Sins of Humanity?' *Sojourners* 9 August.

Greenberg, Irving (1977), 'Cloud of Smoke, Pillar of Fire; Judaism, Christianity and Modernity after the Holocaust', in *Auschwitz: Beginning a New Era*, ed. E. Fleischner. New York: Ktav, 7–55.

Habermas, Jürgen (2008), *Between Naturalism and Religion: Philosophical Essays*, trans. Ciaran Cronin. Cambridge: Polity Press.

'Haiti Raises Earthquake Tolls to 230,000,' *Washington Post* 10 February 2010.

Hammer, Karl (1972), *Deutsche Kriegstheologie, 1870–1918*. Munich: Kösel Verlag.

Hart, David Bentley (2005), *The Doors of the Sea: Where was God in the Tsunami?* Grand Rapids, MI: William B. Eerdmans.

—(2009), *In the Aftermath: Provocations and Laments*. Grand Rapids, MI: Eerdmans.

Henig, Ruth B. (2002), *The Origins of the First World War*. London: Routledge.

The Herald Sun, 12 September 2001, 1.

Heschel, Abraham Joshua (1951), *Man Is Not Alone: A Philosophy of Religion*. Philadelphia: Jewish Publication Society.

Hicks, Edward Lee (1914), *The Church and the War*. London: Oxford University Press.

Hilberg, Raul (1985), *The Destruction of the European Jews*, 3 vols. New York: Holmes & Meier.

Hitchens, Christopher (2010), 'A Fault Is Not a Sin,' *Slate Magazine* 17 January.

—(2007), *God is not Great: How Religion Poisons Everything*. New York: Twelve Books.

Hockenos, Matthew D. (2004), *A Church Divided: German Protestants Confront the Nazi Past*. Bloomington: Indiana University Press.

Holland, H. S. et al. (1914), *To the Christian Scholars of Europe and America: A Reply from Oxford to the German Address to Evangelical Christians*. London: Oxford University Press.

Huntington, Samuel (1993), 'The Clash of Civilizations', *Foreign Affairs* 72.3: 22–49.

Ignatieff, Michael 2004, *The Lesser Evil: Political Ethics in an Age of Terror*. Princeton, NJ: Princeton University Press.

Jenkins, Julian (1989), 'War Theology, 1914 and Germany's *Sonderweg*: Luther's Heirs and Patriotism', *The Journal of Religious History* 15.3, 292–310.

Johannet, René (ed.) (1916), *Pan-Germanism versus Christendom: The Conversion of a Neutral*. London, New York, Toronto: Hodder and Stoughton.

Johnston, Adrian (2008), *Žižek's Ontology: A Transcendental Materialist Theory of Subjectivity*. Evanston, IL: Northwestern University Press.

Jones, Serene (2009), *Trauma and Grace: Theology in a Ruptured World*. Louisville, KN: Westminster John Knox Press.

Juergensmeyer, Mark (2000), *Terror in the Mind of God: The Global Rise of Religious Violence*. Berkeley: University of California Press.

Kaplan, Mordecai (1956), *Questions Jews Ask: Reconstructionist Answers*. New York: Reconstructionist Press.

Karlström, Nils (1967), 'Movements for International Friendship and Life and Work: 1910–1925', in *A History of the Ecumenical Movement: 1517–1948*, ed. Ruth Rouse and Stephen Charles Neill. London: SPCK, 509–44.

Katz, Steven T. (2005), *The Impact of the Holocaust on Jewish Theology*. New York and London: New York University Press.

Kendrick, T. D. (1956) *The Lisbon Earthquake*. London: Methuen & Co.

Kertész, Imre (2002), 'Nobel Lecture – Literature 2002', Nobelprize.org. 5 August 2010 http://nobelprize.org/nobel_prizes/literature/laureates/2002/kertesz-lecture-e.html [last accessed 18 April 2011].

Kettle, Martin (2004), 'How can religious people explain something like this?' *The Guardian* 28 December.

Koenig, Harold G. (2006), *In the Wake of Disaster: Religious Responses to Terrorism & Catastrophe*. Philadelphia and London: Templeton Foundation Press.

Kotsko, Adam (2008), *Žižek and Theology*. London: T&T Clark.

LaCapra, Dominick (1998), *History and Memory After Auschwitz*. Ithaca and London: Cornell University Press.

Leibniz, G. W. (1985), *Theodicy*, trans. E. M. Huggard. La Salle, IL: Open Court.

Lentin, Ronit (2000), *Israel and the Daughters of the Shoah: Reoccupying the Territories of Silence*. New York and Oxford: Gerghahn Books.

Levi, Primo (2007), *Survival in Auschwitz: If This is a Man*, trans. Stuart Woolf. New York: The Orion Press.

Lincoln, Bruce (2003), *Holy Terrors: Thinking about Religion after September 11*. Chicago: University of Chicago Press.

Lindsay, Robert, 'Katrina Dealth Explodes to 1,599' (20 March 2006). Available at: http://robertlindsay.blogspot.com/2006/03/katrina-death-toll-explodes-to-1599. html [accessed 9 January 2011]

Linn, Ruth (1999), 'In the Name of the Holocaust: Fears and Hopes Among Israeli Soldiers and Palestinians', *Journal of Genocide Research* 1.3. 439–53.

Mannheim, Karl (1936), *Ideology and Utopia*. London: Routledge.

Marrin, Albert (1974), *The Last Crusade: The Church of England in the First World War*. Durham, NC: Duke University Press.

Marrus, Michael R. (1987), *The Holocaust in History*. London: Penguin Books.

Mathewes, Charles (2010), *The Republic of Grace: Augustinian Thoughts for Dark Times*. Grand Rapids, MI: Eerdmans.

—(2002), 'Christian Intellectuals and Escapism after 9/11', in *Strike Terror no More: Theology, Ethics, and the New War*, ed. Jon L. Berquist. St. Louis, MO: Chalice Press, 306–15.

McEwan, Ian (2005), *Saturday*. London: Vintage.

McKay, Johnston (2002), *Glimpses of Hope: God Beyond Ground Zero*. Edinburgh: St. Andrew Press.

Mendes-Victor, Luis A., Carlos Sousa Oliveira and João Azevedo (eds) (2009), *The 1755 Lisbon Earthquake: Revisited*. New York and Berlin: Springer.

Merton, Thomas (1968), *Albert Camus' 'The Plague'*. New York: The Salisbury Press.

Metz, Johann Baptist (1980), *Faith in History and Society: Towards a Practical Fundamental Theology*. New York: Seabury Press.

—(1999), *Love's Strategy*, ed. John K. Downey. Harrisburg, PA: Trinity Press International.

—(1998), *A Passion for God: The Mystical-Political Dimension of Christianity*, trans. Matthew Ashley. New York: Paulist Press.

Metz, Johann Baptist and Elie Wiesel (2000), *Hope against Hope*, ed. Ekkehard Schuster and Reinhold Baschert-Kimmig. New York: Paulist Press.

Metz, Johann Baptist and Jürgen Moltmann (1995), *Faith and the Future: Essays on Theology, Solidarity, and Modernity*. Maryknoll, NY: Orbis.

Michael, Robert (2006), *Holy Hatred: Christianity, Antisemitism, and the Holocaust*. New York: Palgrave Macmillan.

Miller, DeMond Shondell and Jason David Rivera (2008), *Hurricane Katrina and the Redefinition of Landscape*. Lanham, MD: Lexington Books.

Moltmann, Jürgen (1974), *The Crucified God: The Cross of Christ as the Foundation and Criticism of Christian Theology*, trans. R. A. Wilson and John Bowden. London: SCM Press.

—(2002), 'Hope in a Time of Arrogance and Terror', in *Strike Terror no More: Theology, Ethics, and the New War*, ed. Jon L. Berquist. St. Louis, MO: Chalice Press, 177–86.

Mombauer, Annika (2002), *The Origins of the First World War: Controversies and Consensus*. London: Longman.

Moore, Michael (2001), 'Death, Downtown' 12 September. www.michaelmoore.com/words/mikes-letter/death-downtown [accessed 15 December 2010].

Moses, John A. (1992), 'State, War, Revolution and the German Evangelical Church, 1914–18', *Journal of Religious History* 17.1, 47–59.

Neiman, Susan (2002), *Evil: An Alternative History of Philosophy*. Princeton and Oxford: Princeton University Press.

Newman, Andy (2010), 'At a Memorial Ceremony, Loss and Tension', *New York Times* 11 September.

Niemöller, Martin (1937), *From U-Boat to Pulpit*, trans. D. Hastie Smith. Chicago and New York: Willett, Clark & Co.

Ochs, Peter (2002), 'September 11 and the Children of Abraham', in *Dissent from the Homeland*, ed. Stanley Hauerwas and Frank Lentricchia. Durham, NC: Duke University Press, 391–402.

O'Neill, J. C. (2002), 'Adolf von Harnack and the Entry of the German State into War, July–August 1914', *Scottish Journal of Theology* 55.1, 1–18.

Ostling, Michael (2001), 'Be Kind to the Antichrist: Millenarianism and Religious Tolerance in the Edict of Pskov', *Studies in Religion/Sciences Religieuses* 30.3–4, 261–76.

Pascal, Blaise (1958), *Pascal's Pensées*. New York: E. P. Dutton & Co.

Pauck, Wilhelm and Marion (1976), *Paul Tillich: His Life & Thought*, vol 1. New York: Harper & Row.

Peek, Lori A. and Jeannette N. Sutton (2003), 'An Exploratory Comparison of Disasters', *Disasters* 27.4, 319–35.

Pereria, Antony (1756), *A Narrative of the Earthquake and Fire of Lisbon*. London. G. Hawkins.

Petrie, Jon (2000), 'The Secular Word HOLOCAUST: Scholarly Myths, History, and 20th Century Meanings', *Journal of Genocide Research* 2.1, 31–63.

The Pew Research Center for the People and the Press, (2001), 'Post September 11 Attitudes', 6 December http://people-press.org/report/144/post-september-11-attitides [last accessed 19 April 2011]

Pope, Alexander (1994), *An Essay on Man and Other Poems*. Mineola, NY: Dover Publications.

Pound, Marcus (2007), *Theology, Psychoanalysis and Trauma*. London: SCM Press.

—(2008), *Žižek: A (Very) Critical Introduction*. Grand Rapids, MI: Eerdmans.

Psychoanalytic Dialogues: special issue on 11 September, 12.3 (2002).

Quarantelli, E. L. (1993), 'Community Crisis: An Exploratory Comparison of the Characteristics and Consequences of Disasters and Riots', *Journal of Contingencies and Crisis Management* 1.2, 67–78.

Rambo, Shelly (2010), *Spirit and Trauma: A Theology of Remaining*. Louisville, KY: Westminster John Knox Press.

Ray, Gene (2005), *Terror and the Sublime in Art and Critical Theory*. Gordonsville, PA: Palgrave Macmillan.

Reno, R. R. (1992), 'Christology in Political and Liberation Theology', *The Thomist* 56.2, 291–322.

Rockmore, Tom, Joseph Margolis and Marsoobian (eds) (2005), *The Philosophical Challenge of September 11*. Oxford: Blackwell.

Rodriguez, Havidan, Enrico L.Quarantelli and Russell Dynes (eds) (2006), *Handbook of Disaster Research*. New York: Springer.

Rorty, Richard (1999), 'Relogion as a Conversation Stopper,' *Philosoply and social Hope*. London: Penguin Books, 168–74

Rothstein, Edward (2005), 'Seeking Justice, of God or the Politicians', *New York Times* 8 September.

Rousseau, Jean-Jacques (1964), *Correspondence complete de Jean Jacques Rousseau*, vol. 4, ed. J. A. Leigh, trans. by R. Spang. Geneva: Institut et Musée Voltaire, 37–50.

Rubenstein, Richard L. (1966), *After Auschwitz: Radical Theology and Contemporary Judaism*. Indianapolis, New York, Kansas City: Bobbs-Merrill Company.

Ruether, Rosemary Radford (1974), *Faith and Fratricide: The Theological Roots of Anti-Semitism*. New York: Seabury Press.

Rumscheidt, H. Martin (1986), 'Doing Theology as if Nothing Had Happened: Developments in the Theology of Karl Barth from 1919 to 1933', *Saint Luke's Journal of Theology* 30.1, 7–19.

Santos, Gabriel A. (2009), *Redeeming the Broken Body: Church and State after Disaster*. Eugene, OR: Cascade Books.

Scott, Frederick George (1934), *The Great War as I Saw it*. Vancouver: The Clarke & Stuart Co.

Sebald, W. G. (2004), *On the Natural History of Destruction*, trans. Anthea Bell. Toronto: Vintage.

Sen, Amartya (2006), *Identity and Violence: The Illusion of Destiny*. New York: W. W. Norton.

Sharpe, Matthew and Geoff Boucher (2010), *Žižek and Politics: A Critical Introduction*. Edinburgh: Edinburgh University Press.

Sloterdijk, Peter (2009), *God's Zeal: The Battle of the Three Monotheisms*, trans. Wieland Hoban. Cambridge: Polity Press.

—(2009), *Terror from the Air*. Los Angeles: Semiotext(e).

Smith, Harry (1917), *Enduring Hardness: A War-time Sermon*. Glasgow: Dunlop.

Smith, Jonathan Z. (1998), 'Religion, Religion, Religious', in *Critical Terms for Religious Studies*, ed. Mark C. taylor. Chicago: University of Chicago Press, 269–84.

Smith, Ryan (2010), 'Pat Robertson: Haiti "Cursed" After "Pact to the Devil"', *CBS News* 13 January. http://www.cbsnews.com/8301-504083_162-12017-504083.html [accessed 10 December 2010].

Snape, Michael (2005), *God and the British Soldier: Religion and the British Army in the First and Second World Wars*. London and New York: Routledge.

Sölle, Dorothee (1984), *The Strength of the Weak*, trans. Robert and Rita Kimber. Philadelphia: Westminster Press.

Sontag, Susan (2003), *Regarding the Pain of Others*. London and New York: Penguin Books.

Spence, Patric R., Kenneth A. Lachlan and Jennifer M.Burke (2005), 'Adjusting to Uncertainty: Coping Strategies among the Displaced after Hurricane Katrina', *Sociological Spectrum* 27.6, 653–78.

Stallworthy, Jon (ed.) (2008), *The Oxford Book of War Poetry*. Oxford: University of Oxford Press.

—(1974), *Wilfred Owen*. London: Oxford University Press.

Stanley, Alessandra (2010), '5 Years on, Katrina Dampens Coverage', *New York Times*, 28 August.

Steele, Michael R. (1995), *Christianity, Tragedy, and Holocaust Literature*. Westport, CN and London: Greenwood Press.

Steiner, George (1967), *Language and Silence: Essays on Language, Literature, and the Inhuman*. New York: Atheneum.

Stern, Jessica (2003), *Terrorism in the Name of God: Why Religious Militants Kill*. New York: Harper Collins.

Stout, Jeffrey (2005), *Democracy and Tradition*. Princeton, NJ: Princeton University Press.

Studdert Kennedy, G. A. (1918), *The Hardest Part*. New York: George H. Doran Company.

Swinton, John (2007), *Raging with Compassion: Pastoral Responses to the Problem of Evil*. Grand Rapids, MI: William B. Eerdmans.

Tillich, Paul (1983), *Briefwechsel und Streifschriften*, ed. Walter Schmidt. Frankfurt am Main: Evangelische Verlagwerk.

—(1994), *Frühe Predigten (1909–1918)*, ed. Erdmann Sturm. Berlin: Walter de Gruyter.

—(1967), *My Search for Absolutes*. New York: Simon & Schuster.

—(1955), *The New Being*. New York: Charles Scribner's Sons.

Tück, Jan-Heiner (1999), *Christologie und Theodizie bei Johann Metz*. Paderborn: Shoeningh.

Tyhurst, J. S. (1951), 'Individual reactions to community disaster', *American Journal of Psychiatry* 107, 764–9.

UN Office of the Special Envoy for Tsunami Recovery, 'The Human Toll'. Available at: http://www.tsunamispecialenvoy.org/country/humantoll.asp [last accessed 19 April 2011].

Updike, John (2006), *Terrorist*. London: Penguin Books.

Urban, Hugh B. (2007), *The Secrets of the Kingdom: Religion and Concealment in the Bush Administration*. Lanham, MD: Rowman & Littlefield Publishers.

Volf, Miroslav (ed.) (2001), *Practicing Christianity: Beliefs and Practices in Christian Life*. Grand Rapids, MI: Eerdmans.

Voltaire (1949), *The Portable Voltaire*, ed. Ben Ray Redman, trans. Tobias Smollett et al. New York: The Viking Press.

Waugh, William L. Jr. (2006), 'The Political Costs of Failure in the Katrina and Rita Disasters', *The Annals of the American Academy of Political and Social Science* 604, 10–25.

Webster, John (2000), *Barth*. London and New York: Continuum.

Wesley, John (1756), *Serious Thoughts Occasioned by the Earthquake at Lisbon*. London.

Wiesel, Elie (1967), 'Jewish Values in the Post-Holocaust Future', *Judaism* 16.3, 266–99.

—(1982) *Night*, trans. Stella Rodway. Toronto, New York, London: Bantam Books.

Wilkinson, Alan (1996), *The Church of England and the First World War*. London: SCM Press.

Williams, Rowan (2005), 'Of course this makes us doubt God's existence', *Daily Telegraph*. London, 2 January. www.telegraph.co.uk/comment/personal-view/3613928/Of-course-this-makes-us-doubt-Gods-existence.html [accessed 3 September 2010].

—(2000), *Lost Icons*. Harrisburg, MA: Morehouse Publications.

—(2005), 'Today is not an occasion for us to focus on fear' *The Guardian* 1 November. www.guardian.co.uk/uk/2005/nov/01/july7.politics [accessed 10 December 2010].

—(2007), *Wrestling with Angels: Conversations in Modern Theology*, ed. Mike Higton. London: SCM Press.

—(2002), *Writing in the Dust: after September 11*. Grand Rapids, MI: Eerdmans.

Winfield, Richard Dien (2007), *Modernity, Religion, and the War on Terror*. Aldershot: Ashgate.

Winter, Jay (1995), *Sites of Memory, Sites of Mourning: The Great War in European Cultural History*. Cambridge: Cambridge University Press.

Wuthnow, Robert (2010), *Be Very Afraid: The Cultural Response to Terror, Pandemics, Environmental Devastation, Nuclear Annihilation, and Other Threats*. Oxford: Oxford University Press.

Young, James E. (1990), *Writing and Re-Writing the Holocaust: Narrative and the Consequences of Interpretation*. Bloomington, IN: Indiana University Press.

Young, Lawrence A. (ed.) (1997), *Rational Choice Theory and Religion*. New York and London: Routledge.

—(2004), *Iraq: The Borrowed Kettle*. London and New York: Verso.

Žižek, Slavoj (2001), *On Belief*. London and New York: Routledge.

—(2003), *The Puppet and the Dwarf: The Perverse Core of Christianity*. London: MIT Press.

—(1994), 'The Spectre of Ideology', *Mapping Ideology*, ed. Slavoj Žižek. London and New York: Verso, 1–33.

—(2002), *The Sublime Object of Ideology*. London and New York: Verso.

—(2002), *Welcome to the Desert of the Real*. London and New York: Verso.

—(1999), *The Žižek Reader*. Oxford: Blackwell.

Žižek, Slavoj, Eric L. Santner and Kenneth Reinhard (eds) (2005), 'Neighbors and Other Monsters: A Plea for Ethical Violence', *The Neighbor: Three Inquiries in Political Theology*. Chicago: University of Chicago Press, 134–90.

Index

7/7 1, 4, 88, 150, 171, 195–7, 202
9/11 4, 10, 85–92, 95–8, 102–6, 108,
       113–18, 120, 123, 124, 126, 127,
       128, 130, 132, 134, 135, 141, 143,
       149, 158, 161, 171, 178, 179, 180,
       182, 183, 185–7, 192, 198

Act, radical 113, 131–3, 137, 139, 143,
       144, 188
Adams, Mary McCord 190–4, 197–9
Adorno, Theodor W 11, 67, 166, 167,
       168, 178, 198, 201–2, 204
Agamben, Giorgio 67, 81
Alexander, David 1 05
Amis, Martin 91
anti-Semitism 65
anti-theodicy 63, 71, 73, 77, 80, 202
atheism 3, 33, 55, 68, 73, 74, 76, 88,
       113, 131, 134, 135, 145, 196, 198
       see also New Atheism
Auschwitz 6 2, 63, 66–9, 72–82, 86–8,
       164–7, 198, 202

Barth, Karl 10, 42–3, 66, 117, 119, 145,
       149–58, 161–3, 164, 165, 166, 168,
       178, 179, 197, 198
belief 3, 7, 10, 34, 47, 52, 88, 91, 94,
       95, 101, 104, 109, 113, 115, 131–9,
       142–5
Benjamin, Walter 166
Berkovits, Eliezer 71, 72, 73
Berman, Paul 115
bin Laden, Osama 85, 90, 98–100, 103,
       107, 117, 128, 133, 195
Bonhoeffer, Dietrich 66, 168

Bush, George W. 31, 90, 92, 98–100,
       103, 108, 128, 130, 133
Butler, Judith 203, 204

Cavanaugh, William 95, 96
chaplain, military 9, 40, 43, 45, 50, 51,
       54–5, 59
'Clash of Civilizations' 97, 98, 101,
       108, 115, 185
Confessing Church 66
Cornell, Vincent 178, 184–6

Dawkins, Richard 10, 27, 91, 95,
       101, 182
deism 20, 34
Delillo, Don 85, 88
disaster research 32, 33

ecumenical 44, 62, 129
Eliott, T. S. 48

Fackenheim, Emil L. 10, 59, 63, 70,
       73–82, 150, 163, 164, 191
'fake passion for the Real' 128, 129,
       130, 133, 137
Falwell, Jerry 102, 103, 107
Freud, Sigmund 3, 117, 194

German Christians 43, 65, 66
God, 'Almighty' 46, 98, 102
       suffering 57–8, 62, 63
Greenberg, Irving 72
'Ground Zero' 2, 10, 100, 107, 116,
       145, 149, 154, 155, 157, 170, 173,
       182, 205

Habermas, Jürgen   4, 115
Haiti   7, 9, 14, 24, 25, 27
Harnack, Adolph von   42–4
Hart, David Bentley   34, 35, 36
Heschel, Abraham Joshua   72
Hitchens, Christopher   27, 91, 95, 101
Holocaust   63–8, 70–7, 80–2
hope   3, 8, 11, 23, 24, 48, 53, 56, 57, 62,
    79, 141, 158, 159, 161, 173, 189,
    192, 197–201, 204
Huntington, Samuel see 'Clash of
    Civilizations'

ideology   9, 10, 43, 51, 59, 64, 65, 67,
    80, 81, 108, 113, 116, 118–25, 129,
    135–7, 139, 141, 144, 145, 149–53,
    156, 159, 160, 167, 171, 172, 178,
    179, 182, 197, 201
Islam   1, 4, 7, 26, 89, 91–6, 98, 99, 115,
    128, 133, 183–5, 201
Israel   25, 63, 74, 77, 80, 81, 133, 155,
    167, 172

Job   17–19, 25, 28, 30, 32, 73, 168, 178,
    194, 199
Jones, Serene   158, 169
Jublilee, Year of   129, 130
Judaism   63, 73, 75–7, 81, 106, 183
Juergensmeyer, Mark   10, 90, 95, 96

Katrina, Hurricane   14, 24–7, 29–32, 35
Kertész, Imre   62
Kettle, Martin   33, 34

LaCapra, Dominick   68, 150, 172
Leibniz, G. W.   20, 21
Levi, Primo   70
Lichtenberg, Bernhard   66, 79
Lincoln, Bruce   92–7, 99–102, 107, 116,
    117, 126, 128, 184
Lisbon Earthquake   13–25, 28, 29, 32,
    34, 62, 82, 87, 88, 102

McEwan, Ian   87, 88, 93
Mathewes, Charles   161, 199
memoria passionis   167–70, 172, 194,
    196, 201, 202, 204

memory   67, 81, 150, 157, 165, 166–72,
    181, 191, 196, 197, 201
Metz, Johann Baptist   10, 150, 165–72,
    178, 181, 194, 197, 199–202
modesty   141–4, 186
Moltmann, Jürgen   168, 198, 199, 201,
    202, 204
Moore, Michael   103
Muselmann   70, 76, 77

Neiman, Susan   62
New Atheism   4, 7, 91, 101, 182

Ochs, Peter   106–8
Owen, Wilfred   47, 48, 55

Pascal, Blaise   134, 134, 138
The Plague   112, 114, 140, 141–3
Pope, Alexander   21, 22

Quran   94

Rambo, Shelly   157, 158, 159, 166, 169,
    170, 173, 191, 204
Rational Choice Theory   3, 160
Real, the   122, 124–7, 129–33, 137, 144
refuseniks   133, 143
road rage   184, 195
Robertson, Pat   27, 102, 103, 107
Rousseau, Jean-Jacques   19, 22–4, 31,
    32, 72
Rubenstein, Richard L.   62, 72

Santos, Gabriel A.   108
Sebald, W. G.   163
September 11 see 9/11
Shoah   62, 68, 72, 74, 75
Sloterdijk, Peter   4, 86, 88, 178, 183–5
Sontag, Susan   150, 170, 172,
    173, 203
Steiner, George   67
Studdert Kennedy, G. A.   40, 52–8, 62,
    63, 72, 75, 192
Swinton, John   35, 36

terrorism   5, 7, 86, 88, 90–2, 99, 115,
    182, 184, 185

theodicy   3, 4, 7–9, 13, 14, 17–21, 24,
   25, 27, 31, 32, 35, 36, 39, 40, 56,
   58, 59, 62, 63, 71–5, 81, 82, 103,
   112, 159, 167, 169, 170, 173, 177,
   190–2, 194, 195, 197, 198
Tikkun   77–9, 164
Tillich, Paul   40, 53–5, 57–9, 62
trauma   32, 67–80, 81, 105, 117, 124,
   126, 127, 135, 150, 153, 157–60,
   165, 166, 169, 172, 173, 178, 189,
   191, 195, 196, 204
Tsunami, Asian Pacific   14, 24–30, 33–5
Tyhurst, J.S.   105, 107–8

Updike, John   91, 93

violence (religion and)   6, 56, 86, 90, 91
   94–8, 152, 155, 158–60, 183, 184,
   195, 196
Voltaire   19–24, 31–4, 39

Wesley, John   17
Wiesel, Elie   62, 68–71, 74
Williams, Rowan   29, 30, 34–6, 177–9,
   181, 182, 183, 185–97, 202, 204
Wuthnow, Robert   3

Žižek, Slavoj   10, 109, 113, 114,
   117–41, 143–5, 149, 152, 153, 161,
   173, 182, 188, 203